When You
Owe the
IRS

When You Owe the Owe the IRS

Jack Warren Wade, Jr.

Macmillan Publishing Company   NEW YORK

Collier Macmillan Publishers   LONDON

Macmillan Publishing Company
866 Third Avenue, New York, N.Y. 10022
Collier Macmillan Canada, Inc.

Library of Congress Cataloging in Publication Data

Wade, Jack Warren.
When you owe the IRS.

Includes index.
1. United States. Internal Revenue Service.
2. Tax collection—United States.   I. Title.
II. Title: When you owe the I.R.S.
KF6301.W33   1983   343.7305′2   83-930
ISBN 0-02-622230-2   347.30352

10 9 8 7 6 5 4

Designed by Jack Meserole

To Gail,
for her love and support

Contents

III THE IRS'S SECRET LAW

IV ADVICE FOR SMALL BUSINESS OWNERS

INTRODUCTION

Fearing and Loathing
the Tax Collector

Why they are the way they are

The day started like any other day. A meeting with the boss, a couple of phone calls, and an exhausting interview. When I got back to my desk, the boss handed me a new assignment. I picked it up for a cursory review and the following letter fell out. It began:

Dear Mr. I.R.S.,

Regarding your recent bill. Up your nose. Bring your guns and we'll settle out of court.

The letter was typed, dated, and signed by the taxpayer. This was not the usual irate taxpayer expressing himself. The question was, was it a serious threat?

I took it to my boss, who read it and laughed. He thought it was a joke, not worth the time to worry about. He told me to forget it. But I didn't think treating it lightly was the responsible thing to do, and so I reported it anyway as a possible threat.

Two IRS inspectors from the Internal Security Division immediately came to investigate. They took the letter for evidence and decided to go visit the taxpayer to determine his true intentions.

The taxpayer wasn't hard to find during the day. He had worked at the same place for nine years. The inspectors tried to see him, but he worked in a restricted area of his company's building. They couldn't go in, and he wouldn't come out. They hung around until 8:00 P.M. that night, but the taxpayer still refused to come out.

The next day was a Saturday, and so the inspectors went to his house. But he refused to answer the door. They knew he was there because they could see him through a window. After a while, they gave up and decided to try again another day.

Two nights later a local police officer noticed that the car in front of him had expired license tags. The red lights and the siren were flipped on and the police officer pulled over the suspect. As the officer approached the car, the suspect pulled out a small gun and aimed it at the officer. When the officer ducked for cover, the suspect floored the accelerator and sped away.

The officer immediately gave chase and radioed for assistance. Forgotten for a moment were two eleven-year-old boys riding in the backseat of the police cruiser as part of the county's "ride-along" program to acquaint young people with police work.

The chase ended at the end of a dead-end street. The suspect jumped from his car and started firing at the police officer. The officer had no time to jump from his cruiser. He returned the fire by shooting at the suspect through his own front windshield.

Within a minute, a second police cruiser pulled in behind the first one. Seeing the gun battle, the second police officer became excited and started firing his shotgun, accidentally blowing out the rear window of the police cruiser in front of him, showering glass on the two boys hunched down on the rear floor.

When the incident was over, it had taken four police officers to make the arrest. Two officers had been shot, one in the knee and one in the ankle. Neither the suspect nor the two boys were hurt. One police officer said the only reason the suspect had been captured alive was that the guy had run out of bullets.

At the police station the only thing the suspect would say was "I thought it was the IRS coming to get me."

That suspect was my letter-writing taxpayer.

THOSE FOLKS BEHIND IT ALL

What is it about the IRS that scares people, and in some cases drives them to acts of madness? Is it the tyranny of taxation? Or is it the frightening reality of a massive bureaucracy whose power and authority are unquestioned and legendary? Or is it simply the fear of the unknown consequences of disobedience?

No other government agency has such a strong and pervasive influence over the way people and businesses conduct their economic life. No other government agency asks so much of the American people—all the way from giving up a part of each paycheck to sitting through that infamous, contemptuous exercise in soul-searching humiliation known as the audit.

To many people thoughts of the Internal Revenue Service conjure up visions of *1984* and "Big Brother." To some, IRS employees are no better than gestapo agents. Others view the IRS as the government's one big stick to keep its citizens in line.

Whatever you may feel about our country, tax system, or politicians, the chances are that your true feelings about the IRS fall somewhere between "fear and respect." But if you have ever had a *bad* experience, your feelings are more than likely to fall somewhere between "fear and loathing." And you probably won't have to look very far to find many people who feel the same way.

The image of the IRS is one of a strong, no-nonsense organization whose power and authority has no equal. It is an image the IRS itself has cultivated over many years. It is also an image that recognizes the success of undertaking one of the most massive jobs in the entire world—making the U.S. government's tax system work.

The IRS states that the "mission of the Service is to encourage and achieve the highest possible degree of voluntary compliance with the tax laws and regulations and to conduct itself so as to warrant the highest degree of public confidence in its integrity and efficiency."

The key words in that statement are "to encourage and achieve . . . voluntary compliance." That phrase may be new to you, but it is the first thing all new IRS employees learn. "Voluntary compliance" is the designation given to the obedience of millions of taxpayers who fulfill their legal tax obligation by voluntarily filing their own tax returns and computing their own tax liabilities.

The size and scope of the voluntary-compliance tax system are uniquely American, and promoting it is an awesome and monumental responsibility. This job is handled by 88,000 IRS employees nationwide at a cost of $2.5 billion. To understand how awesome the job really is, just look at these statistics about the areas of IRS responsibility:

- *Assisting Taxpayers.* The IRS is aware that the preparation of income tax returns is not a simple task for many taxpayers. To enable the American public to comply with the tax law, the IRS provides an assistance program that in 1981:
    —answered 36 million telephone calls;
    —personally assisted 8.7 million taxpayers in local IRS offices;
    —processed 102,000 written inquiries; and
    —furnished over 13 million tax publications.
- *Processing Returns.* The IRS processed 166.5 million income tax returns and supplemental schedules during 1981. It collected gross tax receipts of $606.8 billion, for a $87.4 billion increase over 1980. Total refunds of $63 billion were paid to 73.6 million taxpayers.
- *Collecting Delinquent Taxes.* During 1981 the IRS disposed of 2.2 million delinquent accounts by collecting some $6 billion in overdue taxes. Approximately 1.5 million delinquent tax returns were secured, for additional assessments of $1.8 billion.
- *Auditing Tax Returns.* The IRS examined 1.93 million tax returns in 1981 for an examination coverage of 1.84 percent of all tax returns. The examination program resulted in recommendations for additional tax and penalties of $10.5 billion, of which $2.6 billion was on Forms 1040 and 1040A and $6.3 billion was on corporate income tax returns.
- *Conducting Fraud Investigations.* A total of 5,838 tax-enforcement investigations were initiated in 1981. Prosecutions were recommended in 1,978 investigations and were successfully completed in 1,494 cases. Only 802 taxpayers received jail sentences.

To accomplish this task the IRS is divided into three separate and governing authorities, the National Office, seven regional field organizations, and fifty-eight districts.

The National Office is the headquarters of the IRS, located in Washington, D.C., and the office of the Commissioner of the IRS, who is the chief executive officer of the agency. The Commissioner reports to the Secretary of the Treasury and is the IRS's only political appointee.

The mission of the National Office is to develop broad, nationwide policies and programs for the administration of the tax laws. These officials in Washington also direct, guide, coordinate, and control the operation of the IRS. They issue rulings and regulations, produce the official IRS publications, and issue directives to the field organization through the Internal Revenue Manual (IRM).

The IRM is probably the most comprehensive and precise set of procedures in the entire free world. The portions of the IRM that pertain solely to computer procedures would stack up to fill a complete wall fifteen feet long and eight feet high. It is estimated that the other portions consist of more than fifty thousand printed pages.

The field organizations are divided into seven regions that are composed of districts. Each region is governed by a Regional Commissioner and Assistant Regional Commissioner of each enforcement or administrative function. The mission of the regional office is to execute National Office policies and procedures within the geographical area assigned to the region. This means that regions must establish certain standards and programs to assure the implementation of national policies and procedures.

The districts within the regions are basically organized along state boundaries, except for the larger states of California, Illinois, Texas, Ohio, and Pennsylvania, which have two districts, and New York, which has four. The districts are headed by a District Director who oversees the administrative and enforcement functions within the district. Organizationally, the district is headed by division chiefs of the following divisions:

- Examination Division. Responsible for conducting audits.
- Collection Division. Responsible for collecting delinquent taxes and securing delinquent returns.
- Criminal Investigations Division. Responsible for conducting investigations of tax law violations and making recommendations for prosecution.
- Taxpayer Service Division. Responsible for providing information to taxpayers and assisting them with the completion of their tax returns.

Internal Revenue Service Regions, Districts and Service Centers; Chief Counsel Regional and District Offices

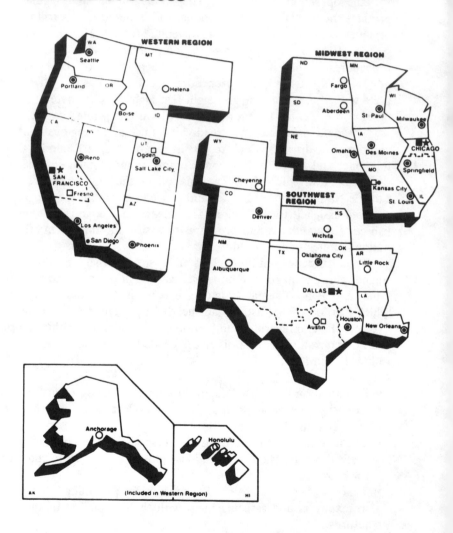

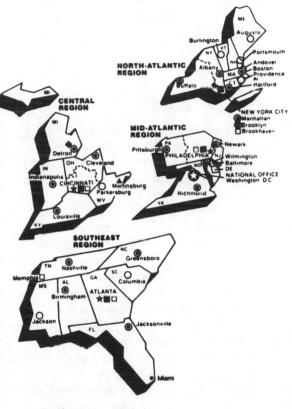

NORTH-ATLANTIC REGION

ME
Augusta
Burlington
Portsmouth
NY VT
NH Andover
Albany Boston
MA Providence
RI
Buffalo CT Hartford

NEW YORK CITY
Manhattan
Brooklyn
Brookhaven

CENTRAL REGION

MI
MI

MID-ATLANTIC REGION

PA
Pittsburgh Newark
PHILADELPHIA NJ
Wilmington
MD Baltimore
DE
NATIONAL OFFICE
Washington DC

Detroit
OH Cleveland
IN
Indianapolis
CINCINNATI Martinsburg
Parkersburg
WV
VA Richmond
Louisville
KY

SOUTHEAST REGION

NC
Greensboro
TN Nashville
SC
Memphis Columbia
MS GA
AL
Birmingham ATLANTA
FL
Jackson Jacksonville

Miami

Legend

▬▬ District Boundary

★ (circle) National Office, Washington, D.C.; Commissioner
Office of Chief Counsel
District Counsel, Washington, D.C. and
District Counsel, International Operations

★ Regional Commissioner/District Director

■ Regional Counsel Office and
District Counsel

○ District Director

● District Counsel

◉ IRS District Director/District Counsel

□ Service Center

▲ National Computer Center (Martinsburg, WV)

◆ Data Center (Detroit, MI)

PUERTO RICO

VIRGIN ISLANDS

(Office of International Operations National Office)

IRS offices are located throughout the district in both cities and towns, large and small. In the major metropolitan areas the local IRS office will have employees from all four divisions. In the smaller offices there are a number of mixes of enforcement employees.

All IRS nonmanagement employees belong to a "group" and are answerable to a group manager or supervisor. In turn, the managers usually report to a branch chief who is responsible for overseeing several groups. The branch chiefs report to the division chiefs, who report to the District Director.

IRS EMPLOYEES

- *Taxpayer Service Representatives and Taxpayer Service Specialists* belong to the Taxpayer Service Division and are involved with assisting taxpayers in preparing their tax returns and resolving various problems. Representatives are generally GS grades 5, 6, and 7, and specialists are GS grades 9 and 10. The specialists are given specialized training in the more difficult areas of income tax law and provide technical assistance to the representatives. If you call or visit your local IRS office, you will first be assisted by a representative. Incidentally, experienced Taxpayer Service Representatives and Specialists frequently know more income tax law than Revenue Agents or Tax Auditors. Their only weakness is that they are not knowledgeable in partnership, corporation, or trust income tax returns.

- *Revenue Agents* conduct audits of tax returns away from the IRS office. They are trained in accounting, and usually audit business income tax returns and more complex individual tax returns, such as 1040's with Schedule C's. An audit by an agent can take anywhere from eight to forty hours depending on the complexity of the return and the scope of the audit. They usually just move right into the offices of the business they are auditing and make themselves at home. With major *Fortune* 500 companies like U.S. Steel, there are whole divisions of agents who are permanently assigned to the auditing project. There have been agents who have practically spent their entire career auditing one firm.

- *Tax Auditors* usually conduct their audits at the local IRS office. If you get a letter from the IRS asking you to come into the IRS office on a certain day to present your documentation for deducting a certain item, you will most likely see a Tax Auditor. Tax Auditors only audit Form 1040, and their work consists mainly of checking the more common types of deductions like medical expenses, charitable contributions, and child care expenses.

- *Special Agents* belong to the Criminal Investigations Division. They do exactly what you would expect: they conduct criminal investigations. They have badges, carry guns, and have the power to make arrests. Their work mostly involves conducting complex financial investigations of taxpayers' business affairs to find evidence of fraud. If you are ever investigated by a Special Agent, you will know it. He's the guy (or gal) who will read you your rights before asking any questions. (It is at this point that you need a lawyer immediately.)

- *Tax Law Specialists* are usually lawyers, CPAs, or ex-Revenue Agents who work in the ivory tower (the National Office) in Washington, D.C. They are usually trained to be experts in extremely minute areas of tax law. Tax Law Specialists are basically responsible for designing the tax forms, writing IRS publications (in legalese), and issuing rulings and IRS regulations.

  You will never see a Tax Law Specialist outside of Washington, D.C. He will not audit your return, seize your car, or help you prepare your tax return.

- *Revenue Officers*, probably the most notorious lot of the entire bunch, are responsible for collecting delinquent taxes and securing delinquent returns. They are also mostly responsible for IRS's bad publicity. They literally possess the most powerful arsenal of weapons within the entire IRS. When Chief Justice John Marshall wrote "the power to tax involves the power to destroy," he was probably thinking of Revenue Officers. Without a court order, they can serve summonses, file tax liens, padlock a business, and seize everything from your paycheck or bank account to the clothes in your closet and the furniture in your house.

  Revenue Officers are taught that their job is to "protect the revenue." The forerunner of the present day officer was the deputy collector, or "revenoor" as he was known, who was responsible for all enforcement functions related to taxes, including busting up stills.

In 1981, Revenue Officers nationwide filed 503,000 notices of federal tax liens, attached 740,000 paychecks and bank accounts, and listed over 8,800 property seizures. Evidence indicates that officers are stepping up enforcement efforts in the collection of delinquent accounts; most statistics show at least a 50 percent increase of enforcement activity in 1981 over 1979, only two years previously.

Most problems with the IRS that do not involve an audit will involve contact with a Revenue Officer at some stage. The following chapters discuss everything they do and everything you need to know to protect yourself from their powers.

- *Revenue Representatives* are collection employees who handle the easiest delinquency cases. They send letters, make telephone calls, and make initial visits to taxpayers in an attempt to collect. If they are not able to close the case within a couple of days, they will turn the case over to an officer. Sometimes this is their greatest threat. They have been frequently heard to tell taxpayers, "If you don't pay up right now, I'll turn this over for enforcement to a Revenue Officer, who will seize everything you've got."

- *Tax Examiners* perform a myriad of different jobs within the IRS. They can be found in the Service Centers, where they either issue correspondence or solve billing problems, and they can also be found in the district offices of the IRS performing various support services for Revenue Officers.

There you have it, a brief sketch of the awesome job the IRS has and a sketch of the people who do that job.

FEAR AND THE IRS

If you asked the IRS commissioner why the public is afraid of the tax agency, he would deny that people are afraid. He would tell you instead that the American people voluntarily comply with the tax laws out of respect for our system of government, sort of a mentality that recognizes "taxes are what we pay for a civilized society."

There is no doubt that there is a certain amount of validity to that argument. A civilized world can exist only as a result of the individual responsibilities of a civilized population. The idea of paying one's fair share has almost universal acceptability. What most people object to is unfairness and inequities in the construction and/or enforcement of the law. One man's justice may be another man's injustice.

You can easily see this in all facets of our society, and no where is it more obvious than in the United States Tax Code. Burdened by the strength of thousands of special interest groups, Congress has written a two-thousand-page document that is a monument to the ability of our society to complicate its affairs to an unintelligible level.

The Tax Code represents the genius of legal fiction. Although the Tax Code was written by lawyers for lawyers, lawyers are unable to agree on what it says. The irony is that the citizens of this country have been conditioned to put their full faith and confidence in the ability of the legal aristocracy to solve their problems and society's ills. For evidence, just look at the overwhelming number of lawyers who are elected to represent the people in state legislatures around the country and in Congress.

What has grown out of the Tax Code, a law so important that it now influences every facet of American business and personal financial life? We know that it has created a billion-dollar society of tax practitioners, accountants, and lawyers who feed off its complexities and obscurities. We know it has left its permanent mark with the withholding deduction in the weekly paychecks of 95 million Americans. We know it has created thousands of special interest groups who lobby long and hard for their piece of the pie. And we know it has created a large bureaucracy with powers so immense that for years and years it was allowed to operate in total secrecy from review of Congress and the American people.

Those years of secrecy gave IRS agents a tremendous psychological power over taxpayers who did not know what their rights were, what the law was, or even what they could do to defend themselves from abusive behavior. And the IRS deliberately took advantage of that power officially and unofficially. It was not uncommon to hear IRS agents say such things as "all taxpayers are liars, crooks, or cheaters" and something to the effect that "delinquent taxpayers really belong in jail."

During the 1960s the media was full of IRS horror stories that gave the impression that taxpayers had no rights. Many taxpayers wondered if the U.S. government had created its own version of a gestapo.

There is no question that the secrecy behind IRS operations was deliberately used to instill fear into the American public. The IRS has never really known why people comply with the tax laws, whether it was because of fear of punishment or out of respect for the political process. So they were not willing to take any chances on upsetting what they referred to as "voluntary compliance." They developed a policy of projecting a "firm enforcement image." They wanted the American public to know they wouldn't tolerate disobedient, recalcitrant, delinquent taxpayers. Revenue Officers became pawns in the game as IRS management pushed them to project that firm enforcement image.

The firm enforcement policy encouraged compliance through fear. Taxpayers were led into compliance by examples of punishment to those who did not obey the law. Projecting this image occurred on all enforcement levels. For example, Revenue Officers were encouraged to make immediate seizures within forty-eight hours of a delinquency, and to top it off, they would invite the press along to witness their enforcement. Naturally it not only gave the press something to write about, but it also served to humiliate the delinquent taxpayer publicly. The real message was "Woe unto anyone who doesn't pay."

Another favorite tactic was to obtain a large number of indictments around the filing deadline of April 15 and to seek big press coverage of those indictments. To this day the IRS public information officers in every district still send out press releases announcing indictments obtained by the IRS. Publicity is still considered a tool to encourage compliance with the law.

For years, while it was able to get away with its campaign of fear, the IRS clearly had the upper hand. Even President Nixon took advantage of IRS's power through the Special Services Staff in Washington, a secret organization within the IRS whose sole purpose was to harass Nixon's enemies.

The secrecy of IRS operations left taxpayers impotent and defenseless. If the IRS said you owed more money, then you had to accept it without question. After all, didn't the IRS know the law? If the IRS seized your property, there was little you could do because the anti-injunction statute in the Tax Code left you powerless to contest it. If IRS agents treated you rudely and contemptuously, you had no place to turn. After all, you were a delinquent taxpayer, weren't you?

And the American people were never to forget the IRS's biggest coup—the imprisonment of the most notorious gangster of all time, Al Capone. Perhaps no other single event in the history of the IRS has had as much impact on the American people as that one case. For decades afterward people would think to themselves that "if the IRS could do that to Al Capone, what could they do to me?"

WHY TAX COLLECTORS ARE THE WAY THEY ARE

Most of the horror stories you may have read are about incidents that occurred while Revenue Officers (tax collectors) were chasing after delinquent taxes.

Revenue Officers are a different breed of government bureaucrat. They have a difficult, thankless job that must be accomplished under difficult and stressful circumstances. The mere exercise of their strong enforcement powers often leads to provocative incidents. After all, it's not easy to remain calm after the IRS has wiped out your bank account, seized your paycheck, or towed away your car.

Revenue Officers in general are not happy creatures either. Their constant exposure to delinquent taxpayers makes them suspicious, cynical, and cautious. People outside the IRS do not understand the difficulties and demands of tax collecting. The serious demeanor of the officer frightens some people while bringing out the hostility in others. It is natural for taxpayers to feel that the Revenue Officer suffers from a lack of sympathy and understanding.

Revenue Officers are truly caught between a rock and a hard place. They not only catch hell from taxpayers, they also catch hell from their own managers who often make impossible demands on them and then berate them for not accomplishing a superhuman task. Morale among Revenue Officers is usually low, especially because of the lack of positive feedback and reinforcement from taxpayers or IRS management.

Three years ago the *Wall Street Journal* quoted a midwestern tax lawyer as saying that Revenue Officers "are the most highhanded, obnoxious bastards I've ever dealt with. They are almost brutal in their approach. They seem to relish their power, and generally they bully the general citizenry. I don't like them, and I don't know anyone in the [legal] practice who does."

But the IRS says that things have changed. There is now supposed to be a new approach to try to help people resolve their problems. That may be, but abuses continue to occur. Until taxpayers know their rights, options, and what alternatives they have, they will continue to be powerless and defenseless against arbitrary and capricious actions of overzealous tax collectors.

Revenue Officers are an "unknown" entity to the American people. While their actions and behavior may receive press coverage, they are not known to the media or the public as "Revenue Officers." They are usually referred to as "Tax Collectors" or "Internal Revenue Agents." But there is a distinct difference between an agent and an officer.

Knowing about the psychology of Revenue Officer behavior will help you immensely as you struggle for survival in your dealings with them. Understanding something of what makes them "tick" may give you the emotional support and self-confidence you need to represent and protect yourself properly.

- *Revenue Officers are the most abused employees within the IRS.* FBI statistics show that 74 percent of all threats and 41 percent of all assaults on federal employees are directed at IRS employees. Two-thirds of these are directed at Revenue Officers.
- *Revenue Officers are not the intellectual giants of the IRS.* Revenue Agents and Special Agents must have college degrees and a minimum requirement of college-level accounting courses. Revenue Officers are *not* required to have college degrees. They are not required to know much tax law either, but they are required to know a lot of procedure.

For these reasons, if you have a messy financial situation or an intricate, complex problem, you will want to make sure that your case is in capable hands. I have seen cases drag on for years simply because the Revenue Officer was not smart enough to figure out how to resolve it.

SURVIVAL RULE ▬▬▬▬▬▬▬▬▬▬▬▬▬▬▬▬▬▬▬▬▬▬▬▬▬▬

Anytime you believe that the Revenue Officer handling your case is not capable of handling it, you should request that your case be transferred to someone else more capable of handling it.

You have a right to have your case handled by someone who knows what he is doing, and you should not have to be the one to suffer just because the IRS has not been hiring the best qualified people as Revenue Officers.

* *The Revenue Officer's job is a high-pressure—production-oriented occupation.* Revenue Officers are under a lot of pressure to close cases according to management standards.

    Even though IRS policy specifically prohibits the managers of officers from compiling production statistics on their employees, they do anyway. The managers from the old school think that is the only way they can measure the performance of their employees. They believe that the number of case closures and seizures is the only barometer of how successful the Revenue Officer has been in "protecting the revenue."

    To succeed in the bureaucratic promotion world the Revenue Officer must make a name for himself. He has to let his superiors know he can project the "firm enforcement image," and he must not be afraid of utilizing those powers and authorities delegated to him, including making a lot of seizures. Managers believe that it makes them look good to have Revenue Officers in their group who make a lot of seizures.

* *Revenue Officers come from diverse backgrounds.* Revenue Officers do not share a common background as do Revenue Agents or Tax Auditors. A few are lawyers who never passed the bar exam and some are "frustrated lawyers" who always dreamed they would but who never made it to law school. A few have owned their own businesses but sought the security of a government job after going broke. Some are retired military men; some have college degrees and some don't. Some fought in Vietnam and some demonstrated against Vietnam.

* *Revenue Officers frequently work for managers who can't manage.* In some districts the only way you can become a manager is to be the meanest, nastiest S.O.B. around. The old school of management believes that fear and not respect is what keeps employees in line. Therefore some of these managers can't distinguish between delinquent taxpayers and their own employees. They treat them both with the same form of tyrannical authoritarianism.

- *Revenue Officers have initial discretion in how their cases are handled, but final authority rests with their management.* Revenue Officers are supposed to be independent employees and as such are paid to make decisions on their cases, using their training, experience, judgment, instincts, and the Internal Revenue Manual for guidelines. Every case is different, and what works for one case may not work for another.

Most Revenue Officers know how to handle almost all of their cases. But their collection techniques not only have to agree with National Office policy, they also have to agree with their manager's philosophy of collection. If the officer starts working a case one way and his manager reviews it and wants it worked another way, then the officer will have to do it the boss's way.

There have been many taxpayers who thought they had an agreement with the officer to do a certain thing, such as make monthly payments, when all of a sudden they experience the seizure of their assets without warning. This problem has typically arisen when the officer did not get the agreement approved by his manager and the manager ordered an immediate seizure. The officer couldn't exactly tell the taxpayer that he had screwed up, so he would go out and seize something. If the taxpayer complained, he would blame it on the boss.

The important point here to remember is that the Collection Division is *not* an efficient well-run organization, and problems not only can arise but most probably *will* arise to cause you harm, grief, or embarrassment. Remember Murphy's law. If anything can go wrong, it will!

SURVIVAL RULE ━━━━━━━━━━━━━━━━━━━━━━━━━━━

Whenever you deal with an IRS collection employee, you should always ask what action is required of you next and what action is next required by the collection employee. Always find out what additional bureaucratic procedures are involved.

- *Revenue Officers have no control over their work load.* The Examination Division has a master plan for its Revenue Agents that enables the division to control how many tax returns will be audited over a year's time. The division controls exactly how many audits there will be across the nation and also how many audits each Revenue Agent will conduct.

The Collection Division has no such ability to control its work load. The number of case delinquencies is more of a reflection on the state of the economy than anything else. When things start getting tight in the business world, especially during a recession, the number of delinquencies soars.

The National Office's Collection Division management has never really been prepared for economic swings in the economy. Obviously, it is not always easy to predict when a recession is going to occur, but even when their computers show an alarming increase in delinquencies, they are more likely to study the problem than they are to resolve it.

But until recently the IRS has been just as victimized by budget cuts as other government agencies, despite the fact that the IRS says that it can recover as much as eight to twenty dollars in additional tax revenue for every dollar spent by the agency for audit and collection expenses.

The Collection Division has tried to deal with budget cuts in several ways, such as increasing computer notices, raising tolerances for enforced collection or personal contact, and by making it easier for taxpayers to obtain agreements to make monthly payments on their liabilities. The fact is, however, the inventory of delinquent cases quickly became out of control. It was so bad in some states that taxpayers could escape paying thousands of dollars in back taxes simply because the IRS did not have enough Revenue Officers to collect them.

The net result is that the government was losing billions of dollars in revenue solely because it wouldn't spend a few million more dollars to keep the revenue flowing in. In the middle of 1982 things changed drastically. IRS received Congressional authority to expand the Revenue Officer force by 50 percent within one year. Practically overnight the IRS began hiring up to 3,000 new tax collectors nationwide.

The IRS is starting to get tough with taxpayers who are not paying their taxes. The number of liens and seizure actions are expected to soar. The battle lines are being drawn for the greatest "war" on delinquent taxes this country has ever seen. If you are a taxpayer who has not filed a tax return, or who has not paid a tax bill, you had better start preparing to protect yourself.

PROTECTING AGAINST AGGRESSION

The first step in self-protection is to know your rights under the Constitution, the tax laws, and IRS policy. Many of the abuses you have heard about occurred under the laws that give the IRS its enforcement powers, and so in a technical sense they were not illegal. The problems arose in the way those powers were used.

The official IRS policy has been to tighten up on those procedures that provided Revenue Officers the opportunity to abuse their powers by making many actions subject to supervisory review. But ironically supervisory review has frequently proved insufficient because *supervisory pressure is probably the main cause of the abuse of taxpayers.*

If left to operate independently, few Revenue Officers would put themselves in a position where they would deliberately abuse or harass taxpayers. Problems seem to arise in those cases where supervisors have given certain marching orders to their Revenue Officers. Whether in a mood to please their boss or in a mood not to displease their boss, they sometimes take actions against their better judgment.

Our system of government operates on checks and balances between the powers of the government and the rights of the people. In the criminal-justice system, every suspect is entitled to legal representation. In the tax system, taxpayers are also allowed to be represented by legal counsel whenever they have dealings with the IRS.

The tax industry has done a remarkable job of helping taxpayers get through the maze of IRS regulations, rulings, and procedures. If you need help in filling out your income tax return, assistance is readily available for a price. If you are audited, you will have no problem finding someone to represent you. If you are investigated for tax fraud, you can turn to an attorney who specializes in tax work to help you. But if you are delinquent in paying the IRS or in filing a tax return, you have no where to go!

The tax industry has forgotten the delinquent taxpayer, and the IRS is aware of it. Every Revenue Officer is aware of it. Every

Revenue Officer's manager is aware of it. There are few accountants, CPAs, tax attorneys, or tax practitioners who are knowledgeable enough in the procedures of the Collection Division to be of service to delinquent taxpayers.

So the balance that exists in every other facet of government authority does not exist for delinquent taxpayers. Because so few taxpayers are aware of their rights under the law and so few of them have the benefit or representation to help them exercise their rights, some individual Revenue Officers will take advantage of them. The following chapters will tell you how to protect yourself from that situation by giving you the information you need to know to balance the equation of power between you and the IRS. You will learn exactly what your rights are in each situation, what the official IRS policy is, and what procedure to expect. Equipped with that knowledge, you will be able to know when you are being abused or harassed unnecessarily or treated unfairly.

The second step in the path toward self-protection is knowing where to turn when you feel that your rights have been abused or that IRS policy has been violated. Many taxpayers don't complain about their treatment because they mistakenly believe they have no rights and therefore must endure whatever the IRS dishes out.

SURVIVAL RULE ▬▬▬▬▬▬▬▬▬▬▬▬▬▬▬▬▬▬▬▬▬▬▬▬▬▬▬▬▬▬▬

Never hesitate to complain about your treatment if you believe that someone within the IRS has violated any of your rights or has overstepped IRS policy.

▬▬▬

There is a natural order of progression in making complaints. The IRS has a program to handle complaints involving problems that aren't resolved to your satisfaction. It is called the Problem Resolution Program, and every district has a Problem Resolution Officer who heads the program. Anyone within the IRS can tell you how to use the program, but complaints of abusive treatment and violations of IRS policy are not within the province of the Problem Resolution Officer. Therefore you may have to proceed along these lines:

- Your first complaint should be with the Revenue Officer's manager. Every Revenue Officer has one, and it would be to your benefit to know who that person is. Since the manager is the one who must approve of the handling of your case, you will find out if your treatment is the result of his marching orders or the result of the Revenue Officers's own doing.

* If that does not work, then you should go to higher-level management. The order of progression then goes to the Field Branch Chief, the Collection Division Chief, the Assistant District Director, and then to the District Director. These officials can often be reached by telephone during an emergency. Any IRS employee can supply you with their phone number or mailing address.

* In a real emergency you may have to call your representative in Congress. He may not be able to get a seizure released right away, but a telephone call from his office to the District Director's office will at least mean that someone higher up must review the case to determine what is going on.

SURVIVAL RULE ▬▬▬▬▬▬▬▬▬▬▬▬▬▬▬▬▬▬▬▬▬▬▬▬▬▬▬▬▬▬▬

If you suspect that what is happening to you involves an integrity problem of the Revenue Officer, a violation of any law, or a serious breach of IRS policy, you should contact the IRS's Regional Inspector in the Office of Internal Security. (See the list at the end of the chapter.)

▬▬▬

Although Regional Inspectors don't like to become involved in spats between Revenue Officers and taxpayers, they do want to know whenever the actions of an IRS employee may be a violation of the law.

One more note: Tax attorneys can be helpful if you are interested in filing a suit against an IRS employee, or in obtaining an injunction to prevent some type of enforcement action, or if you need representation before a court. But they are not necessarily knowledgeable in the procedures of the Collection Division, and so they may not be helpful and can be quite expensive if your problem is not out of the ordinary. And, of course, you may not be able to tell if your problem is out of the ordinary unless you read the chapters in this book that pertain to your problem.

An attorney or a tax practitioner, however, may be able to help you in a subtle way even if he is not knowledgeable in collection procedures. Some Revenue Officers, particularly new ones, are not confident of their own abilities and sometimes back down when the taxpayer's representative intervenes. They have a subconscious fear that the representative may know more than they do and therefore may cause them problems or trouble. But experienced and knowledgeable Revenue Officers don't let tax attorneys or CPAs affect their judgment and often view the taxpayer's expense of having a representative as a waste of money.

DELINQUENT TAXPAYERS DO HAVE RIGHTS

Buried deep within the Internal Revenue Manual are these rights recognized by the IRS as arising from the Internal Revenue Code, IRS policies, and IRS regulations.

You have the right to:

- prompt, courteous, and impartial treatment.
- an explanation of the collection process.
- know certain information as provided under the Privacy Act of 1974.
- confidentiality.
- representation.
- request that your case be transferred to another IRS office.
- request and receive receipts for any payment and copies of any agreement.
- have tax penalties and interest abated if they are not owed.
- file a claim for a refund or a credit.
- file a suit for a refund if the claim is rejected.
- submit an offer in compromise. (See Chapter 7.)
- appeal a decision or an action of an IRS employee to his immediate supervisor.
- designate the application of a payment made voluntarily. (See explanation in Chapter 9 on why this can be important to a corporation.)

USING A POWER OF ATTORNEY

The IRS has to be careful not to violate your rights by disclosing to other persons certain information that is prohibited by law from being disclosed without proper authorization from you. IRS employees can be held personally liable for an unauthorized disclosure of confidential tax return information. It is for this reason that they will require you to sign a power of attorney over to your representative if you want the representative to either negotiate for you or to discuss your tax problem.

The IRS has two different types of powers of attorney. Form 2848, "Power of Attorney," is to be used by you when you want another person to receive confidential information and to perform any of the following acts:

* to receive refund checks
* to execute waivers
* to execute consents extending the statute of limitations
* to execute closing agreements, and
* to delegate authority, or to substitute another representative.

If you give Form 2848 to any person who is not an attorney, a CPA, or an enrolled agent, it must either be witnessed and signed by two disinterested persons or it must be notarized.

IRS Form 2848–D, "Authorization and Declaration," can be used by you in all other circumstances that only involve the *receipt of confidential tax information*. With Form 2848–D you are not really relinquishing any rights. You are only authorizing someone else to receive information from the IRS about your tax problem.

You have the right to select anyone you want to represent you before the Collection Division, even though IRS regulations may indicate otherwise. IRS regulations only allow properly authorized persons to *practice* before the service. This means lawyers, CPAs, and enrolled agents. Enrolled agents are registered with the IRS for the purpose of representing taxpayers before the service. They must qualify either by passing an exam or by virtue of their experience within IRS.

IRS regulations, however, also give the Commissioner the power to authorize any person to represent another without being an enrolled agent. Section 5155.1:(5) of the Internal Revenue Manual states that "unenrolled persons (other than attorneys and CPAs) may qualify for practice before the Service if they present evidence of their qualifications to do so."

This can become a bit complicated, since IRS regulations also restrict to certain categories those unenrolled persons who would qualify. In actuality, though, most Revenue Officers don't pay any attention to those regulations (mainly because they don't know about them, although they are listed in "Treasury Department Circular 230") and will honor any power of attorney properly signed by you.

So it often doesn't matter whom you pick to represent you as long as the IRS hasn't suspended that person from practicing before them, and as long as you have properly authorized such representation.

An original (true) copy of the power of attorney (Form 2848) or a tax-information authorization (Form 2848-D) must be filed with each IRS office in which your representative is to represent you or to receive your confidential tax information. If you need help in completing either form, obtain an instruction sheet from your local IRS office.

(See Form 2848 on the following pages.)

Form **2848**
(Rev. July 1976)
Department of the Treasury
Internal Revenue Service

Power of Attorney

(See the separate Instructions for Forms 2848 and 2848–D.)

Name, identifying number, and address including ZIP code of taxpayer(s)

hereby appoints (Name, address including ZIP code, and telephone number of appointee(s)) (See Treasury Department Circular No. 230 as amended (31 C.F.R. Part 10), Regulations Governing the Practice of Attorneys, Certified Public Accountants, and Enrolled Agents before the Internal Revenue Service, for persons recognized to practice before the Internal Revenue Service.)

as attorney(s)-in-fact to represent the taxpayer(s) before any office of the Internal Revenue Service for the following Internal Revenue tax matters (specify the type(s) of tax and year(s) or period(s) (date of death if estate tax)):

The attorney(s)-in-fact (or either of them) are authorized, subject to revocation, to receive confidential information and to perform on behalf of the taxpayer(s) the following acts for the above tax matters:

(Strike through any of the following which are not granted.)

To receive, but not to endorse and collect, checks in payment of any refund of Internal Revenue taxes, penalties, or interest. (See "Refund checks" on page 2 of the separate instructions.)

To execute waivers (including offers of waivers) of restrictions on assessment or collection of deficiencies in tax and waivers of notice of disallowance of a claim for credit or refund.

To execute consents extending the statutory period for assessment or collection of taxes.

To execute closing agreements under section 7121 of the Internal Revenue Code.

To delegate authority or to substitute another representative.

Other acts (specify) _____

Send copies of notices and other written communications addressed to the taxpayer(s) in proceedings involving the above matters to (Name, address including ZIP code, and telephone number):

and

_____
(Specify to whom granted, date, and address including ZIP code, or refer to attached copies of earlier powers and authorizations.)

This power of attorney revokes all earlier powers of attorney and tax information authorizations on file with the same Internal Revenue Service office for the same matters and years or periods covered by this form, except the following:

Signature of or for taxpayer(s)

If signed by a corporate officer, partner, or fiduciary on behalf of the taxpayer, I certify that I have the authority to execute this power of attorney on behalf of the taxpayer.

_____   _____
(Signature)   (Title, if applicable)   (Date)

_____   _____
(Signature)   (Title, if applicable)   (Date)

(The applicable portion of the back page must also be completed.)   Form **2848** (Rev. 7–76)

REGIONAL INSPECTORS
ADDRESSES AND TELEPHONE NUMBERS

Regional Inspector
Internal Revenue Service
Room 8508
550 Main Street
Cincinnati, OH 45202

Phone: 513–684–3562/64/66

Regional Inspector
Internal Revenue Service
W. J. Green Federal Building
Room 4218
600 Arch Street
Philadelphia, PA 19106

Phone: 215–597–0928/29

Regional Inspector
Internal Revenue Service
4th Floor
221 Courtland Street, N.E.
Atlanta, GA 30043

Phone: 404–221–6543

Regional Inspector
Internal Revenue Service
LB–82
7839 Churchill Way
Dallas, TX 75251

Phone: 214–767–5035

Regional Inspector
Internal Revenue Service
Room 1646
35 E. Wacker Drive
Chicago, IL 60601

Phone: 312–886–5820

Regional Inspector
Internal Revenue Service
Room 1407
26 Federal Plaza
New York, NY 10008

Phone: 212–264–9130/31

Regional Inspector
Internal Revenue Service
Suite 350–S
333 Market Street
San Francisco, CA 94105

Phone: 415–974–7200

I

WHEN YOU HAVE
A PROBLEM

1

Surviving If You Have Not Filed

How to secretly come out of the closet successfully

HOW THE IRS CATCHES NONFILERS

In July 1979 the General Accounting Office issued a report entitled "Who's Not Filing Income Tax Returns?" The study attempted to determine how many taxpayers did not file in 1972, the most current year for which complete data were available. Although 68 million taxpayers were required to file that year, an estimated 5 million taxpayers did not file even though they had a legal requirement to do so. These 5 million taxpayers owed the IRS about $2 billion in taxes. Through various programs the IRS was able to secure delinquent returns from about 600,000 taxpayers, or 12 percent of the nonfiling population. Expressed another way, in 1972 the IRS missed 88 percent of the nonfiling taxpayers.

In 1981 the Collection Division secured over 1.5 million delinquent returns in all tax categories. These were returns that the IRS had to go after, or returns that were filed after the IRS had sent notices of noncompliance, and in many cases after the IRS had telephoned or visited the taxpayers. But this was the tip of the iceberg.

Many more returns were filed after they were due but before the IRS came after them. In 1981 the IRS assessed delinquency penalties on 4 million tax returns. Over one million of these were Forms 1040 and 1040A. As you can see, the extent of the nonfiling problem is enormous. It is also obvious that the IRS cannot put all these people in jail.

Catching nonfilers is a job that depends mostly on computers. The IRS has perhaps the world's most massive computer system, which it uses extensively in a number of nonfiling projects.

* *Information Returns Processing (IRP)*. In the early 1970s the IRS received 300 to 400 million information statements each year. These are W–2 statements, which report income earned and taxes withheld, and 1099's, which report income such as interest, dividends, and royalties. Little did the public know at that time that the IRS was not making full use of those statements. Almost all of the paper information statements sent to the IRS were burned. The IRS publicly admitted that they were not able to file and use all these documents properly because of limited resources. Only a small percentage of information statements were saved and used for various listing and program purposes.

    When Donald Alexander became Commissioner of the IRS and learned of this, he became quite upset. When he told members of Congress, they became upset. When it became public knowledge, the IRS stepped up its program to encourage large businesses to file their information statements on computer tapes.

    For the tax years 1974 through 1977, the IRS processed almost 50 percent of the information statements they received. Because of the high cost of transcription, they only matched 10 percent to 15 percent of the paper documents, but they matched almost all the information statements submitted on computer tapes. Matching entails comparing the information reported on these statements submitted by employers and payers with the information reported on taxpayers' tax returns.

    The IRS now has an arrangement with the Social Security Administration (SSA) to process W–2 documents onto computer tape. The SSA then supplies the income information to the IRS. In 1981 the IRS received over 645 million information statements, of which 336 million were submitted on computer tape and 184 million were W–2's received from the SSA. All the information statements sent in on computer tape and 26 percent of those submitted on paper were matched. The IRS says that in 1982, 84 percent of all information statements will have been matched.

Matching has a twofold purpose. It is done primarily to catch underreporters, or those who do not report all of their income. In 1981 the IRS discovered over 1.2 million discrepancies between income reported on tax returns and income reported on information returns. Each year the IRS collects an additional $500 million this way. Secondarily, matching reveals the names of those taxpayers who have earned income during the year but who did not file a tax return to report that income. These leads constitute the bulk of the resources that the IRS uses to find taxpayers who have not filed. In 1981, 1.6 million taxpayers were discovered not to have filed their tax returns and were sent delinquency notices.

- *Returns Compliance Programs (RCPs).* The IRS uses these programs on a limited scale to focus on a particular area of noncompliance. For example, the Highway Use Tax Program (HUT) has been used for ten to fifteen years to find truck drivers who are liable for the Highway Use Tax but who have not filed Form 2290. Other Returns Compliance Programs are usually oriented around employment or excise taxes. In early 1980 the IRS implemented the Self-employed Professionals Compliance Program in an attempt to locate doctors, dentists, and attorneys who may be nonfilers. Names of persons within these occupational categories are obtained from commercial sources and then matched against IRS records.
- *The Individual Master File (IMF) Stopfiler Program.* This program includes IRS employees, most self-employed individuals and those with capital gains and losses, individuals with credit balances or who requested extensions but did not file, and nonfilers with a high adjusted gross income in the previous tax year.

This program, which begins six months after the due date of Form 1040, essentially matches taxpayers who filed in the most recent year against those who filed in the previous year to discover taxpayers who did not file in the current year. IRS computers are so sophisticated that they are able to target their matching to specific selection criteria based on a high probability of success. For example, selection criteria code 21 is a matching of income tax returns reporting rents and royalties and an income of $20,000 or more.

- *Other Computer Programs.* Various other computer programs use data from a number of sources. For example, the Special Return Association Program identifies nonfilers by associating specific income information to the master file of returns filed. This program identifies:

  —cases in which Forms W–2G, "Statement for Certain Gambling Winnings," could not be associated with payers' returns. (Forms W–2G usually indicate wagering gains from casino gambling winnings or those paid by state-conducted lotteries.)

  —interest income shown on forms filed by Federal Reserve Banks upon redemption of Series H Savings Bonds acquired as a result of the conversion of Series E, F, or J Bonds to H Bonds. (Two of the forms are issued when a taxpayer elects to report interest accrued, and another form is issued when interest is paid upon redemption.)

  —taxpayers who have realized tax-preference income from the exercise of an option. (Forms 3921, "Exercise of a Qualified or Restricted Stock Option," are filed under section 6039(a)(1) of the Tax Code by corporations that transfer a share of stock to any person pursuant to his exercise of a qualified stock option or restricted stock option.)

- *Informants.* The IRS receives a handful of tips every year from individuals who report on others they know or suspect to be nonfilers.

SITUATION: TYPICAL NONFILING SCENARIO

Q. *I did not file my tax return for last year. One of my employers did not send me my W–2 statement until after the April 15 deadline. Now I'm scared and I don't know what to do. What will the IRS do to me if they find out? Will I go to jail?*

Your situation is typical of what happens to many taxpayers each year. You have no need to be scared because your nonfiling was not intentional or "willful." The IRS prosecutes only those nonfiling cases that are "willful." Section 7203 of the Internal Revenue Code makes it a misdemeanor with a fine of not more than $25,000 and/or imprisonment of not more than one year in jail to *willfully* fail to file a tax return.

In order for the IRS to prosecute you under section 7203 they must prove three things:

- You must have been required by law to file the tax return.
- You must have failed to file the return when it was due.
- Your failure to file must have been *willful*.

The first two requirements are not hard for the IRS to prove. The Tax Code specifies that you have a legal requirement to file when your income exceeds a certain level, and it doesn't make any difference if you are due a refund or you have to pay. (Refer to the table on page 36 to see if you were required to file a tax return for a previous year.) Note that the filing requirements change every year. The IRS does *not* want you to file a tax return if you have no tax liability, if your income is below the specified level, and if you are not due a refund. It costs the IRS a lot of money to process a tax return, and so they would rather not tie up their resources processing a lot of paper that does not need to be processed.

The second requirement is easy to prove, too. Obviously, if the IRS has not received your tax return by the due date then there is a failure to file. A due date can be extended very easily. Usually the best course of action for someone who has not received a W–2 statement is:

- to notify the IRS if you have not received the W–2 by the middle of February so that they can attempt to obtain it for you or give you instructions on how to file without it, or
- to request an automatic four-month extension of time to file on Form 4868. Additional time after that can be requested by filing Form 2688. The purpose of filing for an extension of time to file is to prevent the possibility of penalties for failure to file and to establish your intention to file.

FILING REQUIREMENTS FOR EACH CALENDAR YEAR

(Individuals with income at these levels or higher must file a tax return.)

	1965–69	1970–71	1972–74	1975	1976	1977–78	1979–83
1. Single person under 65	$ 600	$1,700	$2,050	$2,350	$2,450	$2,950	$3,300
2. Single person, 65 or older	1,200	2,300	2,800	3,100	3,200	3,700	4,300
3. Married couple filing jointly	1,200	2,300	2,800	3,400	3,600	4,700	5,400
4. Married couple filing jointly with one spouse 65 or older	1,200	2,900	3,550	4,150	4,350	5,450	6,400
5. Married couple filing jointly with both spouses 65 or older	1,200	3,500	4,300	4,900	5,100	6,200	7,400
6. Surviving spouse	600	1,700	2,050	2,650	2,850	3,950	4,400
7. Surviving spouse 65 or older	1,200	2,300	2,800	3,400	3,600	4,700	5,400
8. Married filing separately	600	600	750	750	750	750	1,000
9. Self-employment income	400	400	400	400	400	400	400

The need to prove *willful* intent is usually the most difficult requirement for the IRS in bringing a case to trial. However, unlike a tax evasion case, the IRS does not need to prove an evasion motive. In failure-to-file cases, *willful* means purposeful or intentional, and the IRS must prove that the taxpayer not only knew he was required to file but failed to do so because he did not want the IRS to know how much he owed. To establish willfulness the IRS takes the position that there *must be a substantial tax liability.* It is for this reason that the IRS will not prosecute a failure-to-file case when the government owes the taxpayer a refund or when there is no legitimate tax liability.

If you are expecting a refund, you should go ahead and file for it. The sooner you file, the quicker you will receive your check.

SURVIVAL RULE ▬▬▬▬▬▬▬▬▬▬▬▬▬▬▬▬▬▬▬▬▬▬▬▬▬▬▬

You must file a tax return to get a refund, even though the amount of income you earned was below the legal level requiring you to file.

If you have not filed, you are not more than five months late, and you owe additional tax, you should file as soon as possible to stop the buildup in penalties. The IRS charges 5 percent a month up to a maximum of 25 percent of the unpaid balance for not filing on time.

SURVIVAL RULE ▬▬▬▬▬▬▬▬▬▬▬▬▬▬▬▬▬▬▬▬▬▬▬▬▬▬▬

If you need additional time to prepare your return and can reasonably estimate how much you might owe, pay this estimated amount while requesting an extension of time to file— before *the due date.*

If the entire amount of tax is paid before the due date but the actual filing occurs after the due date, there will not be a penalty for failing to file the return timely. The failure-to-file penalty is based on what is owed on the due date. But be very careful about a particular quirk in the law.

The law states that the failure-to-file penalty will be assessed on the balance owed on the due date and will be assessed each month until the return is filed or five months later, whichever first occurs. If you pay the balance you owe *after* the due date but *before* the return is filed, you will still be penalized the full penalty up to the date of filing or the five months, whichever first occurs. This happens to a few people each year who mistakenly think that they can beat the non-filing penalty by paying before they file, but after the due date.

DECIDING WHOM TO PROSECUTE

You will probably never hear the IRS publicly admit how they choose cases for prosecution, but IRS enforcement employees know the criteria. As in tax evasion cases, the important ingredients are publicity and high visibility. The wealthier the taxpayer, the more established he is in the community, and the more visible he is to the media, the more vulnerable he is to an IRS prosecution. The IRS believes that publicity of enforcement helps to strengthen "voluntary compliance," especially if the publicity occurs during the January-to-April filing season. It is not uncommon to see indictments all across the country issued in the last few weeks before April 15.

The other main criteria are a pattern of delinquency and a substantial liability. The more years that the taxpayer is delinquent and the more tax that is owed, the better the IRS likes the case. All cases involving a criminal violation of the Tax Code are investigated by the Criminal Investigations Division (C.I.D.). Cases that do not conform to C.I.D. criteria are labeled *de minimus*, meaning that the C.I.D. thinks there is not enough money involved to make prosecution worthwhile. The IRS also considers jury appeal as one of its prosecuting factors: The more obvious and the more flagrant the case, the more jury appeal it will have. Cases of low-dollar tax liability are not apt to have high jury appeal.

The IRS is normally interested only in prosecuting those cases for which the nonfiling has occurred at least twice and for which the amount of tax owed is fairly substantial. This helps the IRS to show that the taxpayer perpetrated some harm on the government by failing to file. Obviously, a taxpayer who owes a small amount has harmed the government very little, but there is no guarantee that the IRS won't prosecute a small-dollar or single-year delinquency case.

WHY THERE IS A DELAY IN CATCHING NONFILERS

Even though the IRS relies on several programs to catch non-filers, few cases involved in these programs ever result in a prosecution for nonfiling. In fact, of the 1.5 million delinquent returns secured in 1981, the C.I.D. prosecuted only 409 cases for nonfiling of tax returns. There are probably more people convicted for trespassing than there are for not filing a tax return, even in view of the extensive numbers of nonfilers.

The Collection Division has the primary responsibility for pursuing nonfilers. Revenue Officers who encounter nonfiling cases in which indications of fraud are believed to be evident are supposed to back away and refer the case to the Criminal Investigations Division for investigation. But the C.I.D. is often reluctant to accept nonfiling cases referred to them from Revenue Officers unless the cases show good prosecution potential on the surface. They would rather devote their time and resources to pursuing cases that have already attracted *their* attention. Special Agents in the C.I.D. get their best leads from informants and from working on various projects, but it often takes the C.I.D. several years to find nonfilers.

The Collection Division's compliance programs are designed to catch nonfilers within a couple of years after the delinquency occurs. From six to fifteen months after the due date, the IRS starts sending notices to known nonfilers. Up to four notices are sent during an eleven-week period. If the return is not filed within another couple of weeks after the fourth notice has been sent, the IRS computer prints out an assignment called a Taxpayer Delinquency Investigation (TDI) with a supplemental sheet listing all the information the IRS computer has on that taxpayer.

These assignments are sent to district offices where collection employees, called Process Reviewers and Revenue Representatives, make phone calls to attempt to obtain the delinquent returns. If they are not successful, the assignments are sent to Revenue Officers in the field who then have ultimate responsibility for closing the cases.

Once a case is assigned to a Revenue Officer, he is supposed to be on the lookout for fraud. Trained to identify the "badges of fraud," a Revenue Officer is required to make an initial determination if fraud exists. Some officers think every case has fraud potential, but most experienced ones know that the C.I.D. will only investigate "solid cases."

This is why, on every personal contact, the officer will quietly and nonchalantly observe your house, furniture, and automobile to determine your standard of living. Officers know that an attorney who lives in a $200,000 house and drives a Mercedes Benz 450 SEL would be a more likely prosecution case than a school teacher who earns $15,000 a year, lives in an apartment, and drives a 1974 Volkswagen.

The fraud determination is mostly a farce because officers really don't have the time to look for "badges of fraud" or do the analysis necessary to find them. As long as the taxpayer doesn't admit to willfully not filing and as long as the taxpayer's standard of living is not too far above middle-class standards, the officer almost always assumes that fraud isn't present.

If the Revenue Officer does suspect fraud, he will *not* ask you to file the returns. In IRS parlance asking you to file is known as "solicitation," which can kill a possible referral to the C.I.D. for investigation of criminal prosecution. *IRS policy prohibits prosecuting a nonfiling case when the returns have been solicited.* So if you were ever looking for a clue to determine whether the IRS was interested in prosecuting you for not filing, you should pay attention to what the Revenue Officer or other collection employee does after he asks you why you have not filed. If he says "Fine, thanks," and disappears or terminates the conversation, you should start worrying because it means that he is going to report your statement to the C.I.D. for them to determine if they want the case. If the Revenue Officer asks you to file the returns and gives you a filing date, he has already decided that indications of fraud are not present and that he will not refer your case to the C.I.D.

Cases referred to the C.I.D. are reviewed for prosecution potential. If the C.I.D. decides to pursue a case, an investigation is begun that could take several months or several years depending on the complexity of the case and other priorities. After the case has been worked up by a Special Agent, it is sent through channels for further review within the IRS. This internal review takes several months. Then the case is sent to the Department of Justice for another review, which also takes several months. By the time the U.S. Attorney in the field receives the case, it could be several years after the tax-payer's delinquency was first discovered.

Another reason that could explain why the IRS may not catch a nonfiler for several years lies in the methodology used to catch non-filers. The IRS is aware that there are millions of self-employed tax-payers around the country who have never filed a tax return. Considered part of the "tax underground" or the "subterranean economy," these self-employed nonfilers are rarely caught; their noncompliance is usually discovered accidentally or because an informant has turned them in. For a long time the IRS relied heavily on the Social Security Administration's computers to help find nonfilers. Finding self-employed nonfilers, however, was beyond the potential of the SSA computer system because self-employed individuals must file Form 1040 to earn Social Security credits. Another gap that occurred until the mid-1970s involved employees of the federal government who were not covered under the Social Security System. Some government agencies were not filing W–2s on computer tape, and therefore the IRS was not able to catch those employees who had not filed.

The bulk of the time lost in prosecuting nonfilers is usually caused by the slowly grinding wheels of the bureaucracy. Because the IRS does not like to lose cases, they rarely go out on a limb. Before they take a case to court, they want to make sure that they have covered every angle and that they can win. They believe that their review process has been responsible in helping them win so many cases in court. Cases that do not appear to have a reasonably high chance of success are not prosecuted.

About six years ago a tax protestor publicly prided himself on not filing a tax return for many years and getting away with it. Around April 15 of every year the newspapers and television reporters interviewed him and gave his story a big play. He told boldly how he made $40,000 a year doing consultant work, how he had all of his fees paid in cash, and how he had never filed a tax return and that the IRS could not do anything about it. Meanwhile, several Revenue Officers were trying to collect a substantial sum of tax money from him based on income the Special Agents knew he had received. For some reason the Criminal Investigations Division had decided not to recommend prosecuting him, preferring instead to monitor him year after year. The Revenue Officers who worked the case said that it was difficult to collect any taxes because the protestor was so elusive, but it was clear that the man never earned $40,000 a year.

This went on for several years until IRS Commissioner Donald Alexander saw the protestor on TV and called the local IRS office wanting to know why they had not done anything on the case. I suppose the Special Agents were waiting for the case to come gift wrapped, but after Alexander's call it took less than a month for the protestor to be indicted.

The IRS charged him with six years of willful failure to file. On the witness stand he cried like a baby and claimed he never made enough money to be required to file. The IRS was able to show otherwise and he was convicted. Interestingly enough, even after the conviction and after the jail sentence he was claiming that the IRS had never been able to touch him.

This story is an example of a case that the IRS worked on for several years before charges were brought. To the public it must have appeared that the protestor had slipped by the IRS for many years before getting caught. But the truth was that the IRS not only knew what he had been doing all along but had been putting up with it for many years.

SITUATION: SURVIVING SEVERAL YEARS OF NONFILING

Q. *I have not filed a tax return for the past five years. It started five years ago when I was too busy in my job to prepare my return and I couldn't file on time. After the filing deadline passed, I was scared to file. Each filing season since then I'd prepare the tax return, but I wouldn't file it because I was afraid that they would find out about the year I didn't file. I now have all five years' tax returns in my desk drawer. For the first three years I have refunds that total over $2,000. For the next two years I owe about $200. What should I do? Am I in any trouble for not filing all these returns?*

Cases like yours are not unusual. It is not uncommon for the IRS to eventually find someone like yourself who has not filed for several years. I once located a taxpayer who had not filed for eleven years. Just like you he had kept all his W–2s "just in case," even though he had not prepared the returns. We sat down one day and prepared returns for all eleven years. For the first six years he had more than $700 in refunds that he never got because the statute of limitations had expired. For the following three years he owed money that had to be paid. (Although there is a statute of limitations on getting a refund, there is no statute on owing the tax. A return can be filed twenty years late showing a balance due, and it would have to be paid. The only statute of limitations that applies gives the IRS six years to collect it after filing. After the sixth year it may not have to be paid.) For the next two years his taxes had been over-withheld, and the refunds he had coming back to him not only paid for the three years he owed but gave him some money left over. The following year he came into the office and filed a tax return showing a refund of over $1,000. He admitted that this problem had been bothering him for all eleven years. He had suffered two heart attacks, an ulcer, a nervous breakdown, and countless sleepless nights worrying about what would happen if he ever got caught. I assured him that he had nothing to worry about.

Let me repeat: The IRS is not normally interested in prosecuting nonfiling cases for which there is not a substantial amount owed. Your situation may well turn out to be similar to this one. Obviously, the statute of limitations has expired on the first couple of returns, and so you will not get those refunds. The statute of limitations gives you three years from the due date of the return, including any extensions, to file a return and obtain a refund. If you do not file the returns now, it will only be a question of time before the IRS comes looking for them.

WAYS OF ENFORCING THE LAW

There are two major ways of enforcing compliance with nonfilers: criminal prosecution and civil enforcement.

Criminal Prosecution: There is a statutory period of limitations within which the IRS can bring forth a case for willful failure to file a tax return, under section 7203 of the Internal Revenue Code. The statute of limitations is six years, which means that the IRS cannot prosecute someone for "willfully failing to file" a tax return after the sixth anniversary of the due date of the return.

Civil Enforcement: The IRS also has an enforcement policy for delinquency cases in which no fraud is believed to be present. Every Revenue Officer investigating a delinquent taxpayer is required to:

- determine the extent of the delinquency and the amount of liability owed.
- find out why the returns were not filed.
- determine if there are indications of fraud.
- advise the taxpayer, if there are no indications of fraud, that he is required to file *all* delinquent returns regardless of the number of years in arrears.

At that point the Revenue Officer will set a date by which the returns must be filed. If the returns are not filed as directed, the Revenue Officer must then decide on the *extent of enforcement.* IRM 5(11)41:(3) states:

As a general rule, enforcement should not extend beyond six prior years preceding the date that the investigation is being conducted. Enforcement for shorter or longer periods may be determined where such action appears to be in the best interest of the government from the standpoint of reasonableness, beneficial effect on compliance, and appropriate use of resources.

Revenue Officers are also given the discretion to *not enforce* a nonfiling case when they are "satisfied there would be no 'net tax due' for the period(s) for which the delinquency exists." For self-employed taxpayers this is not possible without preparing the returns. For salaried taxpayers the TDI supplemental sheet usually has a record of the amount of money you earned, the number of exemptions claimed on your last tax return filed, and sometimes how much money was withheld. With this information the Revenue Officer can determine if you would be getting a refund or how much you would owe without allowing for itemized deductions. If the Revenue Officer is convinced that you had no other sources of income, then he may decide not to proceed with enforcement on those cases in which you would have no "net tax due." To have no "net tax due" you would have to have had credits such as withholding or estimated tax payments equal to or more than the amount of your estimated tax liability. If you clearly have a refund coming to you, you must file for it, and the IRS is not going to expend any more resources than necessary to enforce a filing requirement if you do not owe any tax.

Civil enforcement is applied by use of the IRS's summons power. Congress has given the IRS power to issue summonses to persons either to compel them to give testimony or to produce their books and records for the purposes of preparing a return when one hasn't been prepared or to determine the liability of any person for any internal revenue tax. (There are other purposes for the issuance of a summons, and those are thoroughly covered in Chapter 6.)

After the Revenue Officer has determined there is no fraud potential and he has obtained the information he needs to know, he will give you a deadline by which time you must file all your delinquent returns. Usually he will ask you how long it will take you either to prepare the return or to have the return prepared by an accountant or tax practitioner, and the deadline will be based on the time frame you indicate. Be careful not to box yourself into a time period you cannot keep. Allow yourself plenty of time, and if you plan to have someone else prepare the returns, you are advised to find out from the preparer how long it will take to prepare them. Be advised that you may have a very difficult time finding a preparer between January 1 and April 15 who will have the time to prepare them for you. Delinquent returns usually take longer to prepare because the preparer must do more research on the prior years' tax laws to complete them properly.

Revenue Officers will usually give you a deadline that you agree on unless it is perceived that you are unduly delaying your responsibility to file. The deadline is supposed to be far enough into the future to allow you a reasonable period of time to prepare the return. If you are unable to file your delinquent return by the deadline that has been agreed on, it is very important that you communicate this to the Revenue Officer and request an additional period of time.

SURVIVAL RULE ━━━━━━━━━━━━━━━━━━━━━━━━━━━━━━━━━━━

Always request additional time if you cannot meet a Revenue Officer's filing deadline.

━━

If you do not file your return by the deadline and you have not been granted additional time to file, the Revenue Officer must proceed with civil enforcement. Provided that there are no extenuating circumstances in the case, the Revenue Officer will then serve you a summons directing you to appear at a specific date and time at the local IRS office with the books and records specified in the summons. The date of appearance will be at least eleven days from the date the summons is served.

The summons cannot compel you to prepare the return, or returns. It can only require you to give testimony or produce certain books and records. At the time scheduled for you to appear with your books and records, the Revenue Officer will have a Revenue Agent or Tax Auditor standing by that day to prepare the returns, provided they are not too complicated.

Section 6020(a) of the Internal Revenue Code gives the IRS the authority to prepare tax returns from information you furnish. If the return is fairly simple and can be prepared in a couple of hours, the audit employee will prepare the return while you are in the office. Returns that are not any more complicated than a 1040A or a 1040 with a Schedule A may be prepared by the Revenue Officer issuing the summons. If you are a self-employed individual who is required to file a Schedule C, you will have to leave your books and records so that the return can be prepared.

When the return has been prepared, the IRS employee will ask you to sign the return. After you have signed the return, it is sent to the appropriate service center for processing and assessment. Notices are then sent on those returns showing a balance due. By law the IRS has three years to assess the return and six years from the date of assessment to collect any balance due.

The assessment is the legal procedure of recording the tax liability in the IRS's records. It provides the basis for the statutory authority enabling the IRS to collect by seizure. (Assessment is also covered in more detail in Chapters 2 and 5.)

If you refuse to sign the return after it has been prepared, the IRS will not be deterred. Section 6020(b) of the Code allows an IRS employee to sign the return on your behalf. Subsection (2) states that "any return so made and subscribed . . . shall be *prima facie* good and sufficient for all legal purposes." Revenue Officers are not allowed to sign *income* tax returns, but they may sign employment or excise tax returns. Income tax returns can only be signed by a Revenue Agent in the Examination Division.

Before a tax return signed under Section 6020(b) can be assessed, the Examination Division must follow the same appeals procedure as it does for audit deficiency cases. So if you disagree with the proposed assessment, you may contest it through the normal appeals channels.

SITUATION: FILING LATE BUT EXPECTING A REFUND

Q. *I haven't filed or prepared my tax return for last year, but I should have a refund coming because I'm always over-withheld. What kind of a penalty will they sock me with when I do file?*

First of all you should never make an assumption that you are going to receive a refund just because you have in the past. The way the tax rates and the tax withholding tables change so frequently, your tax situation could easily change without your being aware of it. Refunds in prior years are not necessarily a guarantee that you will receive one this year.

If you do file your tax return late and the return shows a refund, the statute of limitations for a refund is three years from the due date of the return. If you send in the return past the third anniversary date, the IRS will keep your refund.

Some taxpayers who have filed late and gotten refunds have also gotten interest paid on that refund because of a strange quirk in the law that was recently corrected. The Code gave the IRS forty-five days in which to process a tax return and issue a refund check without having to pay interest. After the forty-fifth day the IRS was required to pay interest on refunds computed not from the date of filing but back to the date of payment. In the case of employees who had taxes withheld during the year, the IRS computed interest back to the April 15 following the year the taxes were withheld, which is the due date of the return. Taxpayers have been known to receive as much as three years' worth of interest. However, the Tax Equity and Fiscal Responsibility Bill of 1982 changed that, and now interest will only be computed back to the date of filing.

Delinquently filed tax returns are assessed a filing penalty of 5 percent a month up to a maximum of 25 percent of the unpaid balance, computed on the unpaid balance due on the return's due date. For example, if your tax return shows a balance due of $1,000, the IRS can fine you up to $250 for not filing on time. The IRS will also assess a failure-to-pay penalty of 0.5 percent per month up to a maximum of fifty months or 25 percent. Both the delinquency and failure-to-pay penalties are charged per month or on a fraction of a month. On individual income tax returns due on April 15, the month begins on April 16 and follows through on the sixteenth day of each month thereafter. For example, a tax return filed on May 15 would only be assessed one month's delinquency and failure-to-pay penalty, whereas a tax return filed on May 16 would be assessed two month's delinquency and failure-to-pay penalties.

Technically the IRS is not supposed to charge the full 5 percent delinquency penalty when they are charging the 0.5 percent failure-to-pay penalty. The delinquency penalty must be reduced to 4.5 percent. But it doesn't make much difference because either way the penalties can add up to a lot of money.

In addition to the penalties, the IRS also charges interest, which is now subject to fluctuation every six months. A new interest rate took effect on January 1, 1983, with another rate effective July 1, 1983.

SURVIVAL ADVICE FOR NONFILERS

Once the IRS computer has discovered you as a nonfiler, you will be sent up to four notices requesting that you either file delinquent returns or furnish some type of proof that you have filed.

SURVIVAL RULE

If you have not filed by the time the IRS computer starts sending you notices, you should prepare the returns and file them as soon as possible.

This Survival Rule is important. It emphasizes why it is important that you file as soon as possible because the one thing the IRS computer cannot do is to suspect fraud intuitively. Think about that. IRS employees are required to determine if there is any evidence of fraud.

Their guidelines require them to ask you how much you make, how many years you are delinquent, how much tax was withheld or paid through estimated payments, and how much tax you will owe. They are also supposed to survey your life-style to determine if your social status, education, and professional stature would lead one to believe that not only should you have known to file but you didn't file because of some motive of self-interest. All of this can be avoided if the delinquent returns are filed before the computer prints out the TDI assignment and sends it to the field.

Even though every service center has a resident Special Agent whose job is to survey suspicious tax returns and catch possible fraudulent refund schemes, as far as I know the service center does not flag delinquent returns for a Special Agent's review. Therefore the probability that enforcement personnel will become involved in the case when the returns are sent to the service center is very slight. Delinquent returns, just like timely filed returns, are supposed to be sent through the normal processing pipeline. In fact, the General Accounting Office once criticized the IRS for not processing delinquent returns fast enough.

If the service center does have a referral procedure requiring the in-house Special Agent to review delinquent returns, the criteria for referral will probably pertain to either a high level of tax liability or a multiple-year filing of delinquent returns. If you have a high tax liability, you are not going to be able to do much about it. But if you owe more than one return, you should observe the following Survival Rule.

SURVIVAL RULE ▬▬▬▬▬▬▬▬▬▬▬▬▬▬▬▬▬▬▬▬▬▬▬▬▬▬▬▬▬

If you owe more than one year's return, you should file each return in a separate envelope and mail each one at least a week apart.

▬▬

There is no guarantee, of course, that this Survival Rule will keep the Criminal Investigations Division from reviewing your case, but it does minimize the chances that some service center employee will notice your multiple-year filings and refer them directly to C.I.D. Of course, if the IRS computer happens to be programmed to automatically alert the C.I.D. when multiple delinquent returns are filed, even intermittently, there is not much you can do.

Pay particular attention to the next Survival Rule.

SURVIVAL RULE ▬▬▬▬▬▬▬▬▬▬▬▬▬▬▬▬▬▬▬▬▬▬▬▬▬▬▬▬

If you are delinquent for two or more years and you owe a lot of money and would like to file but are afraid of being prosecuted, you should go to an attorney for advice rather than to an accountant.

▬▬▬

An attorney will help to calm any fears you may have by reviewing your situation with you and determining whether or not the facts and circumstances of your nonfiling warrant any concern. Your attorney cannot advise you to not file since that would be illegal and unethical. The big advantage in discussing your problem with an attorney rather than an accountant is that the law protects the attorney-client relationship by making communications between them privileged, whereas the accountant-client relationship does not have that same privilege. In other words, the IRS could not make an attorney testify about what you said if the conversation was for the purpose of obtaining legal advice.

A word of caution: An attorney who does not practice tax law may be under the false assumption that a "voluntary disclosure" affords his client some relief from prosecution. A voluntary disclosure occurs when a taxpayer comes forward and voluntarily discloses to the IRS that he has not filed. Contrary to the belief of many attorneys, the act of voluntary disclosure *does not* prevent the IRS from prosecuting the case, and no Special Agent is allowed to grant immunity to any taxpayer who makes a voluntary disclosure.

You can easily see what you are up against. Statistically, though, there is little need to worry about being prosecuted. In 1981 the IRS only brought forth charges on 1,785 cases for all types of tax violations, and jail sentences were handed out in only 802 cases. These figures represent the entire country for an entire twelve-month period.

WHAT NOT TO SAY TO A REVENUE OFFICER

Repeaters consistently file or pay their taxes late every year. They rarely have a good or a logical excuse for their lack of performance, and some repeaters will say almost anything when Revenue Officers ask them why they have not filed. They will use any inane excuse they can come up with. But the conventional wisdom of many repeating nonfilers is to admit nothing, the theory being that it is better not to tell the truth than to admit wrongdoing. From this conventional wisdom arises the next Survival Rule.

SURVIVAL RULE ▰▰▰▰▰▰▰▰▰▰▰▰▰▰▰▰▰▰▰▰▰▰▰▰▰▰▰▰▰▰▰▰▰▰▰▰

Never admit to deliberately failing to file an income tax return to any IRS employee unless you have first consulted an attorney.

It is important that you do not become confused here. I am *not* suggesting in the slightest that you falsely tell the IRS you have filed when in fact you know you have not. That tactic is used frequently, and all it causes is additional aggravation for both parties. Taxpayers become entrenched in their assertions, and Revenue Officers become firmer in their demands. Eventually the taxpayer loses when the officer begins to suspect that the taxpayer is "jerking" him around.

What I am suggesting is: In the event you are asked by an IRS employee why you did not file, *you should never admit to willfully, deliberately, or intentionally not filing.* An admission of a purposeful violation of the law is the Revenue Officer's indication of fraud that he is looking for. If you have this soul-cleansing urge to admit that you purposely did not file, then you should see your attorney first. Remember: Any excuse is better than no excuse, but don't try to insult an officer's intelligence by reciting a totally unbelievable story.

The question arises that if you file a tax return after the IRS has contacted you, aren't you in effect admitting that you didn't file originally? That may be, but it is unimportant and serves as another reason why you shouldn't persist in asserting that you filed when you know full well that you did not. Many taxpayers will insist that they have filed, but when asked to send a signed copy to be processed, they usually send the original. Original returns are not hard to detect. Some even have the peel-off label in the name and address block. Most have the IRS copy of the W–2 statement attached. That's the real clue. Some are prepared timely but were never filed, probably because the taxpayer couldn't afford to pay what he owed. It is usually easy to tell that they were prepared timely because the date and signature of the preparer show it.

The important point is to file your delinquent returns after you have been instructed to file. Remember that the IRS is only interested in prosecuting cases in which "willfulness" can be proved. Even if all 1.5 million tax returns secured by the Collection Division last year had not been filed timely because of "willfulness," the IRS only could have prosecuted a handful of cases. The IRS's strongest weapon for penalizing nonfilers is the assessment of civil penalties for failure to file, which are asserted automatically unless you can show reasonable cause. (To find out more about reasonable cause and how to get a nonfiling penalty abated, see Chapter 3.)

Surviving When You Cannot Pay

How to legally owe the IRS

THE COLLECTION PROCESS

The set of IRS procedures and methods in collecting delinquent taxes basically follows this sequence of events:

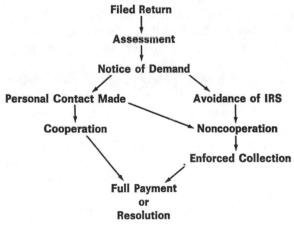

Filed Return

Assessment

Notice of Demand

Personal Contact Made   Avoidance of IRS

Cooperation   Noncooperation

Enforced Collection

Full Payment
or
Resolution

All the actions taken by the IRS during the collection process must fall within the parameters of authority granted by the Internal Revenue Code (IRC). The code gives the IRS authority to make assessments, file liens, enforce collection through seizure actions or whatever enforcement action needs to be taken to collect the tax.

The process begins when a tax return is filed at an IRS service center. Each tax return is processed step by step through the "pipeline," a name depicting the flow of paper through the processing system. The important step is the assessment process, which is the recording of your tax liability into the records of the IRS computer. The assessment starts the legal ball rolling. (The importance of the assessment will be discussed more fully in Chapter 5.)

Assessments for tax, interest and penalties, are posted into the computer where they are matched against credits, such as withholding and estimated tax payments. Any accounts showing a balance due are automatically sent a notice demanding full payment within ten days. From one to four notices are issued over a three-month period. The last notice is boldly entitled "Past Due Final Notice" and is the final warning sent by the IRS computer. It bluntly states that payment must be made within ten days or "enforcement action can be taken at any time." Further warnings specify that "Salary or wages due you may be levied upon . . . by serving a notice of levy on your employer. Bank accounts, receivables, commissions, or other kinds of income you have are also subject to levy. Property or rights to property, such as automobiles, may also be seized and sold to satisfy your tax liability." The warnings are real, and the IRS is not kidding. They can legally do everything they say they can do. And unlike other creditors, the IRS does not need to go to court to attach your paycheck or bank account.

While the computer is spitting out those nasty notices, you may receive several phone calls from various IRS employees, each making a demand for full payment. If your account is not paid in full several weeks after the last notice has been sent, the computer prints out a coded document called a Taxpayer Delinquent Account (TDA). These TDAs serve as assignments to the district and local collection employees. If full collection is not obtained by the employees in the district office, the TDA is sent to a Revenue Officer in a local office, who has the final responsibility for collecting full payment or some-

14

Date of This Notice
OCT 25, 1982

Taxpayer Identifying Number
05X-24-2645

Document Locator Number
02212-273-00703-2

Form Number   Tax Period
1040   DEC 31, 1981

Payment is Due By

ANDOVER, MA 01802

AD 05X242645 30 8112 670 MS20205

JACK H & KATHERINE FROST
1010 FLYNN ST.
ARKHAM, MA 02440

If you inquire about
your account, please
refer to these num-
bers or attach this
notice

Request for Payment

Our records show that a payment is due on your account. Please make the payment by the due date shown
above.

If your records do not agree with the total credits
shown, we may have credited your payment to another
kind of tax. Please help us by completing the information
requested about this payment on the back of this notice
and returning it to us. If more than one payment is involved, attach a list giving the information requested for
each payment.

If the amount due IRS is incorrect for any other
reason, please furnish us an explanation.

In either case, you will need to subtract the payments we haven't included and send us any adjusted
amount due. Make your check or money order payable to
the Internal Revenue Service for the adjusted amount
due. Please show your taxpayer identifying number on
your payment and mail it with this notice in the envelope
enclosed for your convenience.

• Thank you for your cooperation.

Tax Statement

Total Tax on Return . $	722.15
Total Credits	26.08
Plus Penalty*	174.02
Plus Interest*	73.60
AMOUNT Due IRS → $	943.69
Subtract Payments We Haven't Included	
Pay Adjusted Amount Due .... $	

*See these code numbers
on the back for
an explanation of
penalty or interest
charges

01,09

FORM 4162 (PART 1) (REV. 10-81)

• PLEASE ATTACH CHECK OR MONEY ORDER HERE

Balance Due Notice

how resolving the case. The Revenue Officer's desk is literally where the buck stops. He is required to do everything he can within the myriad of legal powers he has available to him "to protect the government's interest" and "maximize the revenue." He has the authority to seize anything from paychecks and bank accounts to cars, houses, and businesses. In fact, Revenue Officers can seize almost anything of value that may have enough equity in it to be sold at auction.

WHEN TO START WORRYING

The Internal Revenue Code provides that a seizure can be made at any time after the following conditions have occurred.

- The tax has been assessed.
- The notice has been sent and demand has been made for payment.
- The payment has not been made within ten days of the date of the notice. (The IRS can waive the ten-day payment period in certain extenuating circumstances and demand immediate payment, as explained in Chapter 5.)

IRS collection procedures are designed to be tough with those who ignore their notices and telephone calls. Some taxpayers have the mistaken impression that if they ignore the computer notices, the IRS will eventually forget about them. In some cases the IRS does forget about them. Policy Statement P–5–72 allows the IRS to stop pursuing collection of accounts "for which the expenses of collection are out of proportion to the amount to be realized from further collection effort." But the IRS refuses to divulge the level at which collection activity stops, and so no taxpayer should feel safe or think that he is off the hook.

Theoretically a seizure can occur at anytime after one notice has been sent and the ten-day period has elapsed without full payment being made. Administrative policy, however, prohibits seizure action on individual income tax delinquencies until after the "Final Notice" has been sent.

Until the TDA is assigned to a Revenue Officer, only monetary assets like paychecks and bank accounts are seized. In fact when the computer prints up the TDA, it searches its memory for the name of the taxpayer's employer and automatically prints up a Notice of Levy addressed to that employer.

Taxpayer Delinquent Account

TAXPAYER IDENTIFYING NO	TAX FORM	PERIOD	BSC	TDA TDI ASSIGNMENT CODE
XX9-64-7792	1040	12-31-80	989	94-01-15-02

VK   MARI

DLN: 94221-074-29508-1   CAF

30-8012

LOC CODE	MICRO BATCH	IDRS CYCLE
9401	9	8133

504 8129
58 8129

STEVEN A. & ALICE MARIES
88 - 8th STREET APT 3
EUREKA, CA 95501

CNC	TDA	IA
N	N	

NOTICE OF LIEN

DATE FILED	LIEN FEE	RELEASE REQUESTED DATE	RELEASE FEE
OFFICE ACTION		DATE	

CODES	ITEMS POSTED	MO. DAY YR	ASSESSMENTS	CREDITS
150	TAX ON RET	05-25-81	1,397.00	
170	ES PEN	05-25-81	52.15	
276	FTP PEN	05-25-81	13.97	
196	NOTICE INT.	05-25-81	18.37	

UNPAID BALANCE OF ASSESSMENTS		$ 1,481.49
LATE PAYMENT PENALTY	09-21-81	27.94
INTEREST ACCRUED TO	09-21-81	57.24
TOTAL DUE ▲		$ 1,566.67

MF 4

HIST

DATE POSTED	TRANSACTION	DATE	AMOUNT	BALANCE	PENALTY	INTEREST

The Notice of Levy is the legal document that is used to attach monetary assets in the possession of someone other than the taxpayer. There are two variations of the form, and one is specially designed for attaching wages, salaries, and other income.

Only Revenue Officers have the authority to seize tangible assets besides monetary sources such as paychecks and bank accounts. IRS policy requires Revenue Officers to make personal contact with taxpayers before proceeding with any seizure action or before filing a Notice of Federal Tax Lien. The tax lien is equivalent to a court-ordered judgment, except that a court order is not needed. It is in effect a legal encumbrance on all your property.

From the time a tax return is filed it is usually several months before the case is assigned to a Revenue Officer. Perhaps it is this long delay that gives some people the impression that the IRS is not going to do anything to them for not paying. Don't be mislead into thinking the same thing. The wheels of bureaucracy may move slowly at first, but eventually the IRS will come around to collect. Many people have been unexpectedly and unfortunately surprised to find their paychecks or bank accounts suddenly seized by the IRS. In 1981 the IRS issued over 740,000 Notices of Levy to attach paychecks and bank accounts.

HOW YOU CAN PREVENT AN IRS SEIZURE

Seizures do not have to happen. You can make it a lot easier on yourself by being more cooperative and responsive, because collection policies exist to make it easier for those who have difficulty in paying. Before discussing what methods or alternatives are available when you cannot pay the IRS, a special point needs to be made.

SURVIVAL RULE ■■■■■■■■■■■■■■■■■■■■■■■■■■■■■■■■■■■■■■

Answer all correspondence from the IRS that requests a reply. Never ignore an IRS notice. If you can't pay the full amount you owe, write or call the IRS address shown on the balance due notice and explain why you can't pay. Communication is all-important.

Form **668-W** (Rev. October 1981)	Department of the Treasury — Internal Revenue Service **Notice of Levy on Wages, Salary, and Other Income**	The taxpayer named at the bottom of this notice owes the United States ▶$804.12

To

```
┌                                    ┐
    IVY BELLS GREENHOUSE
    4000 HOLLOWSTEM LANE
    LEESBURG, VA  20075
└                                    ┘
```

See Part 8 — Instructions for responding

Date
July 26, 1982

Originating district
Richmond, VA

Kind of Tax	Tax Period Ended	Date of Assessment	Taxpayer Identifying Number	Unpaid Balance of Assessment	Statutory Additions	Total
941	12-31-81	03-22-82	54-XX6835X	$ 400.52	$ 35.11	$ 435.63
940	12-31-81	03-08-82	54-XX6835X	336.80	31.69	368.49

Total amount due ▶ $ 804.12

Interest and late payment penalty have been figured to 07-26-82. Additional interest and late payment penalty will continue to be charged until the balance is fully paid.

Demand for the above total amount due was made on the taxpayer, who neglected or refused to pay. The amount is unpaid and still due.

Chapter 64 of the Internal Revenue Code provides a lien for the above tax and statutory additions. Items levied on to pay this liability are: (1) all wages and salary for personal services performed by this taxpayer that you now possess or for which you become obligated, from the date you receive this notice of levy until the liability is fully paid and a

release of levy is issued, and (2) other income belonging to this taxpayer that you now possess or for which you become obligated. The foregoing wages, salary, and other income are levied on only to the extent that they do not include amounts specified as exempt from levy under Code section 6334 *(cited on back of this levy)*.

Demand is made on you for the amount necessary to pay the above tax liability. We will apply amounts received from you as payment on this liability. Please make your checks or money orders payable to the Internal Revenue Service and mail them to the Internal Revenue Service address shown below.

Signature *b. p. Parker*	Internal Revenue Service mailing address
Title Revenue Officer	Telephone number (703) 555-1111	P.O. BOX 111 FALLS CHURCH, VA

Name and address of taxpayer

```
┌                                    ┐
    RICHARD KWANSO
    1788 JOINTFER
    LEESBURG, VA  22075
└                                    ┘
```

Certification of Service

I certify that this notice of levy was served by delivering a copy of it to the person named below.

Name

Title

Date and time

Signature of revenue officer or Service representative

Part 1 — To be returned to Internal Revenue Service

Form 668-W (Rev.10-81)

Silence is almost an open invitation for the IRS to take enforcement action. If your financial situation is such that you have no financial cushion to fall back on, you must take special efforts to respond by either calling the IRS phone number on the notices or going to the local IRS office. Otherwise, a seizure of your assets, such as a paycheck, could result in a serious financial hardship for you and your family.

Although the IRS is interested in collecting full payment, they realize that each case is different and not everyone has the same financial ability to pay. Every single day the IRS seizes paychecks and bank accounts, and every single day they make arrangements for other taxpayers to pay in monthly installments. Every single day someone in the IRS seizes a car, a home, or a business, but every single day they also defer collection activity on other taxpayers in financial hardship.

The difference in the way a case is handled boils down to *communication*. The IRS is doing what they have to by demanding that you pay. You must respond by either paying in full or by communicating to them the reason why you cannot pay. By communicating with them you may find that you may be given an automatic sixty-day extension to pay in full or you may be granted the right under IRS policy to pay in monthly installments. All you have to do is ask. The important factor is you *must ask* for these agreements. If you are unable to pay within sixty days and you do not automatically qualify to pay in monthly installments, special arrangements can *still* be made. Whatever arrangement is followed will depend on your financial status and your ability to pay. In most cases you will have to submit to a collection interview.

SITUATION: TYPICAL FEARS RELATING TO INABILITY TO PAY

Q. *I think I am in a lot of trouble. I just filed my income tax return showing that I owe over $3,000. Last year I was self-employed in the construction business. As you know the recession turned the housing industry upside down, and now I don't have the money to pay this bill. What will happen to me? What can I do? Will I go to jail?*

First let's set your mind at ease. The IRS does not put taxpayers in jail for nonpayment of income taxes. Even though it is a misdemeanor to willfully fail to pay the IRS, this law is almost never used. The IRS would prefer only to apply it against organized crime figures, mainly because the concept of *willfulness* implies a state of mind at a particular point in time, and factual evidence to prove a person's state of mind is difficult to obtain. To win the case in court the IRS would have to show that you knew it was a crime not to pay, that you knew about the law, that you deliberately failed to pay because of an evil motive, and that you had the means to pay as shown by excessive expenditures of money on items not considered to be necessities.

Secondly, as mentioned earlier, there are several methods available to you under IRS policy for resolving your problem. A couple of these methods almost make it as easy as saying "charge it."

IRS policy states that an installment agreement is to be considered when a taxpayer states an inability to pay the full amount of his taxes for financial reasons. There are several courses of action that can occur if you cannot pay in full. (These pertain only to individual taxpayers who owe money on their individual income tax return, Forms 1040 or 1040A. Partnership and corporate tax liabilities are discussed in Chapters 8 and 9.) The IRS can:

- give you a short-term agreement to pay within sixty days.
- give you an agreement to pay in installments over a maximum twelve-month period if you qualify.
- negotiate an agreement with you to pay in installments over a longer period of time, ranging from several months to several years.
- make a determination that collection efforts should be temporarily suspended and no payments need be made now.

Each of these actions has its own criteria for qualification. For instance, the first two agreements may be granted automatically on request but only if you are able to meet certain minor conditions. Usually any collection employee has the authority to make any of these decisions.

DECIDING WHICH OPTION TO TAKE

Basically it is not a matter of choosing, but rather it is a matter of which method fits your financial situation. Until this book was published, you had to rely on the judgment of the Revenue Officer handling your case to determine which course of action you were going to follow. Using the information in this chapter you will be able to determine for yourself how your financial situation fits IRS guidelines for handling your case.

Let's start at the beginning. When you file a tax return showing a balance due, you should immediately begin thinking about how you are going to pay. The IRS handles over 5 million cases of nonpayment each year, and of these the IRS must initiate contact with over 85 percent of them. This results in almost 750,000 Notices of Levy issued each year to attach paychecks and bank accounts. The sad part is that almost all of them could have been avoided.

SURVIVAL RULE ▬▬▬▬▬▬▬▬▬▬▬▬▬▬▬▬▬▬▬▬▬▬▬▬▬▬▬▬▬▬▬

If you have the money to pay the IRS, you should pay as soon as possible.

If you do not have the money, you should start right away to look for borrowing opportunities. Check out as many promising and legal possibilities as you can. Check with your credit union, your bank, your employer, or a rich relative—if you have one. Leave no stones unturned.

SURVIVAL RULE ▬▬▬▬▬▬▬▬▬▬▬▬▬▬▬▬▬▬▬▬▬▬▬▬▬▬▬▬▬▬▬

If you have the means to borrow money to pay your taxes in full, you should do so.

You need to try to borrow before you talk to anyone at the IRS. Since borrowing money takes time, you should start trying as soon as you determine that you cannot pay what you owe. When you do talk to the IRS, the first question you will be asked is "Have you tried to borrow?" If you say no, you will be told to go try. If you say yes, they will ask you where you tried. Don't be intimidated by this line of questioning. Revenue Officers are forbidden to require you to produce documentation showing you have been turned down for a loan.

Once the borrowing question has been settled, the Revenue Officer must determine whether you are truly unable to pay. There are always people who have the ability to pay but, for whatever reason, try to delay paying as long as they can. Revenue Officers frequently encounter this situation, and it results in making them suspicious of many of the stories they hear. Sometimes they carry the hard line a little too far, making it more difficult for those who do have a true financial hardship.

Because of IRS's enforcement power and the ease with which it can be used, you are better off owing money to a bank or a finance company than to the IRS. But if owing the IRS is your only alternative, you should be prepared to do whatever is necessary to protect your interests. To do so you need to know your financial status inside and out, what options are available to you concerning your ability to pay, the enforcement powers that can be used against you, and how to prevent enforced collection from occurring in the first place.

INTEREST AND PENALTY CHARGES

On all delinquencies the IRS makes two assessments: one for interest and another for failure to pay. The interest charge is an ever-changing percentage rate that is initially based on the original unpaid balance of the tax but is also charged on unpaid penalties after they are assessed. The Tax Equity and Fiscal Responsibility Bill of 1982 made several changes in the method that the IRS uses to assess interest. Beginning on January 1, 1983, the IRS will make semiannual adjustments to the interest rate. From January 1, 1983, to July 1, 1983, the interest rate will be 16 percent. In addition, all interest accruing after December 31, 1982, will be *compounded daily*.

The failure-to-pay penalty is assessed only on the unpaid tax and is computed at 0.5 percent per month or a fraction of a month. (More information on the interest and penalty charges can be found in Chapter 3.)

SITUATION: MAKING PARTIAL PAYMENTS

Q. *I have recently received a bill for $982 that I can't pay in full now. I do have $300 that I could send. Should I send the $300 and try to borrow the rest, or should I wait until I have the full amount?*

That's a good question. There have been many taxpayers in your position who never sent the IRS anything at all. They assumed that the IRS either wanted it all or none at all. Many times it is advisable to send what you have as a partial payment because it shows your good faith by attempting to liquidate the liability.

However, and unfortunately, if you make a partial payment without following up to make arrangements to pay the remaining balance, you may not be doing yourself any favors. The IRS will record the name of the bank on which the check is drawn and use that information as a levy source. Taxpayers who do not want the IRS to know where they bank use cashier's checks and money orders, but even these negotiable instruments sometimes cause problems. People often send them without enclosing enough information so that the IRS can apply the money to the proper account.

SURVIVAL RULE ▬▬▬▬▬▬▬▬▬▬▬▬▬▬▬▬▬▬▬▬▬▬▬▬▬▬

If you pay by cashier's check or money order, make sure that you send the payment to the IRS in the envelope sent you and that you have enclosed a copy of the notice with the payment. Also be sure to write your name, address, and social security number on the payment and to keep a copy of the cashier's check or money order readily accessible in your files.

▬▬▬▬▬▬▬▬▬▬▬▬▬▬▬▬▬▬▬▬▬▬▬▬▬▬▬▬▬▬▬▬▬▬▬▬▬▬▬

SHORT-TERM PAYMENT AGREEMENT UP TO SIXTY DAYS

If after analyzing your own financial status, you believe you can borrow the money, you should immediately call or write to your local IRS office and ask for an extension of time to pay. The IRS will give you a short-term extension of time in which to negotiate a borrowing arrangement.

The Revenue Officer will input a code into the IRS computer system that will effectively stop any more delinquent notices from being sent to you during the extension period. The computer will also be suppressed from issuing any automatic Notices of Levy to attach your paycheck or bank account. It will also suppress the printing of a Taxpayer Delinquent Account, thereby preventing an assignment from being issued for enforced collection action.

A short-term payment agreement up to sixty days may be available to *any* taxpayer for *any* type of tax owing any amount of money. The extension is specifically allowed to provide extra time for borrowing the money to *fully pay* the tax. An office visit is not necessary to obtain this extension because the information needed by the IRS to approve the extension can be given over the phone.

This agreement provides for an extension up to sixty days but can be shorter depending upon the circumstances of the case. The Revenue Officer will ask you how much time you need. If you say two weeks, then that is what you will be given. If you say thirty days, you will be given the thirty days. If you ask for the entire sixty days it will be granted to you, but you may also be asked to pay a portion of the liability within the first thirty days.

The number of days extended must be mutually agreed on. It is probably a good idea to ask for the entire sixty-day period, since you never know what kind of contingency could arise that would delay your ability to pay within the time period.

SURVIVAL RULE ▬▬▬▬▬▬▬▬▬▬▬▬▬▬▬▬▬▬▬▬▬▬▬▬▬▬▬▬

If you can pay in full within sixty days, ask for the entire sixty-day period anyway to allow you additional time for unforeseen contingencies.

A sixty-day agreement requires the Revenue Officer to complete Form 433–D, "Installment Agreement." If your request is made in person, you will have to sign the form. Some offices may require both signatures of a joint liability. You can get around this easily enough either by bringing your spouse into the office with you or by making the request over the telephone, since agreements made by phone do not require your signature. If you want, they can send you the form for both signatures and you can mail it back.

Form **433-D**
(Rev. October 1980)

Department of the Treasury — Internal Revenue Service

Installment Agreement

Name and address of taxpayer(s)	Social security or employer identification number 587-13-1234	(Check as appropriate)
PATRICK & HELENA WOODRUSH 1398 CRISPIN WAY SPRINGFIELD, MISSOURI 65807	Kinds of taxes (Form numbers) 1040	☑ Individual
	Tax periods 12-31-81	☐ Corporation
	Amount of tax owed $1,522.00	☐ Partnership

The undersigned agrees that the Federal taxes shown above, plus any interest and penalties provided by law, will be paid as follows:

$ **338.00** to be paid on **Oct. 15, 1982** and $ **338.00** to be paid

on the **15ᵗʰ** of each **MONTH** thereafter until the liability is paid in full and also agrees that the above tax

installments will be increased as follows:

Date of increase	NONE			
Amount of increase	$			
New installment amount	$			

Conditions of this agreement

- This agreement is based on your current financial circumstances and is subject to revision or cancellation if subsequent financial statements required by IRS reflect a change in your ability to pay.
- This agreement may require managerial approval. If it is not approved, you will be so notified.
- All Federal taxes that become due during the term of this agreement will be paid on time.
- All Federal tax returns that become due during the term of this agreement will be filed on time.
- Any refunds that might otherwise be due will be applied to this liability until this liability is satisfied.
- Permission to make installment payments may be withdrawn, and the entire tax liability may be collected by levy on income or by seizure of property if the conditions of this agreement are not met, or if it is determined that collection of these taxes is endangered.

Additional conditions

Your signature *Patrick Woodrush*	Title (if corporate officer or partner)	Date 10-15-82	For assistance, contact
Spouse's signature (if joint income tax return) *Helena Woodrush*		Date 10/15/82	(Telephone)
Agreement examined and approved by (signature)		Date Oct 22, 1982	Interviewer Eden Taylor

General Information

Employer (Name and address) RAMSHEAD LEATHERS, 52118 POWDER MILL RD., SPRNGFLD	Taxpayer's Telephone Number(s) ▶	(Home) 389-6218 (Business) 580-1621

Banks (Names and addresses)

MARTENS NAT. BK. , 2324 BRIGHTSEAT RD., SPRNGFLD

Notice of Federal tax lien filing determination (check one)

☐ Notice of tax lien filed   ☑ Notice of tax lien not required

☐ Notice of tax lien to be filed—taxpayer notified   ☐ Notice of tax lien not filed (Form 3991 attached)

To obtain this extension you will need to supply the following information:

- The name and address of your employer and your spouse's employer if the money is owed on a joint return.
- The amount of your take-home pay and the dates of paydays.
- The names and addresses of your bank accounts. You are not required to supply the account number, even if you are asked.
- A description and license number of each motor vehicle you own.
- The location, description, equity, and mortgage holder of all real estate.

Just because you have been given sixty days to fully pay doesn't mean that you should wait until the sixtieth day to pay. You should make it a point to pay as soon as you can. During the entire time of the extension, interest and penalty charges continue to build. Also you never can tell when your payment will arrive at the IRS. Sometimes mail can take ten days to go across town.

AUTOMATIC INSTALLMENT AGREEMENT
UP TO TWELVE MONTHS

Under the provisions specified in Section 5231.3 of the Internal Revenue Manual (IRM), individual income taxpayers who *request* additional time to pay may be granted an *automatic installment agreement of up to twelve months to fully pay*, provided that the account is still in notice status and the total amount outstanding is less than the secret tolerance amount specified by the IRS. (More about these tolerance levels follows.) The request may be made in person or by mail.

The IRS, however, will *not* give you this automatic installment agreement privilege if one or more of the following apply:

- You are delinquent in filing a tax return and there is a Taxpayer Delinquency Investigation of your case (see Chapter 1).
- There is already an installment agreement outstanding.
- The account was previously in installment agreement status but you defaulted.
- Your account has a Taxpayer Delinquent Account outstanding.

This privilege will be granted only to individual income taxpayers who owe taxes on Form 1040 or 1040A. It does not apply to any other type of tax liability. The payments must be in equal installments, and you must sign IRS Form 433–D or Form 2159, "Payroll Deduction Agreement."

There are several important points that should be re-emphasized with the automatic installment agreement.

- The privilege is available only by *request*. The IRS will not set up monthly billing until *after* you have contacted them and asked for the arrangement.
- You will be granted up to twelve months to pay based solely on *your determination of your ability to pay.* You will *not* have to submit to a complete collection interview, and you will *not* have to furnish a financial or information statement showing all your assets, liabilities, and monthly expenses.
- You will have to furnish certain information, such as where you work, how much you make, the dates of your paydays, the places where you bank or save money, the make and model of any automobiles you own, and the location and value of any real estate you are buying or own. In the event that you default on the installment agreement, the IRS will use this information in seizing those assets.
- This privilege is only automatic while your delinquent account is in *notice status*, which means you have until the third week after the date of the final notice to *request* and be granted this privilege. Once the account goes to TDA status you will have to submit to a complete collection interview in order to qualify for a negotiated installment agreement.
- The maximum amount that must be owed to qualify for this automatic installment privilege cannot be divulged by anyone from the IRS. This is "Official Use Only" information protected from public disclosure, even under the Freedom of Information Act.

In order to qualify for this privilege you must request it, and the IRS will tell you if you do not qualify. You have absolutely nothing to lose by asking. Either by letter or in person you should phrase your request this way:

Automatic Installment Agreement

"I am requesting an automatic installment agreement under the provisions of IRM 5231.3. I owe $(fill in amount here). Do I qualify?"

SURVIVAL RULE ▬▬▬▬▬▬▬▬▬▬▬▬▬▬▬▬▬▬▬▬▬▬▬▬▬▬▬▬▬▬

You should request an automatic agreement, under the provisions of IRM 5231.3, even though you do not know if your total amount outstanding is lower than IRS's secret tolerance level.

▬▬

If the answer is yes, you are in fat city. If the answer is no, you should ask this question: "How much would I have to pay now to bring the 'total amount outstanding' down to meet the tolerance criterion qualifying me for the automatic installment agreement?"

This is one of the IRS's catch-22 problems. The IRS manual does not require that your amount owed be the "original assessed amount." It only requires that the "total amount outstanding" be lower than the tolerance criterion figure. This means that at some point between your original assessment (reflected on your *first* notice) and the last notice you received, the original balance could be reduced by subsequent payments in order to allow you to qualify for the installment privilege.

If the Revenue Officer will not tell you how much you need to pay to reduce your "total amount outstanding" down to the qualifying level, you should try the strategy of making small payments you can afford and *then* asking if you qualify. Eventually the officer is going to have to tell you.

But if you are in this situation, you are also up against *time*: You must make your request before the end of the third week after the date of your final notice. Once your account goes to Taxpayer Delinquent Account status and is assigned to the district or local office for collection, you will have to submit to a collection interview and tell the IRS everything about your financial life that you would not want them to know.

NEGOTIATED INSTALLMENT AGREEMENTS
OF VARYING DURATION

A negotiated agreement to pay in monthly installments over a lengthy period of time is now within the recognized policy guidelines of the IRS. IRS Policy Statement P–5–14 (approved on March 3, 1976) states: "Although there is no specific authority for allowing a taxpayer to liquidate a delinquent account by installment payments, installment agreements are to be considered, and may be entered into, when appropriate."

The type of negotiated installment agreement discussed in this section is different from the automatic installment agreement discussed previously. Policy Statement P–5–14 refers to all types of taxes and taxpayers by virtue of the fact that it mentions none specifically. Installment agreements can be made with partnerships, corporations, sole proprietorships, or any other type of entity for any type of tax, whether excise taxes, income taxes, or withholding taxes. This chapter focuses on the individual income taxpayer who owes taxes from Form 1040 or 1040A. (Business owners who would like to know more about how they can pay their taxes in installments should refer to Chapter 8.)

Specific IRM guidelines for installment agreements are loosely drawn. Each region and district has its own policies regarding installment agreements, and so one taxpayer's experience in one district may differ from another taxpayer's experience in another district. Basically the installment agreement is used when there are no other means of collection. Sometimes the district or regional policies are so strict that they result in acceptances of few agreements. Revenue Officers are seldom free to make negotiated arrangements without supervisory approval on various levels, and the review process is never perfunctory. Supervisory reviewers are in a position to nitpick the case and usually do. Although it is often difficult to put cases into a mold to fit a set of arbitrary rigid guidelines, Revenue Officers are often required to do just that.

THE COLLECTION INTERVIEW

In the event you do not qualify for an automatic installment agreement and you do not have the money to fully pay and you know that you cannot borrow the money because you have tried, you should contact your local IRS office and be prepared to bare your financial soul. You will be told that you must come in for a collection interview because lengthy installment agreements cannot be negotiated over the phone.

SURVIVAL RULE ▬▬▬▬▬▬▬▬▬▬▬▬▬▬▬▬▬▬▬▬▬▬▬▬

If you are unable to borrow the money to fully pay your taxes and you do not qualify for an automatic installment agreement, you should go to your local IRS office, fully prepared to submit to an interview, and attempt to negotiate an arrangement to pay in installments.

▬▬▬▬▬▬▬▬▬▬▬▬▬▬▬▬▬▬▬▬▬▬▬▬▬▬▬▬▬▬▬▬▬▬▬▬▬▬

The purpose of the collection interview is to determine your ability to pay by evaluating your financial condition. For this you will have to furnish the information necessary for a Revenue Officer to complete Form 433–A, "Collection Information Statement for Individuals" (see pages 81–90).

The collection interview will be very comprehensive, and, unless you are dealing with a rookie, it is doubtful that your encounter will be termed "pleasant." Revenue Officers are taught to be assertive and firm in taxpayer interviews and "they've heard it all before." It is not wise to come on like gangbusters, and it is equally unwise to assume an over friendly posture. Either approach will arouse suspicion and mistrust, a result counterproductive to your aims of trying to portray yourself as a cooperative and communicative taxpayer.

Your objective should be to negotiate the best arrangement you can—to pay your taxes in a manner that creates the least amount of stress on your wallet, bank account, and style of living. To achieve this objective you must come to the interview fully prepared. This means that you must take the time to review your entire financial situation and compile sufficient data to reflect that financial situation as truthfully and as accurately as you can. You should be fully prepared to answer any and all questions about your financial situation because good preparation will save you a lot of time and aggravation.

Experience has shown that most taxpayers have no accurate idea of how much money they spend each month for many of the items listed on the form. Most know how much they make, and how much is left over at the end of the month, but practically little about where it all went. For example, although groceries are a major household expense, most *men* have no idea how much is spent for the family's groceries because their wives are traditionally the shoppers in the family.

In order to prepare for the collection interview you will need to assemble the following data:

- Your Social Security number and your spouse's number if your return was jointly filed.
- Name, address, phone numbers, and paydays of employers.
- Name, address, and telephone number of next of kin.
- Ages and relationships of dependents living in your household.
- Your date of birth and that of your spouse.
- How many exemptions or withholding allowances you are claiming on your W–4 form filed with your employer.
- The tax year of your last filed income tax return and the adjusted gross income on your return (your best bet is to take a copy of the return to the interview with you).
- Names and addresses of all bank and savings accounts, the type of account, the account number, and the balance in each account.
- Names and addresses of all financial institutions to which you owe money, including charge cards, the amount of your monthly payments, the credit limits, balances owed, available credit lines, dates money was borrowed, and dates of final payments.
- The location, box number, and contents of any safe deposit box you may be renting.
- Name of your life insurance company, the policy number, type of policy, face amount, and available loan value.
- Information about any court proceedings, bankruptcies, repossessions, transfers of assets, condition of your health, anticipated increase in your income or assets, and participation in trusts, estates, or profit-sharing plans.
- Description and location of all real estate owned or being bought.
- A listing of your assets and liabilities, including the amount of cash you have, how much is in your bank accounts, the value of your stocks, bonds, or other investments, and so on. For everything you own, including automobiles and real estate, they need

to know its present value, the amounts still owed on the property, and the same information relating to financial institutions specified above.

- A monthly income and expense analysis that shows the sources and amounts of all family income and lists the amounts of all "necessary living expenses," including rent, groceries (for the entire household), utilities, transportation, insurance (car, medical, life, home), medical, and estimated tax payments. List any other item that you incur monthly and consider to be a necessary living expense.

Form 433–A will be completed by the officer from answers that you give about your financial status. Taxpayers are rarely allowed to complete their own forms.

Once the form has been completed and you and your spouse have signed it (under penalty of perjury), the officer will determine a course of action. The officer could:

- Require you to make immediate payment from such monetary assets as your checking account or savings account. IRS policy requires immediate payment whenever a taxpayer has cash equal to the tax liability.
- Require you to liquidate available assets to raise the money to apply to the taxes. Assets that can be readily converted to cash include stocks and bonds, the loan value of life insurance policies, and so on. Unencumbered assets, equity in encumbered assets, interests in estates and trusts, and lines of credit are examples of sources from which money can be obtained.
- Give you a sixty-day payment agreement and direct you to borrow money on assets that have enough equity to be used as collateral.
- Give you an installment agreement to make monthly payments over a long period of time.
- Recommend enforcement action unless you pay in full by a given date. A seizure of a paycheck or a bank account does not require the filing of a federal tax lien. Seizures of assets such as automobiles and houses first require the filing of the lien. Liens can only be filed by revenue officers.
- Recommend that all collection action be suspended based on your inability to pay now or in the immediate future. IRS policy

provides for stopping all collection efforts when the taxpayer can demonstrate financial hardship and for resuming collection when his ability to pay improves. Studies have shown that many deferred cases are later collected by offsets from future refund checks.

When the Revenue Officer's analysis of your assets reveals no obvious solution for liquidating the liability, the monthly income and expense analysis is used as the basis for determining how much you will be asked to pay monthly. IRM 5223:(4)(g) states that "the amount to be paid monthly on an installment agreement payment will be the difference between the taxpayer's net income and allowable expenses rounded down to the nearest five-dollar increment."

It is this process of determining what is an "allowable expense" that has probably caused more problems between officers and taxpayers than any other rule or policy relating to collection procedures. Over the years "allowable expenses" have been called "ordinary and necessary" and just simply "necessary" living expenses. Until recently these terms were not defined, and it was up to local managers to use their own judgment in determining what was "ordinary and necessary."

IRM 5223 now provides some guidelines for Revenue Officers in deciding what constitutes an allowable expense item. It is important that you follow this closely because any monthly expenditures you are now making will be disallowed by the IRS if they are not within these guidelines, and the net result will be a higher monthly payment to the IRS to the exclusion of the disallowed item.

In deciding what constitutes an allowable expense item, Revenue Officers must follow IRM 5223:(4)(a):

(4) When analysis of the taxpayer's assets has given no obvious solution for liquidating the liability, the income and expenses should be analyzed.

(a) When deciding what constitutes an allowable expense item, the employee may allow:

1 expenses which are necessary for the taxpayer's production of income (for example, dues for a trade union or professional organization; child care payments which allow a taxpayer to be gainfully employed);

2 expenses which provide for the health and welfare of the taxpayer

and family. The expense must be reasonable for the size of the family and the geographic location, as well as any unique individual circumstances. An expense will not be allowed it if serves to provide an elevated standard of living, as opposed to basic necessities. Also, an expense will not be allowed if the taxpayer has a proven record of not making the payment. Expenses allowable under this category are:

a rent or mortgage for place of residence;

b food;

c clothing;

d necessary transportation expense (auto insurance, car payment, bus fare, etc.);

e home maintenance expense (utilities, home-owner insurance, home-owner dues, etc.);

f medical expenses; health insurance;

g current tax payments (including federal, state and local);

h life insurance, but not if it is excessive to the point of being construed as an investment;

i alimony, child support or other court-ordered payment.

3 Minimum payments on secured or legally perfected debts (car payments, judgements, etc.) will normally be allowed. However, if the encumbered asset represents an item which would not be considered a necessary living expense (e.g., a boat, recreational vehicle, etc.), the taxpayer should be advised that the debt payment will not be included as an allowable expense.

4 Payments on unsecured debts (credit cards, personal loans, etc.) may not be allowed if omitting them would permit the tax-payer to pay in full within 90 days. However, if the taxpayer cannot full pay within that time frame, minimum payments may be allowed if failure to make them would ultimately impair the taxpayer's ability to pay the tax. The taxpayer should be advised that since all necessary living expenses have been allowed, no additional charge debts should be incurred. Generally, payments to friends or relatives will not be allowed. Dates for final payments on loans or installment purchases, as well as final payments on revolving credit arrangements after allowing minimum required payments, will be noted so the additional funds will be applied to the liability when they become available. If permitting the taxpayer to pay unsecured debts results in inability to pay or in only having a small amount left for payment of the tax, the taxpayer should be advised that a portion of the money available for payment of debts will be used for payment of the taxes and that arrangements must be made with other creditors accordingly.

(b) As a general rule, expenses not specified in 5223:(4)(a) above will be disallowed. However, an otherwise disallowable expense may be included if the interviewing employee believes an exception should be made based on the circumstances of the individual case. For instance, if the taxpayer advises that an educational expense or church contribution is a necessity, the individual circumstances must be considered. If an exception is made, the case history will be documented to explain the basis for the exception.

(c) The taxpayer will be required to verify and support any expense that appears excessive based on the income and circumstances of that taxpayer. However, proof of payment does not automatically make an item allowable. The criteria in 5223:(4)(a) apply.

(d) In some cases, expense items or payments will not be due in even monthly increments. For instance, personal property tax may be due once a year. Unless the taxpayer substantiates that money is being set aside on a monthly basis, the expense will be allowed in total in the month due and the payment agreement adjusted accordingly for that month. Expense items with varying monthly payments should be averaged over a twelve-month period unless the variation will be excessive. In such instances, exclude the irregular months from the average. For example, if a utility bill will be excessive during the three winter months, average the other nine months. Use the remarks section of the CIS [Collection Information Statement] to explain the expected increase in expenses, and decrease any related installment agreement accordingly during the affected months.

(e) In arriving at available net income, the interviewer should analyze the taxpayer's deductions to ensure that they are reasonable and allowable. The only automatically allowable deductions from gross pay or income are federal, state and local taxes (including FICA or other mandatory retirement program).

1 Other deductions from gross pay or income will be treated and listed as expenses, but only to the extent they meet the criteria in 5223:(4)(a) above;

2 To avoid affording the taxpayer a double deduction for one expense, the interviewer must ensure that such amounts remain in the total net pay figure and are also entered on the expense side of the income and expense analysis.

IRM section 5223:(4)(a)4 states that "payments on unsecured debts may not be allowed if omitting them would permit the taxpayer to pay in full within 90 days." Sometimes when taxpayers only owe a couple of hundred dollars, Revenue Officers use that reference to suggest to them that they delay making a payment on another debt and use the money to pay the taxes. Most taxpayers don't understand why, but the IRS reasoning is simple. A delay of one or two months to most creditors usually results only in late-payment penalties. It can take months for a creditor to claim default on an obligation and go to court to get a judgment. The IRS, however, has almost immediate seizure authority without the requirement to go to court to get a judgment. A paycheck or bank account can be attached without the requirement to even file a federal tax lien, and so there are no delays in making those kinds of seizures.

Another policy you should pay particular attention to concerns monthly payments to other creditors. If you are making periodic payments on obligations that will be paid in full during the period of time you are making monthly payments to the IRS, you will be asked to increase the IRS payments by the same amount you were paying the other creditors.

The interview with the officer can be difficult and time consuming. You must be prepared to protect your own interests and not make any commitments you cannot keep. If you are lucky enough that the IRS will accept your proposal for a monthly installment agreement, you may want to consider using a payroll-deduction arrangement. In fact, the IRS would prefer that payments be made through a payroll-deduction agreement since agreements made this way seldom default. The officer will fill out Form 2159, "Payroll Deduction Agreement," and give you a copy for your employer to sign.

HOW TO HANDLE A DISAGREEMENT

Obviously not every interview can go smoothly, and there are many circumstances under which problems can arise. Sometimes personality clashes—or even an age difference—play a part. For example, an older taxpayer may resent demands or threats from a younger IRS employee whom he considers still "green" and "wet behind the ears." Or a taxpayer may not agree with how his case is being handled.

The first level of review is the employee's immediate supervisor.

SURVIVAL RULE ▬▬▬▬▬▬▬▬▬▬▬▬▬▬▬▬▬▬▬▬▬▬▬▬▬

If you reach an impasse with the Revenue Officer regarding your liability or your ability to pay, you are entitled to and should request that your case be reviewed by a supervisory official.

▬▬▬▬▬▬▬▬▬▬▬▬▬▬▬▬▬▬▬▬▬▬▬▬▬▬▬▬▬▬▬▬▬▬

The next higher officials are the branch chief, the division chief, and the district director.

If the conflict gets too bad, it will be to everyone's benefit to have the case transferred to another employee. Assignments are not etched in stone, and a good supervisor will reassign a case if you make the request based on a conflict between you and the employee handling your case.

SITUATION: HOW THE IRS HANDLES
A FINANCIAL HARDSHIP

Q. *My husband is a self-employed consultant. We owe $2,500 for last year's income and self-employment tax. He has not held a job in five months, and we can't pay all our bills on the assistance we receive. Do you think the IRS would consider our case a hardship and leave us alone for a while?*

Your question brings up another option: *A determination by the IRS that collection efforts will be temporarily suspended and no payments need be made now.* There are times when a tax liability simply cannot be collected, either because the taxpayer or any of his assets cannot be located or because payment would create a hardship on the taxpayer and his family by preventing the taxpayer from meeting necessary living expenses. In these cases the Revenue Officer makes a report on IRS Form 53, "Report of Taxes Currently Not Collectible," and recommends that further collection efforts be temporarily suspended. The Collection Division refers to these cases as "currently uncollectible" because the taxpayer still owes money and will be asked to pay at a later date. Revenue Officers refer to the procedure as "53ing" a case.

Before a case can be reported as uncollectible, Form 433–A must be completed in full, signed by both spouses, and certain items may have to be verified. Some offices may require that a check of real property and personal property records be conducted at the local courthouse to verify that you do not have other assets that you are not showing on the form. The IRM requires a review of your latest income tax return prior to reporting uncollectible cases exceeding two thousand dollars. So if you owe more than that amount be sure to take a copy of your last income tax return to the interview.

A federal tax lien must be filed on all cases reported uncollectible of $1,000 or more. A filed federal tax lien is equivalent to a judgment, and a court order is not needed prior to filing. (For more information on the tax lien see Chapter 5.)

When Form 53 is prepared, the Revenue Officer must decide when your case is to be reactivated for a financial review or for a presumed ability to pay. Usually this is done by inputting a code into the computer that will reactivate the case when you file an income tax return showing an adjusted gross income of a predetermined level. The Revenue Officer will select an adjusted gross income level that represents a large enough increase in your income to warrant additional collection efforts. For example, if you cannot pay your taxes on an income of $15,000 a year, the case may be deferred until your earnings are $17,000 to $18,000 a year.

The uncollectible determination is made by the officer and his supervisor. You cannot demand that collection efforts be suspended, but you can make a convincing case when a true hardship exists. The IRS used to say that an "undue hardship" had to exist, but they never defined what an "undue hardship" was. Now the IRS has a policy defining the circumstances under which an account may be reported uncollectible based on a financial hardship. Policy Statement P–5–71 (approved on November 19, 1980) says:

As a general rule, accounts will be reported as currently not collectible when the taxpayer has no assets or income which are, by law, subject to levy. However, if there are limited assets or income but it is determined that levy would create a hardship, the liability may be reported as currently not collectible. A hardship exists if the levy action prevents the taxpayer from meeting necessary living expenses. In each case a determination must be made as to whether the levy would result in actual hardship, as distinguished from mere inconvenience to the taxpayer.

Because of the rapid appreciation of real estate in the past few years a lot of taxpayers have been able to borrow money on their increasing equity by obtaining a second mortgage. If you have income sufficient to make payments on a second mortgage, the case cannot be reported uncollectible. But if your income has been temporarily disrupted, as happens to millions of wage earners during a recession, no one will loan you the money for a second mortgage. In this instance, the IRS can suspend collection and file a federal tax lien to protect its interests in the real estate.

Most hardship cases involve taxpayers who do not own real estate, who have no savings, whose incomes are barely sufficient to meet expenses, and whose only assets are an automobile, which they need to get to and from work. The IRS will not seize your automobile if you have a true hardship case and have demonstrated such by submitting to a collection interview and completing Form 433–A. Instances in which the IRS has seized property in hardship cases have arisen because taxpayers have failed to fully respond and cooperate with the IRS. It must be emphasized again: *If you want to prevent the IRS from conducting a seizure to collect the money, you must respond to the IRS notices and you must follow the proper procedures to have your case handled according to IRS guidelines.*

In order to determine if your case is a hardship based on IRS criteria, you should be able to answer *no* to *all* the questions that follow:

- Do you have the money to pay in full now?
- Do you have the potential to borrow enough money to pay the taxes?
- Do you have any assets that can be used as collateral for borrowing money?
- Do you have sufficient income exceeding your necessary living expenses that will enable you to keep an installment agreement?

UNDERSTANDING FORM 433–A

Form 433–A, "Collection Information Statement for Individuals," is the Collection Division's most widely used form. It is used in analyzing your financial status to determine your ability to pay. Once it is determined that you do not have the money to pay or the means to borrow, the Revenue Officer will require you to give your financial profile on a Form 433–A.

Revenue Officers and some Revenue Representatives can arrange an appointment at your convenience and at either your house or place of employment. At other times you may be required to come into the office for the collection interview. It really depends on the stage of the collection process. If your account is in notice status, you will have to come into the local IRS office without an appointment. If the account is in Taxpayer Delinquent Account status and the case is assigned to someone from collection, an appointment can be arranged.

Form 433–A is a multipurpose form. It is not only used to determine your ability to pay, but it serves as an information source for collection or seizure action and will be useful in providing clues to your whereabouts if you were to leave town suddenly.

Revenue Officers are resourceful. If they try hard enough, they can find out anything about anyone from the sources that are available to them. In the following discussion you will learn how resourceful they can be in using the information on this form. Form 433–A is divided into six sections, beginning with the entity section.

Entity Section: Identifies you by name, address, home phone number, and marital status. The correct address and Zip Code are important because they tell the Revenue Officer where the federal tax lien is to be filed.

Section I: Lists the names and addresses of your employers. If both you and your spouse are employed, both sections must be completed if your tax liability arose from a jointly filed return. The dates of the paydays are used to determine the best timing for seizing a paycheck. For example, if you get paid on Friday, the Notice of Levy to attach the paycheck would be served before Friday in order to guarantee attachment.

Section II: Requests personal information related to your next of kin and any dependents you may have. This information is very

Form **433-A**
(Rev. April 1981)

Department of the Treasury – Internal Revenue Service

Collection Information Statement for Individuals

(If you need additional space, please attach a separate sheet.)

1. Taxpayers' names and address (including County)	2. Home phone number	3. Marital status
PATRICK + HELENA WOODRUSH 1398 CRISPIN WAY SPRINGFIELD, MISSOURI 65807	417-389-6218	MARRIED

	4. Social Security Numbers	a. Taxpayer 587-13-1234	b. Spouse 580-15-4321

Section I. Employment Information

5. Taxpayer's employer or business (name and address)	6. Business phone number	7. Occupation
RAMSHEAD LEATHERS, INC. 5211S POWDER MILL RD. SPRINGFIELD. MISSOURI 65804	580-1621	SALES

	8. Paydays FRIDAYS	9. (Check appropriate box) ☒ Wage earner ☐ Sole proprietor ☐ Partner

10. Spouse's employer or business (name and address)	11. Business phone number	12. Occupation
SKY BLUE ENTERPRISES, INC. 43211 HUDSON AVE. SPRINGFIELD, MISSOURI 65803	291-1583	SECRETARY

	13. Paydays MONDAYS	14. (Check appropriate box) ☒ Wage earner ☐ Sole proprietor ☐ Partner

Section II. Personal Information

15. Name, address and telephone number of next of kin or other reference

WIFE'S MOTHER : NORMA RAE CARDINAL, 1512 LOVELACE CT., SPRINGFIELD, MO. 65800   620-1732

16. Age and relationship of dependents (exclude husband and wife) living in your household	17. Number of exemptions claimed on Form W-4
2 SONS, 3 +5 1 Daughter, 7	5

18. Date of birth	a. Taxpayer ▲ 05-20-48	b. Spouse 06-03-50

Section III. General Financial Information

Form 433-A (Rev. 4-81)

19. Latest filed income tax return (tax year)	20. Adjusted gross income on return
1981	$25,000+

21. Bank accounts (Include Savings & Loans, Credit Unions, IRA and KEOGH accounts, Certificates of Deposit, etc.)

Name of Institution	Address	Type of Account	Account No.	Balance
MARTENS NAT. BK.	2324 BRIGHTSEAT RD.	CHECKING	12-75-183	$1,400

Total (Enter in Item 28) ▲ $114.00

22. Bank charge cards, Lines of credit, etc.

Type of Account or Card	Name and Address of Financial Institution	Monthly Payment	Credit Limit	Amount Owed	Credit Available
MASTERCARD	MARTENS NAT. BK. 2324 BRIGHTSEAT RD. SPRNGFD.	$45.00	$1,500	$780	$720
CHARGE	JASON CLOTHIERS 196 S. ARGONNA DR. SPRNGFD.	$35.00	$600	$440	$160
CREDIT UNION	UNION CREDIT UNION #4 PLAZA SQ. SPRNGFD	$50.00	$2,000	$1,990	-0-
FINANCE CO.	B+C FINANCE SERVICES #3 PLAZA SQ. SPRNGFD	$45.00	$2,590	$2,200	$300

Totals (Enter in Item 34) ▲ $175.00 | | $5,410 | $1,180

23. Safe deposit boxes rented or accessed (List all locations, box numbers, and contents)

NONE

24. Real Property (Brief description and type of ownership)	Address (Include County and State)
a. NONE	
b.	
c.	

25. Life Insurance (Name of Company)	Policy Number	Type	Face Amount	Available Loan Value
NONE				

Total (Enter in Item 30) ▲

(over)

Section III — continued

General Financial Information

26. **Additional Information** *(Court proceedings, bankruptcies, repossessions, recent transfers of assets for less than full value, anticipated increases in income, condition of health, etc.; include information on trusts, estates, profit-sharing plans, etc., on which you are a participant or beneficiary)*

(Please note: The interviewer will help you complete Sections IV and V.)

Section IV.   Asset and Liability Analysis

Description (a)	Cur. Mkt. Value (b)	Liabilities Bal. Due (c)	Equity in Asset (d)	Amt. of Mo. Pymt. (e)	Name and Address of Lien/Note Holder/Obligee (f)	Date Pledged (f)	Date of Final Pymt. (g)
27. Cash							
28. Bank accounts							
29. Stocks, Bonds, Investments							
30. Cash or loan value of insur.							
31. Vehicles *(Model, year, license)*							
a.							
b.							
c.							
32. Real property a.							
b.							
c.							
33. Other assets							
a.							
b.							
c.							
d.							
e.							
34. Bank revolving credit							

35. Other Liabilities (Include judgments, notes, and other charge accounts)				
a.				
b.				
c.				
d.				
e.				
f.				
g.				
36. Federal taxes owed				
37. Totals	$			$

Section V.   Monthly Income and Expense Analysis

	Income (a)		Necessary Living Expenses (b)	
Source	Gross	Net		
38. Wages/Salaries (Taxpayer)	$	$	46. Rent	$
39. Wages/Salaries (Spouse)			47. Groceries	
40. Interest - Dividends			48. Allowable installment payments	
41. Net business income (from Form 433-B)			49. Utilities	
42. Rental income			50. Transportation	
43. Pension (Taxpayer)			51. Insurance	
44. Pension (Spouse)			52. Medical	
			53. Estimated tax payments	
			54. Other expenses (specify)	
45. Total	$	$	55. Total	$
			56. Net difference (income less necessary living expenses)	$

Certification

Under penalties of perjury, I declare that to the best of my knowledge and belief this statement of assets, liabilities, and other information is true, correct, and complete.

57. Your signature	58. Spouse's signature (if joint return was filed)	59. Date

GPO 986-322

Form **433-A** (Rev. 4-81)

important to Revenue Officers. Many taxpayers who otherwise may not have been found have been located through addresses or information supplied by their next of kin. The ages and relationships of your dependents is useful too. If you have school-age children, their school records will have to be transferred if you move, and the IRS can always serve a summons on the school board to obtain the forwarding address of the records.

Section III: Requests general financial information, starting with the year you last filed an income tax return and the adjusted gross income reported on the return. For this information it is probably a good idea for you to have a copy of your tax return with you when you go for your interview.

Your income tax return is a very valuable source of information not only for collecting but also for locating you if you move without leaving a forwarding address. For instance, this is some of the information that can be obtained from your tax return.

- The W–2s give the names and addresses of your employers for levy sources, and sometimes employers have forwarding addresses or can supply other information that will help locate you.
- Income sources such as rents, royalties, and pensions are listed.
- Depreciable business assets may be levy sources.
- Medical deductions are frequently listed by names of doctors who may have a current address or name of your current employer.
- Listed dividend and interest income are obvious levy sources.
- Interest deductions will provide clues to where you bank.

In block 21 you must list all your bank, checking, and savings accounts. You need to know the name and address of each financial institution you deal with and the account number and the balance in each account. The IRS can seize the entire amount in any checking or savings account.

Block 22 is a listing of all bank charge cards or other lines of credit. You will need to supply the name and address of each financial institution from whom you receive credit, the type of account it is, your monthly payments, the credit limit, total amount owed, and available credit balance of each account.

Block 23 is for listing any safe-deposit boxes you rent, the address of the box, and the contents of the box. Believe it or not, the

IRS can seize the contents of your safe-deposit box. The information you supply here is almost their only source of knowledge in locating a safe-deposit box. Because so few taxpayers use safe-deposit boxes, IRS agents and officers are *not likely* to go from bank to bank serving summonses to locate potential safe-deposit boxes unless the case is exceptionally important or the balance due is tremendously large *and* there is good reason to believe that a safe-deposit box exists. But remember that if you do rent a safe-deposit box and store taxable-income-producing stocks, bonds, or other investment-related papers and documents in the box and take a deduction on your income tax return for the rental of the box, the officer handling your case may see the deduction on your tax return, thereby discovering the existence of the box. Many taxpayers do not even bother taking the deduction for the simple reason that they do not want any government agency to know where they store their valuables.

A brief description and the location of any real property you own or are buying are recorded in block 24. A seizure of a house is probably the easiest seizure a Revenue Officer could make. You must list all your real property; you can't hide it from the IRS. The real property records are always researched for true title of ownership and to determine if there are any other liens having priority over the federal tax lien.

You must list your life insurance policies in block 25. The IRS wants to know the name of the insurance company, your policy number, the type of policy (term, whole-life, or universal), the face amount of the policy, and your available loan value. Your right to the cash surrender value of your insurance policy is "property" or "rights to property" subject to the tax liens. State laws exempting the "cash surrender value" from garnishment or attachment by creditors do not apply to the IRS. The "cash surrender value" is the amount you would receive by turning in your policy to the insurance company. As a matter of policy the IRS only seizes the "cash loan value," which will not affect your policy coverage. The cash loan value is the amount you can borrow from the company by using the policy as security and still maintain the policy coverage. The IRS can attach the cash loan value by simply serving a Notice of Levy form on the insurance company, but to collect the "cash surrender value" of the policy the IRS must go to court in a suit to foreclose on the federal tax lien. Because suits take a lot of time and money, it is much more effective for the IRS to levy the cash loan value.

Block 26 is used to record any general information on your financial affairs. The Revenue Officer will ask you questions about everything from court proceedings, bankruptcies, repossessions, and recent transfers of property to the condition of your health and your participation in any trusts, estates, or profit-sharing plans. Some taxpayers may be offended about revealing details of their health, but in this case it is actually to your benefit to go into every little detail of every little ache and pain you may have, particularly if your health pertains to your ability to obtain and/or retain employment. The information could be especially useful when the Revenue Officer needs to document why your taxes are currently uncollectible.

Section IV: Lists all your assets and liabilities. This is in the basic balance sheet format. The blocks are self-explanatory. It is important to the IRS that each block be filled in completely. Even though you do not prepare the form you will have to supply the officer with all the information needed to fill in every block. It is important to be as precise as you can, not only with the balances due on your indebtedness but also with the dates the debts were incurred and the dates of final payments. In recessionary times taxpayers often fall behind in their obligations, particularly with unsecured creditors such as companies with whom you have charge accounts. A tough interviewer may disallow those debts for which you are not currently making payments by claiming that they cannot be counted if they are not being paid. This is particularly unfair if you are in the position of performing a juggling act, paying one bill one month and paying another the next month. Even though Form 433–A does not provide space, you should indicate somewhere on the form those bills that are behind in payments and indicate how many months the payments are overdue.

The reason some officers do not want to list monthly payments of debts that are not being paid is that the monthly income and expense analysis in section V would show a negative net difference, meaning that more money is being spent than is being earned. Some supervisors contend that a taxpayer cannot spend more than he makes if there are no resources to draw from, but they forget that at times people can become so overextended that they cannot make all their payments. Stick to your guns. Make your collection interviewer count all your payments even though some are not being paid.

Line 31 lists the description and license number of each vehicle you own. Obviously this information is used to reveal assets that IRS can seize. Automobile seizures are quite effective in obtaining full payment, especially if the taxpayer has only one car and needs it for transportation. Before making the seizure, the officer must verify all the information listed here and also obtain the vehicle's ID number from the state authority licensing motor vehicles.

On line 34 you must list all your liabilities including those previously listed in block 22. The IRS wants to know specifically how much you owe, how much you are paying each month, the date you borrowed the money, and the date of your final payment.

Section V: Is the Monthly Income and Expense Analysis. On the left side you list all your monthly sources of income for the entire family and on the right side you list all your "necessary living expenses" for the entire family. The items specifically included here are rent, groceries, allowable installment payments, utilities, transportation, insurance, medical, and estimated tax payments. It is very important that you account for all your monthly expenses because any expense that you do not tell the IRS about will not be recorded and the money that otherwise would go for the expense item would have to go to the IRS.

The one area that taxpayers probably underestimate the most is their spending on groceries. Very few people keep track of the total amount of money they spend on food. They often forget about the many trips they make for small purchases, such as bread, milk, and cigarettes. These small purchases often go unnoticed, but they do add up.

The very bottom of Form 433–A is the affidavit section for you to sign under penalty of perjury. The perjury statement is on the form to intimidate you so that you will give an accurate statement. The IRS wants you to think that if you deliberately omit or falsify statements on the form that you are in a "heck of a lot of trouble." The fact is that this is another one of IRS's scare tactics. Taxpayers make misrepresentations on the form all the time by leaving out sources of income, overstating expenditures, and omitting assets. Telling you this is not meant to encourage deception; it is merely meant to put to rest any fears that you may have. It would be almost impossible for the government to spend the resources needed to try a court case on a deceptive or fraudulently completed form like the 433–A. If the IRS were conducting a large criminal investigation against you and already had enough evidence to bring several charges of fraud against you, they could easily throw in another one of making a false statement just to add fuel to the fire, but even that isn't likely. Revenue Officers have their own way of handling taxpayers who deliberately deceive them. They just start seizing everything in sight. So be as honest as you can in supplying financial information.

Fighting Interest and Penalty Bills

And who isn't interested in interest?

TYPES OF PENALTIES

The number of taxpayers who do not file tax returns because they owe money is quite high. My experience as a Revenue Officer leads me to believe that about 90 percent of the tax returns not filed on time owe additional taxes. The Internal Revenue Code provides for *criminal and civil* penalties for those who do not file or pay timely. Chapter 1 thoroughly covers the circumstances under which the IRS would most likely prosecute for *not filing* on time, and Chapter 2 discusses the circumstances under which the IRS would most likely prosecute for *not paying* on time. This discussion will concentrate on the *civil* penalties that the IRS imposes. Civil penalties are handled administratively, and court review is not required.

For the fiscal year ending September 30, 1981, the IRS assessed over 22 million penalties totaling $3 billion. The Internal Revenue Code provides for a myriad of civil penalties. There are penalties for failing to file a tax return on time, for failing to pay the tax on time, for passing a bad check, for negligence, for fraud, and for a number of other situations that will not be discussed here. Each penalty has its own rates and method of computation.

Before beginning the discussion, there is a need to clarify some IRS terminology. Our tax system is one of self-assessment. You actually compute your own tax liability and charge yourself when you complete and file your tax return. The act of *assessment* is the official recording by the IRS of the charges against you. When a tax liability is assessed, applicable penalties and interest are assessed at that time in the same manner as the tax. You are then sent a computer-printed bill, dated the day of assessment, asking for full payment of tax, penalties, and interest.

Another term discussed is *accrued* penalties—penalties that will continue to run or build up until the tax liability is paid. Penalties are first accrued between the time the tax return or payment becomes delinquent and the moment of assessment. After the assessments of tax, the appropriate penalties, and interest have been made, the failure-to-pay tax penalty becomes the only penalty that continues to accrue. And it continues to accrue, or build up, until the balance of assessed tax has been paid.

A term frequently used in IRS offices is *asserting a penalty*. Assertion of a penalty must occur before assessment: This is the decision-making process of first determining your liability for the penalty and then computing the amount of penalty to be assessed. Assertion of a penalty is normally thought of as an act performed by an IRS employee as opposed to the assessment process, which is normally computer controlled. Without a specific decision made by an IRS employee *not* to assert penalties, the IRS computer automatically asserts penalties by assessing them. Except for the element of human determination, the process of assertion is synonymous with assessment.

In order to help you determine how much additional money it will cost you for not filing and paying on time, each penalty that may apply to your situation will be discussed.

INTEREST

Of course interest is not a penalty, but it is an additional charge nonetheless. From January 31, 1982, through December 31, 1982, the effective rate that the IRS charged was 20 percent. It was changed to 16 percent on January 1, 1983, and it is revised every six months thereafter.

- An individual income tax return *filed and paid* by April 15 will not be charged interest.
- Interest is compounded on a daily basis and is computed not only on the unpaid balance of tax but also on any penalties that have been assessed and not paid within ten days of notice and demand.
- Interest charges are assessed at the same moment the tax liability is assessed on tax returns that are not paid in full by the due date of the return (April 15 for 1040s). Notices demanding payment are automatically issued when the assessments are made. If the bill is paid within ten days, no other interest charges will be due. If payment is made *after* the tenth day, further interest will be charged for the entire period, including the previous ten days.
- There is no authority for waiving interest on delinquent taxes or for refunding interest that has been legally collected.
- The Tax Code authorizes the IRS to abate interest on all or any part of an assessment that was caused by a mathematical error of an IRS employee who prepared the tax return. That IRS employee must have been acting in an official capacity to provide taxpayer assistance in preparation of income tax returns. The interest may be abated within the thirty-day period after the date of the notice and demand made for payment of the related assessment.
- An extension of time to file does *not* grant an extension of time to pay. Therefore any tax that is shown to be due that was not paid by the due date of the return will be charged interest from the due date of the return to the date of final payment.

FAILURE-TO-PAY PENALTY

The Tax Code also provides for a penalty to be charged for failure to pay the tax on time. The penalty is computed on amounts shown as tax at 0.5 percent per month or a fraction of a month, from the due date of the return until date of final payment. It accrues solely on the amount of tax owed and is not computed on interest or other penalties. The penalty is limited to a maximum of 25 percent or fifty months.

The method of computation includes charging a full 0.5 percent on each fraction of a month. For example, a payment received one month and one day late is treated the same as a payment two full months late.

A failure-to-pay penalty can also arise as the result of an additional assessment of tax from an audit. But the failure-to-pay penalty on an audit assessment does not compute back to the due date of the tax return; it only arises when the tax assessed from the audit has not been paid in full within the ten-day notice-and-demand period. In other words, it only arises on the eleventh day after assessment.

The failure-to-pay penalty will be charged unless you can show that the failure to pay was due to reasonable cause and not willful neglect. (This penalty may be compromised under the offer-in-compromise procedures discussed in Chapter 7, and at the end of this chapter.)

FAILURE-TO-FILE PENALTY

The Tax Code provides a penalty for failure to file any tax return on or before the prescribed due date unless you can show that the failure was due to reasonable cause and not willful neglect. The amount of the penalty is 5 percent of the unpaid tax for each month or a fraction of a month that the tax return was not filed, up to a maximum of 25 percent.

- The filing penalty is computed on the balance of tax owed as of the filing due date. It is *not* computed on the total assessed tax but only on the unpaid *balance of assessed tax*. Credit is given for estimated tax payments and for withheld income tax.
- The failure-to-file penalty is charged not only on the balance of tax due on the filing due date, but it will also be prorated on any additional tax later shown to be owed.
- The IRS says that "if reasonable cause does not exist, but it is determined that the delinquency in filing a return was not flagrant, willful, or due to gross negligence, the taxpayer may be informed of the privilege of submitting an offer in compromise of the Failure to File Penalty . . ." (See Chapter 7 and the section in this chapter on how to submit an offer to reduce penalties.) But don't

hold your breath waiting for someone from the IRS to tell you to submit an offer in compromise.

- The failure-to-file penalty is computed on the amount owed as of the filing due date and accrues until either the tax return is filed or until the penalty has accumulated to 25 percent. Tax payments made *after* the filing due date but *before* the tax return is filed do not lower the amount of tax on which the penalty is computed.

- The Tax Equity and Fiscal Responsibility Bill of 1982 imposes a minimum $100 penalty for returns that are past due by 60 days or more, provided that there is tax due on the return. In the event the tax due is less than $100, the penalty will be equivalent to the amount of the tax.

- Also, just to make things a little more confusing, the Tax Code provides that when the failure-to-pay penalty is charged at the same time as the failure-to-file penalty, the failure-to-file penalty must be reduced by an equivalent amount so that both penalties together do not exceed 5 percent per month. Over the years the IRS computers have handled this in different ways. Now the computer charges a full 5 percent per month when both penalties apply and codes the assessment charge to both penalties.

If you have not filed your tax return for the sole reason that you do not have the money to pay the tax, then you should read Chapters 1 and 2 for help in determining what course of action you should follow. *You should realize that the IRS frowns on nonfilers who claim an inability to pay as an excuse for not filing.*

DISHONORED-CHECK PENALTY

Unlike other creditors who may have the right to press charges against you for writing a bad check, the Tax Code currently does not give the IRS that right. Several years ago the IRS studied the idea of asking Congress to change the law to make it a misdemeanor for writing a bad check, but the idea has not made any progress. Some IRS officials believe that the problem of bad checks is serious and that the government should protect itself from an activity that in all other respects would be considered criminal. In 1981 the IRS assessed more than 296,000 civil penalties against taxpayers for writing "bad checks."

The Tax Code levies the penalty at 1 percent of the amount of the dishonored check with a minimum penalty of five dollars. If the check was written for an amount less than five dollars, the penalty will be for the amount of the check. The penalty will also be asserted against anyone who submits a money order that is subsequently not paid. (For example, if the money-order company were to go bankrupt and not pay the holders of the money orders.)

This penalty is mainly levied to compensate the government for the additional clerical expense of processing a dishonored check and to serve as a deterent to those who would freely write a "bad check." Although the term *bad check* is used rather freely in describing this penalty, the IRS will actually assess the penalty whenever the tax-payer's bank does not honor the check for *any* reason. It actually makes no difference why the check was not honored.

The penalty for a dishonored check will be abated by the IRS if you can convince them that you wrote the check in good faith and had reason to believe that it would be duly paid. Less than 3 percent of bad-check penalties are abated because few taxpayers are aware of the condition under which IRS will abate the penalty.

SURVIVAL RULE ━━━━━━━━━━━━━━━━━━━━━━━━━━━━━━━

If you are assessed a penalty for a dishonored check but wrote the check in good faith, believing it would be paid, you should write the IRS a letter requesting abatement and outlining the circumstances under which you believe it should be abated.

━━━

NEGLIGENCE PENALTY

A penalty is asserted when a Tax Auditor or a Revenue Agent discovers that there has been either negligence or an intentional disregard of published rulings and regulations in the preparation of a tax return. It is not applicable when there has been a mere error or where there may be a difference of opinion on some controversial question. It can only be asserted when there is no evidence to indicate or substantiate that you have willfully intended to commit tax evasion. (Criminal and civil penalties can arise from a willful intent to evade taxes.)

The negligence penalty is computed at 5 percent of any under-payment assessed as a result of the audit plus an amount equal to 50 percent of the interest due on that portion of the underpayment for which the negligence was determined. The 50 percent addition to the interest is based on the interest assessed at the time the additional tax is assessed, computed back to the original due date of the tax return without any regard for extensions of time to file.

The following are examples of situations in which the IRS may determine that there has been negligence:

- You have continued to make substantial errors in under-report-ing income or claiming disallowable deductions year after year, even though you have been audited previously and the same mis-takes have been brought to your attention.
- You have failed to maintain proper records after having been warned of improper record keeping in the past, and you have continued to file tax returns with substantial errors.
- You have made careless and exaggerated claims of deductions that cannot be substantiated by the facts.
- You have failed to offer any explanation for under-reporting your income or for failing to maintain proper books and records.

If you intend to challenge the IRS's assertion of the negligence penalty, you must do so during the appeals process that follows a proposed audit assessment of additional taxes. After the appeals process has terminated, or the time to make the appeal has expired, and the additional tax and negligence penalty have been assessed, the tax and the penalty cannot be abated unless they are first paid. Revenue Officers are not allowed to abate negligence penalties, and neither are the examiners in the service centers.

In 1981 the IRS assessed 126,000 negligence penalties in the amount of $21 million.

CIVIL-FRAUD PENALTY

Fraud is a word that is most assuredly associated with the en-forcement image of the IRS. It is also a word that will make the hearts of millions of taxpayers skip a beat. The word immediately conjures up visions of bars, stripes, and jail cells. Yet, despite the ferocious reputation of the IRS, few taxpayers are ever charged with criminal fraud. In 1981 the IRS only prosecuted 1,494 cases nationwide for a wide range of criminal activity. Only 802 taxpayers in the entire nation even received jail sentences.

Your real concern should be with how IRS's fraud enforcement can affect you in a civil way. (If you are ever faced with a charge of *criminal* fraud you are in serious trouble and you should get a lawyer right way.) Most taxpayers are not aware that *the IRS can charge fraud as a civil administrative procedure that does not involve prosecutors or courts.*

The civil-fraud penalty, even if it began with a routine audit examination, can be recommended only after a criminal investigation has been conducted by Special Agents of the Criminal Investigations Division. Both civil and criminal sanctions may be imposed for the same fraudulent act, and a decision not to prosecute or an acquittal in a criminal case has no bearing on the imposition of the civil-fraud penalty.

The reason is that the burden and measure of proof is different in civil and criminal cases. In criminal cases "the Government must prove every facet of the offense and show guilt beyond a reasonable doubt. In civil cases, the Commissioner's determination of the deficiency is presumptively correct and the burden is placed on the taxpayer to overcome this presumption. When fraud is alleged, the Government has the burden of establishing such fraud by clear and convincing evidence" (Section 411:(6) of IRM 9781, *Special Agent's Handbook*).

IRS Policy Statement P–9–5 states: "The civil fraud penalty will be recommended for each taxable period where clear and convincing evidence is available to prove that some part of the underpayment of tax was due to fraud. Such evidence must show intent to evade the payment of tax which the taxpayer is believed to be owing as distinguished from mistake, inadvertence, reliance, or incorrect technical advice, honest difference of opinion, negligence, or carelessness."

If the IRS discovers you have committed a fraudulent act, you will be investigated for criminal prosecution. The IRS has the right to impose a civil-fraud penalty concurrently with prosecution of criminal fraud and also has the right to recommend assertion of a civil-fraud penalty where prosecution is not undertaken.

Regardless of how the IRS proceeds with the criminal case, if a determination is made that you have under-reported your tax liability "with intent to evade tax," the IRS will impose a fine equal to 50 percent of the under-reported tax plus an amount equal to 50 percent of the interest due on that portion of the underpayment attributable to fraud. The 50 percent addition to the interest is computed the same as the 50 percent addition to the interest where a negligence penalty is asserted. The Tax Code does not allow the IRS to assert a negligence penalty and a fraud penalty at the same time.

The timing of filing your tax return is a consideration in computing the fraud penalty. If the tax return was filed on time (by its due date including extensions), the underpayment on which the fraud penalty is based is the difference between the corrected liability and the amount of tax originally reported on the return. If the tax return was filed late, the fraud penalty is based on the entire recomputed tax liability.

Unlike other penalties, civil-fraud penalty assessments are not necessarily made against both persons who may have signed the tax return. When a joint tax return is filed, both spouses are held liable for payment of any portion or even all the tax, interest, and penalties that are incurred by the filing of that joint tax return; however, when a 50 percent civil-fraud penalty is assessed, Tax Code section 6653(b) states that only the spouse who has committed the fraudulent conduct is liable for payment of that penalty. In the event both spouses have participated in the fraudulent activity, then and only then would they both be held responsible for its payment. If a husband and wife file separate tax returns, then only the spouse filing the fraudulent return is liable for payment of the civil-fraud penalty.

In 1981 the IRS assessed 12,178 civil-fraud penalties for a total of $58 million. A civil-fraud penalty cannot be abated administratively. It must be challenged during the audit-appeals process before assessment. After assessment you will have to pay the tax and penalty and then file a claim for refund if you want to challenge it again.

PENALTY FOR FAILURE TO PAY ESTIMATED TAX

Prior to January 1, 1983, certain taxpayers were required to file Form 1040–ES, "Declaration of Estimated Tax for Individuals," *and* to pay estimated taxes up to four times a year. Paying estimated taxes is the method self-employed taxpayers use to pay income and Social Security taxes when they have no withholding. Estimated tax payments are also required of salaried individuals who may not have enough income tax withheld.

The Tax Equity and Fiscal Responsibility Bill of 1982 eliminated the requirements to *file declarations* of estimated tax for any taxable year beginning after December 31, 1982. The bill, however, did not eliminate the requirement to *pay* estimated taxes. All payment requirements are still in effect as if the requirements relating to the declarations of estimated tax were still in effect. This means that you must still pay your estimated taxes as before or else the IRS will impose a penalty for insufficient payments, just as before. The estimated tax penalty is computed in the same manner as before and at the same rate as interest.

The estimated tax penalty is automatically imposed if you do not pay in full the correct amount of estimated tax by the due dates of the installments. Installments are due on April 15, June 15, September 15, and January 15 of the succeeding year. *Unlike other penalties, this penalty cannot be abated for reasonable cause.* But the IRS will not assert the penalty if any one of these four situations exist:

- You make estimated payments and have tax withheld at least equal or more than equal to last year's tax liability.
- You make estimated payments and have tax withheld equal to or more than 80 percent of the tax due on your annualized taxable income.
- You make estimated payments and have withheld tax equal to 90 percent of the tax due, using current year's tax rates applied to the actual income prior to the month in which the installment is paid.
- You make estimated payments and have tax withheld equal to or more than what would have been due on your previous year's income using current year rates.

The tax bill of 1982 also prohibits the IRS from imposing a penalty for failure to make estimated tax payments for any taxable year if all of these pertain to you:

—You did not have any tax liability for the preceding tax year.
—The preceding tax year was a taxable year of twelve months.
—You were a citizen or resident of the United States throughout the preceding taxable year.

If you qualify for an exception to the penalty under any of the five situations discussed above, you should follow this survival rule.

SURVIVAL RULE ▬▬▬▬▬▬▬▬▬▬▬▬▬▬▬▬▬▬▬▬▬▬▬▬

The only way to prevent the assessment of a penalty for failing to pay estimated tax is to complete Form 2210, "Underpayment of Estimated Tax by Individuals," and send it with your tax return at the time of filing.

Form 2210 is designed specifically for you, either to compute the amount of estimated penalty that you think you would owe or to claim nonassessment of the penalty due to the existence of one of the five special situations. The method of computation is rather complicated, and so few taxpayers ever complete Form 2210 on their own. Accountants and tax practitioners usually know this and charge more to complete one.

If you decide that you want to complete Form 2210 yourself, you can go to your local IRS office for assistance. Otherwise you may have to pay an accountant or a tax practitioner to help you. That is why a lot of taxpayers just pay the penalty and forget about trying to fight it. In fact, a lot of tax practitioners tell their clients to do that, too, because Form 2210 takes up too much of their time to complete.

If the IRS has already assessed a penalty for failing to make adequate estimated tax payments, you can still request an abatement without having to pay the tax first.

SURVIVAL RULE ▬▬▬▬▬▬▬▬▬▬▬▬▬▬▬▬▬▬▬▬▬▬▬▬▬▬

To request an abatement of a penalty for failure to pay estimated tax, you must complete Form 2210 showing that you meet one of the situations that exempt you from having to pay the penalty and return it to the appropriate IRS service center with a copy of your bill.

▬▬▬

SITUATION: FIGHTING PENALTY BILLS

Q. *I recently got a bill from the IRS charging me $500 worth of penalties. I don't think it's fair. I filed my tax return late, but I had a good reason. My husband died in early April, and it took me several months before I could attend to the family's financial affairs. Then it took me quite a while before I could find all the material to prepare the return. I think the IRS ought to be more understanding of people's problems and not fine them under circumstances like mine. What should I do?*

You are right. The IRS should be more understanding and compassionate with taxpayers' problems, and in some cases they are. But the IRS needs to be told when there has been a problem before they can possibly do anything about it. Unfortunately, the IRS does not like to publicly acknowledge that taxpayers can be "officially excused" for not filing or paying on time. Nowhere in the IRS income tax instructions is there a mention of what to do in a circumstance like yours. Yet the IRS deals with problems and situations like yours every day.

In 1981 the IRS assessed 12.2 million penalties against *individual* income taxpayers but abated only 1.2 million of them, or roughly 10 percent of all individual penalties assessed. More than likely the IRS either could have or would have abated more penalties if more taxpayers had not given in so easily.

And just how does the IRS decide when to abate a penalty and when not to abate? The Tax Code repeatedly provides that penalties will be assessed unless "such failure is due to reasonable cause and not due to willful neglect." This almost seems to say that willful neglect will be presumed automatically in the absence of reasonable cause. Therefore it is standard procedure for the IRS to automatically assess penalties whenever a deliquency to file or pay has occurred and the taxpayer has not presented reasonable cause. There are several problems here that pertain to millions of situations or circumstances similar to the one in the example above:

- The IRS has not specifically defined "reasonable cause" for the public.
- The IRS has not clearly told taxpayers what to do if the reason for failure to perform was somewhere in between reasonable cause and willful neglect.

Because IRS publications are not clear on either of these situations, most taxpayers are left totally in the dark, not knowing if the IRS will abate penalties or the circumstances under which they can be abated.

IRS regulations are not much help either. For example, Regulation 301.6651(3)(c)(1) states:

- "If the taxpayer exercised *ordinary business care and prudence* and was nevertheless unable to file the return within the prescribed time, then the delay is due to a reasonable cause."
- "A failure to pay will be considered to be due to reasonable cause to the extent that the taxpayer has made a satisfactory showing that he exercised *ordinary business care and prudence* in providing for payment of his tax liability and was nevertheless either unable to pay the tax or would suffer an undue hardship . . . if he paid on the due date."

As you can see, the regulations are general enough to leave plenty of room for discretion. And the IRS would prefer that the public know only the definitions given to them in the regulations. But the truth is that the IRS has developed a specific set of guidelines called "reasonable cause criteria," which is a list of circumstances that helps IRS employees decide if your personal situation allows them to recommend either nonassessment or abatement of the penalties.

The IRS has attempted to shield the reasonable cause criteria from public disclosure by placing it in an obscure provision of the Internal Revenue Manual (IRM) on computer procedures. They believe that if the information became public, it would be widely abused.

But as clever as the IRS has tried to be, they have inadvertently retained the reasonable cause criteria in various places in the IRM. On pages 106–107 are reproductions of those portions of the IRM relating to reasonable cause criteria.

SURVIVAL RULE ▬▬▬▬▬▬▬▬▬▬▬▬▬▬▬▬▬▬▬

If you have already been sent a bill for penalties and you believe that you have reasonable cause that they should be abated, you should either write to the IRS service center that sent the bill or visit your local IRS office. In either case you should submit a written request for abatement and outline your reasons why your request is being made.

▬▬▬▬▬▬▬▬▬▬▬▬▬▬▬▬▬▬▬▬▬▬▬▬▬▬▬▬▬▬▬▬

Each tax return is processed through an IRS service center where tax examiners read and act upon correspondence from taxpayers. These tax examiners are not computers; they are humans who have the authority and the responsibility of handling requests for abatements by taxpayers and other IRS employees. During a telephone conversation with one of these tax examiners about an abatement of a penalty, I was told that about all a taxpayer had to do was to ask for an abatement and he got it. A lot of abatements were being made even though taxpayers did not show reasonable cause. The point was made that reasonable cause consisted of almost any "good, understandable, and believable" explanation that did not clearly show "willful neglect." The reason why the tax examiners were so lenient in abating penalties was that the IRS had a bad enough reputation, and as a public relations gesture it made good sense to have taxpayers think that there were "sympathetic and compassionate" employees within the service. Another reason was that many taxpayers who felt that the IRS was being too harsh with them would write to their representatives in Congress to complain. Even though intervention from Capitol Hill consisted merely of a written inquiry, the unwritten rule within most government agencies is to please members of Congress so that they can please their constituents. So in an attempt not to anger Congress, the service center would abate taxpayers' penalties under a loose interpretation of reasonable cause.

The point is that you have little to lose by writing to the service center and requesting that the penalty be abated. If you would rather talk to someone about your problem, then you can go down to your local IRS office and talk with either a Taxpayer Service Representative or a Revenue Officer in the Collection Division. Either employee has the authority to request abatement of penalties, and tax examiners in the service center are not allowed to overrule abatement requests from these two IRS employees.

A sympathetic representive or officer will complete Form 3870, "Request for Adjustment," and see that it is sent to the appropriate service center for processing.

A word of caution is presented in the next survival rule:

SURVIVAL RULE ▬▬▬▬▬▬▬▬▬▬▬▬▬▬▬▬▬▬▬▬▬▬▬▬▬

If you have already been billed for a penalty that you think you should not have to pay, make your request before the Past Due Final Notice for payment is sent to you.

As you might expect, Revenue Officers are not normally as "sympathetic and lenient" as are other IRS employees. Revenue Officers constantly work in a hostile environment in which lies, deception, and fraud characterize a good many of their cases. This makes them cynical, unresponsive to taxpayers' problems, and a lot less understanding than other employees. What is reasonable cause to one officer may not be so to another, IRS guidelines notwithstanding.

This problem mainly arises because not all Revenue Officers have access to an Internal Revenue Manual, and many who do have access to manuals just do not take the time to read them. Many officers like to show their muscle by telling taxpayers to "pay it and file a claim later." For this reason the IRS has instituted a procedure whereby you can appeal a decision by an IRS employee who refuses to abate a penalty.

PENALTY APPEALS

You can use the IRS penalty-appeals procedure after an IRS employee—a tax examiner at the serivce center, a Taxpayer Service

4562.2 *(10-25-78)*

Reasonable Cause for Delinquent Filing

(1) In accordance with policy statement P-2-7, the following eight specific causes for failure to file a return within the time prescribed by law, if clearly established by the taxpayer, will be accepted as reasonable.

(a) Return was mailed in time (whether or not the envelope containing the return had sufficient postage). A return is considered mailed in time if the date of the postmark stamped on the envelope falls on or before the due date. If the due date falls on Sunday or a legal holiday, the following business day is within the legal period.

(b) Return was filed within the legal period but in the wrong district, or directly in the Regional Commissioner's or Commissioner's office.

(c) Delay or failure to file was due to erroneous information given the taxpayer by an internal revenue officer or employee.

(d) Delay was caused by death or serious illness of the taxpayer or a death or serious illness in his/her immediate family. In the case of a corporation, estate, trust, etc., the death or serious illness must have been of an individual having sole authority to execute the return or of a member of such individual's immediate family.

(e) Delay was caused by unavoidable absence of the taxpayer. In the case of a corporation, estate, trust, etc., the absence must have been of an individual having sole authority to execute the return.

(f) Delinquency was caused by the destruction by fire or other casualty of the taxpayer's place of business or business records.

(g) Taxpayer, prior to the time for filing return, made an application to the District Director's office for proper blanks and these were not furnished him/her in sufficient time to permit the executed return to be filed on or before its due date.

(h) Taxpayer proves that he/she personally visited the office of the District Director or a subordinate office before the expiration of the time within which to file return for the purpose of securing information or aid to properly make out his/her return, and through no fault of his/her own was unable to see the representative of the Service.

(2) If the cause does not fall within one of the reasonable causes enumerated above, the District Director will decide whether, in his/her opinion, the statement of facts submitted by the taxpayer establishes a reasonable cause for delinquency. A cause for delinquency which appears to a person of ordinary prudence and intelligence as a reasonable cause for delay in filing a return and which clearly negatives a willful intent to disobey the taxing statutes, or gross negligence, will be accepted as reason-

able. In cases where ignorance of the law is claimed, reasonable cause should not be presumed. Each case must be determined on its own merit. Ignorance of the law can be considered for reasonable cause if other facts support this contention, such as first-time filers, sudden first-time FTD depositary requirements, etc. The taxpayer should evidence ordinary business care and prudence and the case should be judged on its own merits.

P–2–7 (Approved 12–29–70)
Reasonable cause for late filing of return or failure to deposit or pay tax when due

Any sound reason advanced by a taxpayer as the cause for delay in filing a return, making deposits under the Federal Tax Deposit System, or paying tax when due, will be carefully analyzed to determine whether the applicable penalty should be asserted. Examples of sound causes for delay which, if established, will be accepted as reasonable cause are shown below.

(1) Death or serious illness of the taxpayer or a death or serious illness in his/her immediate family. In the case of a corporation, estate, trust, etc., the death or serious illness must have been of an individual having sole authority to execute the return or make the deposit or payment or of a member of such individual's immediate family.

(2) Unavoidable absence of the taxpayer. In the case of a corporation, estate, trust, etc., the absence must have been of an individual having sole authority to execute the return or make the deposit or payment.

(3) Destruction by fire or other casualty of the taxpayer's place of business or business records.

(4) Taxpayer was unable to determine amount of deposit or tax due for reasons beyond the taxpayer's control. However, this cause will be acceptable for taxpayers required to make deposits or payments of trust fund taxes only when the taxpayer was unable to have access to his/her own records.

(5) The facts indicate that the taxpayer's ability to make deposits or payments has been materially impaired by civil disturbances.

(6) Lack of funds is an acceptable reasonable cause for failure to pay any tax or make a deposit under the Federal Tax Deposit System only when a taxpayer can demonstrate the lack of funds occurred despite the exercise of ordinary business care and prudence.

Other explanations may be acceptable

Acceptable explanations of delinquency are not limited to the examples given above, since any reason for delinquency in filing or making deposits or payments which established that the taxpayer exercised ordinary business care and prudence but was nevertheless unable to comply within the prescribed time will be accepted as reasonable cause.

Representative, or a Revenue Officer—has refused your request to abate a penalty or penalties. This appeals procedure only pertains to penalties that have already been assessed or after a bill has been sent. It does not apply to requests made for nonassessment at the time a delinquent return is filed. Even though you can make a request for nonassessment at the time you file a delinquent return, a decision by the collection employee to assess the penalty anyway cannot be appealed through formal channels.

If you disagree with the penalty determination prior to assessment, you will be informed that a postassessment appeal procedure will allow you the opportunity to appeal the determination at a later date. This policy can be detrimental to you because there may be a mix-up during the billing period and a seizure might be made on your bank account or paycheck before you have had an opportunity to appeal the assessment. These kinds of incidents do occur quite regularly.

The penalty-appeal procedure can begin at any time after you have been billed for the penalty. It is *not necessary* and it is *not required* that a payment be made on the penalty before beginning the penalty-appeal procedure. This is an administrative process totally separate from any other claim procedure that may require you to first pay the tax and then file a claim. A formal claim is *not* necessary in this case.

In the event that your request to the IRS employee for a penalty abatement is denied, the employee is required to notify you of the appeal procedure. If you decide to proceed with the appeal, you will be given fifteen days to submit a written request. No special form is provided, and the request can be handwritten on stationery. It will be sent directly to the appeals office.

If the penalty amount is already in the delinquency stage (that is, it has already been assigned to a Revenue Officer for collection), enforced collection action will not be taken within the fifteen-day period or during the time that the case is under consideration by the appeals office.

You should know, however, that the IRS is prepared to continue with enforced collection action if they have reason to believe that the penalty appeal is being used solely to delay collection and the circumstances indicate that enforced collection action should be continued.

The appeals officer will review the case, your written request, and any information from the denying employee that may be available. He has forty-five days to act on the request. This is the final administrative appeal avenue available to you. The only recourse after this is to pay the tax, file a claim for a refund, and sue in court for reimbursement if the claim is denied. For that you will need an attorney.

SITUATION: PREVENTING PENALTY BILLS

Q. *I want to go ahead and file my tax return even though it will be filed late and I owe several thousand dollars. It looks like I'll be hit with quite a few penalties for failure to file, failure to pay, and failure to make estimated tax payments. I believe that I had a good enough reason for not filing and that I shouldn't have to pay all those penalties. I don't want to wait until I get billed before I start to fight this thing. What should I do?*

Before we discuss your problem, let's discuss how you could have prevented some of those problems in the first place. First, if it appears that you will not be able to file on time, the IRS regulations provide that you should request an extension of time to file regardless of the reason needed for the extension. You can get an automatic four-month extension of time to file your tax return by filing Form 4868, "Application for Automatic Extension of Time to File U.S. Individual Income Tax Return." Remember, though, that *an extension to file is not an extension to pay.* You are required to compute your total tax liability, or estimate it as close as you can, and pay any balance due with Form 4868, which must be filed by the due date of your tax return (April 15 for most people).

If you need longer than four months to file, you should either write to the IRS outlining the reasons you need an extension or file Form 2688, "Application for Extension of Time to File U.S. Individual Income Tax Return." The IRS requires that you first use Form 4868 before using Form 2688 unless your case is a "hardship." (What is a "hardship"? The IRS doesn't say.)

To obtain an extension you need to tell the IRS the following information:

- The reason why you are requesting the extension.
- How much additional time you need.
- The tax year to which the extension applies.
- Whether you have already filed another extension of time to file.
- Whether you filed your tax returns on time for the preceding three years and, if not, the reasons why.
- Whether or not you filed and paid timely any estimated tax that may have been due.

As you already know, nothing is simple with the IRS. Most people would prefer not to answer all those questions and to say the heck with the whole thing. But if you end up owing a hefty tax liability and didn't have an extension to cover you until you file, you could be hit with an enormous penalty for failing to file on time.

Some taxpayers don't even bother requesting the automatic four-month extension, thinking that if they have to go through the trouble of figuring what they owe, then they might as well complete their tax return and file it on April 15. There's probably something to that argument.

SURVIVAL RULE ▆▆▆▆▆▆▆▆▆▆▆▆▆▆▆▆▆▆▆▆▆▆▆▆▆▆▆

If you cannot file your tax return by the due date, then you should always file a request for an extension of time to file.

At the time you file the tax return, you can make a plea for nonassessment of any penalties you would otherwise be liable for. The two penalties for which you should present reasonable cause and attempt a nonassessment are the failure-to-file and the failure-to-pay penalties.

The IRS does allow nonassessment of penalties during assessment of the tax liability. There are several ways in which this can be handled.

Taxpayer service employees (either representatives or specialists) are required to determine if reasonable cause exists or if a penalty should be assessed when taxpayers hand deliver delinquent returns to them. If the representative or specialist concludes that reasonable cause exists for nonassessment of a penalty or penalties, they should

SURVIVAL RULE ▬▬▬▬▬▬▬▬▬▬▬▬▬▬▬▬▬▬▬▬▬▬▬▬▬▬▬▬▬▬▬

*If you mail a delinquent return to the service center that shows
you still owe tax, you should attach a letter explaining your
circumstances for being delinquent and request that no penalties be assessed due to reasonable cause. Trying to head off
a penalty assessment in the first place is the best strategy.*

SURVIVAL RULE ▬▬▬▬▬▬▬▬▬▬▬▬▬▬▬▬▬▬▬▬▬▬▬▬▬▬▬▬▬▬▬

*If you want to make personal contact with an IRS employee
to request nonassessment of penalties, then you should personally file your tax return at your local IRS office with a
Taxpayer Service Representative or a Taxpayer Service Specialist. Avoid, if possible, contact with Revenue Officers or
other collection employees.*

complete Form 4571, "Explanation for Late Filing of Return or Late
Payment of Tax," and attach it to the tax return. A written statement
of explanation by you is also preferable and, if available, should be
attached to Form 4571. Otherwise you can make an oral statement,
and the explanation will be written on Form 4571. The representative
or specialist must also notate on the tax return that reasonable cause
exists for nonassessment of the penalty. For Forms 1040 and 1040A
this is done by completing Form 4364, "Delinquency Computations,"
and attaching it to the return. You will want to make sure this is
done, and so observe the representative or specialist carefully.

If the representative or specialist decides that reasonable cause
does not exist and that the penalties should be assessed, you will be
informed that you will have to pay the penalty and file a claim for a
refund on Form 843, "Claim," if you want to challenge the decision.

Although it is best to avoid contact with a Revenue Officer when
requesting a nonassessment of penalties, it is not possible to do so
after the IRS computer has already sent you up to four notices
requesting that you file a delinquent return and has printed a computer paragraph called a "Taxpayer Delinquency Investigation"

(TDI). A TDI is a case assignment requiring a Revenue Officer either to secure the delinquent return or to find out if you are not liable for filing. Once the TDI assignment has been made, the IRS expects that officer to vigorously pursue the case, including deciding when a delinquent return is secured, whether or not reasonable cause exists, and whether penalties should be assessed.

However, since nothing is engraved in stone, some taxpayers are crafty about avoiding contact with an officer even after they have been personally contacted and directed to file their delinquent return with a specific officer. There is no law that says you cannot bypass the officer and send the return directly to the IRS service center. When this happens the IRS computer automatically sends a notification to the officer telling him that the return has been filed and the case is closed. At that point the officer does not care whether you had reasonable cause or even whether penalties should be assessed. The officer is usually happy, in fact, because the case is closed without expending more of his time.

COMPROMISING A PENALTY

Earlier it was mentioned that penalties can be abated only if the failure to act was due to reasonable cause and not to willful neglect. What happens if your excuse falls somewhere in between—the IRS does *not* consider it to be reasonable cause, but it certainly is not willful neglect?

The answer to that question can be found in Chapter 7 relating to the compromise provisions of the Tax Code. An "offer in compromise" is an amount of money offered by you in an attempt to bring about a legal reduction in your tax liability or penalties.

There are two situations under which you can compromise a tax or penalty liability: when there is a reasonable doubt that the IRS will ever be able to collect your tax or penalty, or when there is a reasonable doubt that you may be liable for the tax or penalty. Although penalties can be compromised on either of these conditions, it almost always occurs based on doubt of liability.

This discussion will focus on compromising two *delinquency* penalties, the failure-to-pay penalty and the failure-to-file penalty.

If the IRS guidelines show that your failure to act (thereby incurring a penalty or penalties) was due to reasonable cause, then your penalty should be abated, and you should not have to pay it. If the delinquency was flagrant, willful, or involves gross negligence, the delinquency penalty cannot be compromised on the liability issue.

The concepts of gross negligence and willfulness involve subjective interpretations by the Revenue Officer handling the case. A court or judicial determination is not necessary because the assessment and collection of civil penalties are administrative and civil matters, not criminal or judicial ones.

The Internal Revenue Manual (IRM) does not define *gross negligence*, but previous editions stated that "any case in which a taxpayer has been delinquent several times would usually be considered as a sufficient basis for the rejection of a compromise . . . ," meaning that a past history of negligence would lose support for compromising your penalty or tax.

The IRM defines *willful* as "meaning intentional, deliberate, voluntary, knowing, without reasonable cause, as distinguished from accidental. It is construed to be the attitude of a person who, having a free will or choice, either intentionally disregards the statement, or is plainly indifferent to its requirement."

So if your reason, explanation, or excuse falls somewhere in between reasonable cause and gross negligence or willfulness, then you may have grounds for compromising the penalty. Just so that you clearly understand at this point: Compromising a penalty means that you will have to give in a little by paying a certain amount. The amount that you think you should have to pay is called the *offer*. An offer always involves a certain sum of money, even if it is only ten cents on each dollar owed. Chapter 7 explains the compromise procedure in depth and should be read before proceeding with this section on compromising penalties.

* * *

It is the opinion of the IRS that tax, interest, and penalty constitute one liability and that the penalty and interest may not be divorced from the tax. Known as the "one liability principle," this is really not contradictory, as it may first seem, to the statement made earlier that penalties can be compromised even though the tax is not being compromised.

An offer in compromise relates to your *entire* liability of tax, penalties, and interest. When a compromise is submitted to compromise the tax, it also covers those penalties and interest that pertain to the tax liability. But an offer can be submitted to compromise a penalty, or penalties, separate from the tax. The reason it is important for you to know this is because the IRS has imposed a condition before they will allow you to submit an offer to compromise a penalty: The tax and interest *must* be paid first, along with any *other* penalties that are not being compromised.

If the tax and interest are not paid when a penalty offer is submitted, the IRS will withhold any action on the offer until the tax and interest *are* paid. The IRM requires Revenue Officers to reject a penalty offer when the outstanding tax and interest are not paid within a reasonable period of time.

Another important fact you should know is in IRM 5792.3:(1): "A penalty offer will not be favorably considered if the penalty itself is already paid. Since there is no outstanding liability subject to compromise, the offer should be rejected immediately."

SURVIVAL RULE ■■■

You should not pay a penalty if you intend to submit an offer to compromise it.

If you have never heard of the compromise provision before, don't be surprised. The IRS has deliberately kept a low profile on it, not wanting to be deluged by offers from taxpayers. Each offer submitted becomes a full-scale case requiring an investigation by another officer who has been trained in offers, and the approval of each offer requires the study, review, and signature of a number of officials within the chain of command. Because of all the staff time involved in investigating and processing offers, the IRM only allows officers to inform you of the right to submit an offer to compromise "when the offer is in the best interests of the government."

Several important points need to be made about submitting a penalty offer, and these relate to the IRS's hesitation in publicly inviting taxpayers to follow the compromise route:

- Under the one liability principle an acceptance of a penalty offer by the IRS effectively, conclusively, and finally settles all matters of the *entire* liability for tax, penalty, and interest for the years or periods being compromised. This means that after a penalty offer has been accepted the IRS cannot assess additional taxes on the tax return being compromised, and you can never file an amended tax return for an adjustment that may result in a refund.

SURVIVAL RULE ▰▰▰▰▰▰▰▰▰▰▰▰▰▰▰▰▰▰▰▰▰▰▰▰▰▰▰▰▰▰▰

Do not file an offer to compromise a penalty unless you are willing to forgo your right at some future time to submit an amended return for the tax liability on which the penalty has been assessed.

IMPORTANT: Before submitting a penalty offer, you must be convinced that you have claimed all the deductions that you are entitled to claim and that you have legitimately reduced your tax to the lowest amount possible.

- The IRM requires that the tax return for the period being compromised by a penalty offer *must* be audited or accepted on "survey" and closed. A survey occurs when an IRS auditor merely "looks over" the tax return without calling you in to explain what you have put on the return. The "look-over" is done as a spot check to see if anything appears amiss. If something looks unusual or out of the ordinary, the IRS auditor can then pull the tax return for an audit. If everything looks okay, the tax return is sent back to the service center for storage, and you will never even know about the "look-over."

SURVIVAL RULE ▰▰▰▰▰▰▰▰▰▰▰▰▰▰▰▰▰▰▰▰▰▰▰▰▰▰▰▰▰▰▰

If you are afraid of being audited, then you should not file an offer to compromise a delinquency penalty.

- A compromise entails a contract between you and the IRS, and the contractual terms are spelled out on IRS Form 656 (see pages 202–203). Paragraph 3(b) of Form 656 specifically bars refunds that might otherwise be allowable. This means that the IRS can keep any future refunds that may be due you for the tax year to which the penalty offer applies, any refunds due you for prior tax years, or for any refund due you during the calendar year in which the offer is being submitted. The waiver of refunds does not make much sense on doubt-of-liability offers because in effect the IRS could collect more taxes than the amount being offered. By crossing out the waiver of refunds on Form 656, you are preventing the IRS from taking any future refunds you may be entitled to.

SURVIVAL RULE ▬▬▬▬▬▬▬▬▬▬▬▬▬▬▬▬▬▬▬▬▬▬▬▬▬

When submitting an offer to compromise a penalty based on the premise that the facts lie somewhere between reasonable cause and willful neglect, cross out line 3, subparagraph (b) of Form 656, "Offer in Compromise."

The IRS has had problems with this procedure in the past, because the one liability principle prevents them from auditing a tax return closed by a penalty offer, but yet taxpayers have sued to recover refunds based on carrybacks of net operating losses and investment credits. So in order to protect your rights to receive future refund checks on tax years not closed by the penalty offer and in order to protect the one liability principle that effectively closes the tax liability compromised by a penalty offer, the IRS has devised Form 2261–D, "Collateral Agreement—Delinquency Penalty Offer," to be used when compromising penalties.

Form 2261–D clarifies the waiver provisions of Form 656 and precludes your getting any refunds due to a carryback of either a net operating loss or an investment credit only from the tax year of the penalty compromise. This form must always be used on offers to compromise a delinquency (failure-to-file and/or failure-to-pay) penalty involving an income tax return.

HOW MUCH SHOULD YOU OFFER?

The IRM does not say how much of an offer is acceptable to the IRS to compromise penalties based on doubt of liability. It only says "the degree of doubt in each particular case as supported by the evidence will determine the dollar amount acceptable." But as you already know, the measure of a degree of doubt is always a subjective determination by an IRS official, who may be influenced by the degree of pressure that he may feel in his role to "protect the government's interest."

The IRS management basically dislikes the offer statute. Management officials like to see things in black and white, without gray areas. I would imagine that if more taxpayers began submitting offers, and the offer statute became public knowledge, that the IRS would push Congress to abolish it. At present there are too few offers submitted and too few people who know about it for the IRS to worry. So far it has not proved to be a danger to voluntary compliance.

The general IRS dislike of the offer statute may be manifested in a certain amount of resistance that you may experience. For instance, the Revenue Officer may not even suggest it even though he may quietly think to himself that your situation would be a perfect offer case. Or he may try to discourage you by telling you that the boss does not like offers and never approves any.

Even if you persist, the officer may tell you that it is useless to submit one because he won't approve it and that if he does not approve it, then no one else will. He may even tell you that he does not know anything about offers, that special officers work them, and that he cannot help you.

A Revenue Officer may try to dissuade you from submitting an offer in a number of ways. This is where your own instincts come in. You have to develop a feel for the situation and the negotiation process. Obviously it is possible that the officer is being honest with you in telling you that you do not have a chance to have an offer approved. Do not try to push the issue if deep down you know your excuse for not filing or not paying indicates gross negligence or willfulness. Even if you are able to convince the officer, there are many more officials with more years of experience who must also be convinced. But if your discussion with the officer leads you to believe otherwise, then follow your instincts and pursue it. You may have to go directly to the officer's boss for discussion and negotiation; this is perfectly proper and many times it is the only way to get results.

If you are fortunate enough not to experience any resistance, or fortunate enough to overcome some initial resistance, then you have taken the first big step. The next step is to try to determine how much

SURVIVAL RULE ▬▬▬▬▬▬▬▬▬▬▬▬▬▬▬▬▬▬▬▬▬▬▬▬▬▬▬

> *If you reach an impasse with a Revenue Officer who tries to convince you, against your better judgment, that you have no grounds for compromising a penalty, then you should go directly to his manager.*

should be offered to ease your pain of having to pay what they say you owe. Even though the IRS may accept offers as low as ten cents on the dollar, they certainly do not do it in every case and more than likely they will not do it for a penalty offer based on doubt of liability. A nominal 10 percent offer would probably be accepted only in a doubt-of-collectibility case with slim prospects for future recovery. We can almost imagine the IRS only accepting a 10 percent offer from a taxpayer on his deathbed.

In a doubt-of-collectibility case, the determination of what to accept is more objective because it is based on the value of your assets. A doubt-of-liability case is different because there is no objective way to measure the degree of doubt. My own guess is that for the lack of a gut feeling one way or another, the IRS may be prone to just split the difference down the middle, fifty-fifty.

Again, the whole process requires discussion and negotiation. Other factors may play a role, such as the amount of money involved, the kind of evidence that exists to support the facts, your credibility, your past history, your attitude, the Revenue Officer's attitude, the attitude of the officer's boss or the boss's boss, the credibility of witnesses to substantiate the event or nonevent, or a whole host of other factors.

One suggestion would be to start the negotiation process by sitting down with an officer and outlining the relevant facts in writing and placing a numerical value (say 1 to 10) next to each fact. This numerical value would be a subjective determination of how closely the fact appears to meet a reasonable-cause criterion. Of course, to do this you need to know what the reasonable-cause criterion is, since it is obviously part of the negotiation process.

The next step would be to list all the evidence or documentation or supporting facts that may exist. Next to each one, place another numerical value (using the same scale) representing the degree to which that item supports the facts listed previously.

The third step would be to average each category by adding up the total scores and dividing by the number of items listed to obtain an average for that category. After you have obtained an average from each category, then you average the two categories to arrive at one final score. Subtract this score from the highest numerical value used (say either 10 or 100 percent) and the remainder represents the percentage of the amount that should be offered. For example, if the remainder is 3 or 30 percent, then you would offer 30 percent of the total penalty being assessed.

Because the Internal Revenue Manual does not define the degree of doubt in objective terms, in the event of a disagreement a process needs to be worked out, and if fifty-fifty is unacceptable, and my suggestion either does not work or apply to your situation, then you must try to find a way that will. The intent of the negotiations is to produce a result compatible with your best interests and to arrive at a fair and equitable solution.

Avoiding Hidden Pitfalls
of an IRS Audit

*Some serious matters you will otherwise
learn the hard way*

VISIBLE ENFORCEMENT

The tax return audit is the IRS's most visible enforcement program. It receives the most media attention, more books have been written about audits than any other IRS program, and it is generally considered by many taxpayers to be IRS's biggest weapon in promoting voluntary compliance. Perhaps nothing causes as much large-scale anxiety and as many sleepless nights as the friendly letter of invitation from the IRS requesting taxpayers to come into the office for an *examination* of their tax return. (The IRS no longer uses the word *audit*, preferring the word *examination*. Since *audit* is the more commonly understood term, it will be used here.)

There is a great deal of mystique surrounding the audit process. The average, law-abiding, middle-class, middle-income taxpayer is usually "scared to death" the first time he is audited. He is always afraid that the IRS may know something about him that he doesn't want the IRS to know or that the IRS may discover he made some "silly error" and send him to jail for it. Or he may wonder if somehow, for whatever reason, he has been personally selected by the government to go through "this humiliating, soul-searching experience" to "teach him a lesson." For these taxpayers, it is not the audit procedure itself that produces the anxiety, it is the fear of the *consequences of the audit*.

Some taxpayers are too complacent about the audit process and make a game of trying to beat the IRS. They deliberately falsify deductions, under-report income, or claim deductions they know are not allowable, figuring that they save money each year they are not audited and not caught. This approach is often referred to as the "audit lottery," because the players know that their chances of being audited are less than one in fifty. With normal odds and even probabilities, this taxpayer reasons that he may only be audited once every fifty years. And if he is audited, the additional tax, penalties, and interest he will have to pay will probably not even come close to the money he has saved by deliberately cheating on his tax return.

If you are worried about being audited and are afraid of the possible consequences, you should become familiar with the entire audit procedure—from how your tax return is selected for an audit to how to appeal an audit—and you should definitely study the information in this chapter that discusses some of the financial consequences of an audit and what you can do to protect yourself from them.

THE AUDIT IN A NUTSHELL

The audit process actually begins when you file your tax return. At each IRS service center a tax examiner will edit and code your return for computer processing. This is a manual check for completeness, accuracy, and obvious errors. The information on the tax return is then placed on magnetic tape for computer processing. The service center's computers check the accuracy of your arithmetic and then pick up other errors not discovered by the tax examiner.

If you have made an *obvious error* on your tax return—such as claiming a partial dependent, making duplicate deductions, or claiming your full medical expenses without regard to subtracting the required 3 percent of your adjusted gross income—the computer will automatically correct it as a mathematical error and will adjust your refund check or bill you accordingly.

During this initial processing your return may also fall into the "Unallowable Items Program," identified as a "Correspondence Correction Program" with the express purpose of identifying and correcting items unlawfully deducted on the returns. Common examples are deductions for personal living expenses, a loss on the sale of a personal residence, utility taxes, personal legal expenses, federal excise taxes, and deductions for life insurance premiums. If you are expecting a refund, the IRS will adjust it and send you a smaller check based on the tax value of your unallowable item.

During processing, IRS computers classify each income tax return for audit potential. This is done by a mathematical technique called "Discriminate Function," or DIF as it is known in IRS terminology. DIF is a computer program that assigns weights to certain characteristics on the tax return. These weights are added together to obtain a composite score for each return. The higher the score, the greater the probability of a significant tax change. The returns that have the highest scores are selected first for audit.

The computers also identify certain nonbusiness income tax returns with minor issues that can be audited by correspondence from the service centers.

Returns are also selected randomly for audit, as part of the IRS's Taxpayer Compliance Measurement Program (TCMP). This is a *full-scale audit* of *all* income items and deductions on the tax return. The IRS has several other programs that help select tax returns for audit.

The audit may be conducted by correspondence from the service center, at an IRS office with a Tax Auditor, or in your home, place of business, or accountant's office with a Revenue Agent. Tax Auditors usually audit wage earners and small businesses. Agents usually audit the more complex individual, partnership, and corporation income tax returns.

In 1981 the IRS audited 1.93 million tax returns, of which 1.77 million were audits made by Tax Auditors and Agents and 161,000 were service center audits. An additional $10.5 billion in tax and penalties were recommended for assessment, of which $2.6 billion were from Forms 1040 and 1040A.

AUDIT-APPEAL PROCEDURES

When the audit has been completed, the auditor will explain his findings, ask you to sign a form agreeing to the findings, and ask you to pay any additional tax found due. Although audits can result in refunds, more than 94 percent of them do not. Any proposed deficiency assessment can be appealed without paying the deficiency first. But once you sign the form agreeing to the deficiency assessment, the die has been cast. You will lose all your appeal rights until you have paid the tax in full.

SURVIVAL RULE ▬▬▬▬▬▬▬▬▬▬▬▬▬▬▬▬▬▬▬▬▬▬

Don't sign any forms agreeing to a proposed deficiency assessment if you do not agree with the findings and intend to appeal your case.

There have been a number of taxpayers who have signed the forms agreeing to the assessment and then later claimed that they did not know what they were signing. A signature on the agreement form is as good as gold, and a denial of knowing its purpose or understanding what the form says will not save you from having to pay the deficiency assessment in full. Never think that just because you have been a "good, cooperative, taxpayer" and agreed to the auditor's findings that you are entitled to special consideration in paying the tax on *your* terms. The IRS does not see it that way. Once you sign the form agreeing to the proposed assessment, the tax is then assessed and you must pay within ten days of receiving a balance due notice or suffer the consequences of being treated as a delinquent taxpayer.

If you do not sign the form agreeing to the proposed deficiency assessment, you will be sent a letter notifying you of your right to appeal within the IRS bureaucracy to the appeals office. This letter is called the thirty-day letter because it gives you thirty days to file your appeal. A *written* protest will be required if the proposed change in tax is more than $2,500.

Most problems are resolved at the appeals level, but in the event that you are not satisfied there, you may take your case to the Tax

Court after you have received a ninety-day letter, or notice of deficiency. This is a formal letter giving you ninety days to file your appeal with the Tax Court (150 days if it is addressed to you outside the United States).

One of the auditor's selling points in getting you to sign the agreement form is that it automatically stops the running of interest for at least thirty days on the proposed tax deficiency. Otherwise, interest accumulates on any proposed deficiency during the entire period the tax is unpaid, even while it is under appeal. It is computed on the balance of tax due from the due date of the return until paid.

You may wish to pay your proposed tax deficiency to stop the accumulation of interest while your case is pending before the Tax Court, since it may be quite a while before your case is even heard. If you wish to do this before you have received your notice of deficiency, you must take certain precautions to protect your right to petition the Tax Court. Normally, full payment made *prior* to the notice of deficiency constitutes an agreement to the proposed deficiency assessment and precludes issuance of the notice of deficiency.

Receiving a notice of deficiency is an essential requirement enabling you to petition the Tax Court. Without it, the Tax Court will not accept your case.

SURVIVAL RULE ▬▬▬▬▬▬▬▬▬▬▬▬▬▬▬▬▬▬▬▬▬▬▬

In order to protect your right to petition the Tax Court while you are paying the tax prior to the issuance of the notice of deficiency, you must give the IRS a statement that you want the payment treated as a "cash bond" for the payment of any taxes later found due by the Tax Court.

This cash bond will stop the accumulation of interest, and if you win in Tax Court it will be returned with interest. Without the signed statement the IRS will not issue the notice of deficiency subsequent to a full payment.

Be aware, though, that if you make this "cash bond" deposit with the IRS, once the notice of deficiency has been sent, you will not see it again until the Tax Court renders its opinion: The IRS will make an assessment for the tax in the amount of the deposit and apply it as a payment of tax.

Any payment made *after* the notice of deficiency has been sent does not affect your right to petition the Tax Court for a review of your case.

Additional avenues of appeal include the U.S. District Courts or the U.S. Court of Claims. These courts normally only hear claims for refunds, and so these avenues are only available *after* you have paid the tax. The procedure requires that you first file a claim with the IRS for a refund, and if the IRS rejects your claim or does not act on it within six months, you can then file your suit.

JEOPARDY AND TERMINATION ASSESSMENTS

Besides the inconvenience of having to take off from work to appear with the auditor and of spending countless hours reconstructing your tax return and trying to find a multitude of receipts and documents, the consequences of the audit can be "financially embarrassing." The IRS may not only hit you for additional taxes, but there are a number of penalties you may be liable for, as well as several years' worth of interest. As it was pointed out earlier, once the tax has been assessed and notice and demand have been made, you have only ten days to pay, just like everyone else. (If you are unable to pay in full, you had better read Chapters 2 and 5.)

The power of the IRS is awesome. As discussed throughout the book, these powers must be respected because the IRS has the power under the law to be as demanding as it wants in almost any situation that involves the Internal Revenue laws. Nothing else in the Tax Code, however, compares with the fierce and overwhelming power given the IRS under the *jeopardy and termination procedures*. These are powers given the IRS to enable it to protect the government's interest in certain unusual circumstances, but it is also a power that if not used judiciously can literally *destroy* a taxpayer.

Section 6861 of the Tax Code reads in part:

If the Secretary believes that the assessment of a deficiency, as defined in section 6211, will be jeopardized by delay, he shall, notwithstanding the provisions of section 6213(a), immediately assess such deficiency (together with all interest, additional amounts, and additions to the tax provided for by law), and notice and demand shall be made by the Secretary for the payment thereof.

That little bit of legal jargon gives the IRS the authority to immediately assess you *any* amount of income taxes they *think* you might owe, without any prior rights of appeal. That means *no* audit interview with an auditor, *no* chance to appeal to the appeals office, and *no* chance to petition the Tax Court for a hearing. And how fast is immediately? As fast as it takes to make one phone call to the assessment officer at a service center.

And that is not the end of it. While the Revenue Agents are swooping down on you to assess your back taxes, Revenue Officers are right behind them like vultures after a carcass. Code section 6331(a) gives them the right to make *immediate demand for payment*, totally without regard to the normal ten-day notice-and-demand period. If full payment is not made immediately—and it never is in a jeopardy situation—the Revenue Officer can legally *seize everything you have*, and you have no choice but to stand by and watch helplessly!

(Think it can't happen in America? Just ask your accountant or your representative in Congress about these powers.)

To top it off, the jeopardy assessment power is not restricted to audit deficiency assessments on tax returns already filed. The regulations pursuant to Code section 6211 allows the IRS to exercise its jeopardy assessment powers *even if you haven't filed a tax return.* The IRS gets around a nonfiling by making up a tax return for you.

IRM 4584.2 states that "all jeopardy assessments have the common characteristic that prior to assessment it is determined that *collection* will be endangered if regular assessment and collection procedures are followed."

According to IRS Policy Statement P–4–88, at best *one* of the following conditions must exist:

- You must be or appear to be making plans to quickly depart from the United States or to conceal yourself from the IRS.
- You must be or appear to be quickly placing your property beyond the reach of the government either by removing it from the

United States, concealing it, dissipating it, or transferring it to other persons.

• Your financial solvency must be or *appear* to be imperiled.

SURVIVAL RULE ▬▬▬▬▬▬▬▬▬▬▬▬▬▬▬▬▬▬▬▬▬▬▬

You must be careful what you say to an auditor concerning any of those three situations; otherwise, you may find yourself the subject of a brutal IRS enforcement power.

▬▬▬▬▬▬▬▬▬▬▬▬▬▬▬▬▬▬▬▬▬▬▬▬▬▬▬▬▬▬▬▬▬▬▬▬

The auditors' manual requires them to be on the alert for any conditions where a jeopardy assessment may be necessary to protect the government's interest. The IRS doesn't miss a trick. Although the jeopardy assessment power is used after the end of a tax year, the IRS will not be deterred by the fact that collection of the tax may be in jeopardy *during* the tax year, before the tax year has even ended.

Code section 6851 allows the IRS to *terminate* your tax year at *any* point and immediately assess your taxes with immediate notice and demand for payment. Obviously, then, no tax return is needed for the termination assessment either. By terminating your tax year, the IRS just figures out how much you owe up to that point, assesses it, demands it, and collects it, all in the same action.

There are *subsequent* appeal procedures for jeopardy and termination assessments, and they are both basically the same. In a nutshell, you have the right to have the assessment reviewed by the appeals office, and then you have the right to appeal to either a U.S. District Court or the U.S. Tax Court, depending on the tax being assessed.

Even though the IRS may have immediately assessed your tax and immediately enforced collection of the tax, the Revenue Officers are prohibited from selling the seized property until after your appeal has resulted in a final decision or the time allowed for you to file a court appeal has expired.

The Revenue Officer, however, can sell your seized property at any time if you consent to the sale, if he considers your property to be perishable goods, or if he determines that the expenses to conserve and maintain the property will greatly reduce the net proceeds to be received from sale of the property.

SURVIVAL RULE ▬▬▬▬▬▬▬▬▬▬▬▬▬▬▬▬▬▬▬▬▬▬▬▬▬▬▬▬▬

If the IRS hits you with a jeopardy or termination assessment you must seek legal assistance immediately.

The appeals procedures in jeopardy and termination assessments give you a limited time to act. Failure to appeal these IRS actions timely and vigorously may result in the loss of your assets. In several cases taxpayers have been left virtually bankrupt by the power of IRS's jeopardy and termination authority. It is not advisable to treat the situation lightly.

THE INNOCENT SPOUSE RULE

Most married taxpayers file joint tax returns because the government gives them an incentive to do so: The tax rates on a joint filing are usually less than the tax rates for married, filing separately. But few joint filers are aware of the financial ramifications of a joint filing when their tax return is audited.

The rule is that both spouses signing a joint return are equally liable for the full payment of any audit deficiency assessment. The Tax Code allows the IRS to collect any tax due on a joint filing from any assets owned jointly or from the individual assets of either spouse owned separately.

After an audit examination has been conducted on a jointly filed return, the notice of deficiency is required to be sent to the taxpayers' last known address. If both spouses are living together there usually is no problem with both of them knowing about the deficiency assessment. But if the spouses are not living together, because of separation or divorce, a *serious* problem can arise for the spouse who does not know about the audit examination.

A lot of separated married couples will get together briefly for the purpose of filing a joint return. This typically happens when one spouse, who is usually the husband, initiates the idea on the premise that it will save them both money. The wife agrees and signs the return in good faith, believing in her husband's ability to prepare a correct tax return.

When the tax return is subsequently pulled for audit, the IRS sends the notification letter to the address shown on the tax return, which is usually the husband's, since it was he who initiated the joint filing. For some reason, and it may be caused by a communication problem (such as they aren't speaking to each other), the husband doesn't tell the wife (or ex-wife, as the case may be by the time of the audit) about the audit and doesn't tell the auditor about their separate residences.

Auditors are supposed to obtain the signatures of both spouses of a joint filing, but many audit deficiencies are assessed by default; that is, the taxpayers never sign anything and never appeal the proposed assessment to the Tax Court. So when the time for appeal has elapsed, and there has been no response, the auditor sends the case forward for assessment without the necessary signatures. It is under these circumstances that separated or divorced wives may become liable for a tax liability they know nothing about.

The horror story begins when the tax is assessed and notice and demand is sent to the address of the husband, who then neglects or refuses to pay the bill. As explained in Chapter 2, the IRS computers will print out Notices of Levy to seize the paychecks of any taxpayer who does not pay in full or communicate his problem to the IRS after four notices have been sent. Since both spouses are liable for any tax assessment on a jointly filed tax return, the computer will send Notices of Levy indiscriminately to attach the paychecks of either spouse. Unfortunately, it is easier for the IRS computers to discover where a wife works than it is for an IRS auditor to discover where a wife lives (particularly if the auditor is unaware of separate residences).

Most people go into mild shock when their employers tell them the IRS has seized their paycheck, particularly for a tax liability they know nothing about. For separated or divorced spouses trying to rebuild their lives, the incident can be devastating, financially and emotionally.

Legally the IRS feels it is on solid ground in attaching the assets of a separated or divorced spouse whose only "crime" was that she signed a tax return jointly with her husband. But most Revenue Officers are compassionate enough to look beyond the legalities to the moral and ethical issues and will issue a Release of Levy to any spouse in this situation. But a Release of Levy is only temporary, because the tax must be paid sooner or later.

SURVIVAL RULE ▬▬▬▬▬▬▬▬▬▬▬▬▬▬▬▬▬▬▬▬▬▬▬▬▬▬

If you are a separated or divorced spouse, and the IRS has seized your paycheck or bank account for a tax liability that you know nothing about, you should immediately contact the Collection Division at your nearest IRS office and try to get the seizure released.

▬▬▬

The tragedy is further compounded when the wife later discovers the basis for the deficiency assessment. Frequently, as it turns out, the deficiency arose because the husband did not report all *his* income, overstated *his* deductions, or failed to prove *his* expenses. Even though the wife was totally innocent in these matters and actually had no responsibility in the improper preparation of the tax return, she became liable for her husband's actions, or inactions, solely by virtue of signing the joint tax return. The obvious fact is that she would have been much better off filing her own tax return separate from her husband's.

Once the case is assigned to a Revenue Officer for collection, he may try to work something out between the spouses for paying the tax, even though he is not obligated to do so. Some of the more eager Revenue Officers may tell the wife to "pay the tax and file a claim for a refund."

The Revenue Officer knows that he can collect the full amount from both spouses or he can collect it from either of them. If they are not communicating and trying to work it out, he may decide to enforce collection against the spouse who has the better financial situation, even if it happens to be the wife who had no actual responsibility in the preparation of the return or any responsibility for the deductions or expenses claimed on the return. This is because responsibility is not the key issue with the Revenue Officer—the key issue is liability. And as far as the IRS is concerned, a wife who signs a joint return is just as liable as her husband.

The unfairness of this situation is obvious. Many years ago Congress acknowledged this and exempted *certain* spouses from the liability of an audit deficiency assessment. Code section 6013(e) is known as the "innocent spouse" rule. Although a spouse may actually be "innocent" of many aspects of a partner's financial affairs and may be even more ignorant of tax laws and the financial ramifications of filing jointly, Congress only exempted from liability those spouses who can meet these three conditions:

* The deficiency assessment must arise from the discovery of unreported gross income in excess of 25 percent of the original amount reported on the return.
* The spouse must establish that in signing the return, he or she did not know of, or had no reason to know of, the under-reporting of income.
* The spouse must not have "significantly benefited," either directly or indirectly, from the amounts omitted from the gross income reported on the return.

The innocent spouse exemption only applies to situations in which gross income was omitted from the tax return. *It does not apply to increased taxes from the disallowance of deductions or expenses claimed on the return.*

SURVIVAL RULE ▬▬▬▬▬▬▬▬▬▬▬▬▬▬▬▬▬▬▬▬▬▬

If you have filed a joint tax return on which an audit deficiency assessment was made and the "innocent spouse" criteria apply in your case, you have the right to demand an abatement of your liability.

You can ask for an abatement of the liability at *any* time after it has been assessed. And, of course, if the innocent spouse rule applies to your case and you are in the process of being audited, you can make a request for exemption from the liability by quoting the innocent spouse rule.

If you are lucky enough to obtain an abatement or nonassertion of the liability, your spouse will then become *solely* liable for the full amount of the unpaid taxes.

II

WHEN THE IRS GETS TOUGH

Preventing a Seizure of
Your Assets

How to keep the IRS from getting it all

INTRODUCTION

The point has been repeatedly emphasized that seizures can be avoided through prompt communication with the IRS. The IRS will collect delinquent taxes without resorting to seizures if *you* take the initiative and responsibility to explore available alternatives and to propose a payment arrangement compatible with your financial situation. Almost *all* of the IRS's 750,000 levies or seizures in 1981 could have been avoided or prevented had those taxpayers either cooperated more fully or quickly communicated their problems to the IRS.

If the IRS has already sent you the computer notices and someone from the IRS is talking tough about enforced collection, do not despair. Payment arrangements are still possible at any time, even after a seizure has already been made. In fact, a large number of payment arrangements are made *after* a levy or a seizure. Many taxpayers do not take the IRS computer notices or phone calls seriously until it is too late.

SURVIVAL RULE ▬▬▬▬▬▬▬▬▬▬▬▬▬▬▬▬▬▬▬▬▬▬▬▬▬▬▬▬

Never ignore an IRS notice or call, and never wait for the IRS to come to you. Always go to the IRS first.

▬▬

THE SEIZURE PROCESS

During the filing of a tax return, the corrected tax liability shown on the return is "assessed" as the return flows through the processing pipeline in the service center. "Assessment," the recording of the tax liability onto IRS records, is officially accomplished when an assessment officer at the service center signs Form 23–C, "Assessment Certificate." The assessment starts the legal basis for any enforcement action. The assessment date is important because:

- It begins the six-year statutory period for collection.
- It is the date that the statutory lien provided by Code section 6321 arises.

The statute of limitations gives the IRS six years to collect any overdue tax. If the tax cannot be collected within that period of time, the IRS will ask you to sign a waiver to extend the statute. If a waiver cannot be obtained and the tax fully collected by seizure, the IRS can initiate legal proceedings to obtain a judgment that is valid in some states for up to twenty years.

Code section 6321 gives the U.S. government a lien on all property and rights to property, whether real or personal, belonging to any person who neglects or refuses to pay after demand has been made for payment. The federal tax lien, sometimes referred to as the "general" or "secret" lien, is the basis for all IRS enforcement actions.

A lien is a charge on one person's property in favor of another person. Mortgages on houses and cars are forms of liens. So if you have not paid your taxes, the IRS has a charge on all the property you own. The federal tax lien also attaches to any property you may subsequently acquire while the taxes remain unpaid.

It is important to know that if the taxes are not paid within ten days after a notice has been sent demanding payment, the IRS has the legal right to make a seizure and file a Notice of Federal Tax Lien in the courthouse where you live. This notice is a public document and, once filed, establishes priority over subsequent creditors who may obtain judgments against you. The filed notice of lien informs the public that taxes are owed and serves to protect the IRS's rights on your property. Once filed, the Notice of Federal Tax Lien cannot be released until either the tax is paid in full or the statutory period for collections has expired.

The IRS is *not required* to file a Notice of Federal Tax Lien before making a levy or a seizure, but as a matter of policy the IRS will file one before making a seizure of tangible personal property or real property. The only conditions that must exist prior to levy or seizure are that an assessment must be made, notice must be sent, and there must be a neglect or a refusal to pay. Code section 6331 does, however, give you ten days to fully pay before the IRS can take any enforcement action against you, unless the IRS can show it must act more quickly because the collection of the tax is in jeopardy.

Section 6331 of the Tax Code provides the statutory authority to make a *levy*, a legal term describing the administrative means of collecting taxes by seizure of property, which may then be appropriated by the government to satisfy delinquent taxes. For most practical purposes the terms *levy* and *seizure* are interchangeable. In IRS parlance, *levy* usually means taking possession of property in the hands of a third party, for example, a paycheck or a bank account. Confiscating an automobile, business assets, or real property is considered a *seizure* by the IRS.

The IRS has the power to seize *all properties* or rights to property (except those specifically exempt) belonging to the person liable for the tax—whether the property is real, personal, tangible, or intangible.

Chapter 2 contained a brief discussion of the collection process up to the time a Tax Delinquent Account is printed and sent to the district office. After the account reaches delinquency status, collection employees in the district collection office methodically and routinely try to determine the best way to collect the money you owe. The collection employees will phone taxpayers while at the same time looking for sources of levy. If you are contacted during this stage, you will not only be asked to fully pay, you will also be asked where you work and where you bank.

The collection employee will try to negotiate a short-term arrangement or an installment agreement like those discussed in Chapter 2. Should you not cooperate by failing to give the information asked of you or by not making a firm arrangement or commitment to pay the tax, the collection employee will then initiate levy action against any known source. This will also occur when the IRS has been unable to contact you or you haven't responded within a reasonable period of time since the notices were sent.

Many of the delinquency notices sent to the district office by the service center will already have computer-printed Notices of Levy attached to them. The information on financial resources comes from W–2 statements and 1099 forms filed with tax returns and an IRS data base called LEVYE, which stores information obtained from phone calls, previous installment agreements, or from a collection interview. Remember that any time you tell the IRS where you work or bank, it may become a part of IRS records.

The district offices routinely initiate levy notices to seize paychecks and bank accounts by the thousands each day. Most of the time they are successful in obtaining either full payment or an immediate response from the levied taxpayers. "Full pay" is the major objective, but in the absence of an ability to collect in full, the IRS strives to collect as much as it can in the shortest period of time possible.

WARNINGS PRIOR TO SEIZURE

IRS policy allows taxpayers a reasonable opportunity to pay voluntarily and comply with the tax laws before taking any seizure action. IRM 5311:(5) states that "before levy or seizure is taken on an account, the taxpayer should be informed, except in jeopardy situations, that levy or seizure will be the next action taken and given a reasonable opportunity to pay voluntarily. Once the taxpayer has been advised and neglects to make satisfactory arrangements, levy action should be taken expeditiously."

Code section 6331(d) requires that a *written* notice be sent before making a seizure of your salary, wages, or other property. The IRS's last computer notice, titled "Past Due Final Notice," serves as official notification of such possible seizure action. The last computer notice states that "enforcement action can be taken at any time after

10 days. . . . Bank accounts, receivables, commissions, or any other kind of income you have are also subject to levy. Property or rights to property, such as automobiles, may also be seized and sold to satisfy your tax liability."

The Tax Code requires that the written notice either be given in person, left at your residence or usual place of business, or sent by certified or registered mail to your last known address. Sending the final notice to your last known address fulfills the written notification requirement, even if the notice is returned to the IRS as undeliverable. Consider the final notice your *first serious warning*.

The second warning usually comes a few weeks later via a phone call from the collection interviewer, who will probably try to put "the fear" into you by telling you that if you don't pay they will either send a Revenue Officer out to start seizing your assets or they may send out a levy notice to attach your paycheck or bank account. For many taxpayers this is the second but last, serious warning. At this point, though, immediate seizure activity will only be made on paychecks and bank accounts.

Seizures of other types of property, such as businesses, automobiles, and real estate, can only be made by Revenue Officers who are also required to warn you if they are contemplating any such seizure action. The warning from the Revenue Officer may well be your third and final serious warning.

As you can see, the warnings can occur at any stage of the collection process, either from the final notice, subsequent phone calls, or the collection interview.

SURVIVAL RULE ▬▬▬▬▬▬▬▬▬▬▬▬▬▬▬▬▬▬▬▬▬

Any warning of possible seizure action, whether made orally or by correspondence, should not be taken lightly. If you do not respond promptly, you will most likely have your paycheck(s) or bank account(s) seized.

The IRS keeps a record of when each warning is made to protect itself from charges by taxpayers that they didn't know the IRS was going to make the seizure and to assure itself that IRM procedure is being followed.

Taxpayers who comply with the instructions in IRS notices to respond promptly, or who comply with the demands of collection employees, *will avoid having their property seized.* If you can't pay your taxes in full, attempt to arrange an installment agreement, an extension of time to borrow the money, or a determination that you cannot pay at the current time.

SURVIVAL RULE

If you do obtain an extension of time to pay, make sure that you either comply or communicate why you cannot. If the IRS gives you an installment agreement, make sure you make every payment promptly or tell someone at the IRS why you are late.

SEIZURES OF PAYCHECKS

The Tax Reform Act of 1976 made several important changes in IRS's powers to seize wages and salaries. In the past the IRS was allowed to keep the entire paycheck and the taxpayer got nothing. But the IRS always had to come back with another Notice of Levy to seize additional paychecks. Under the present code provisions you will be able to keep a part of your paycheck, even if it is just barely enough to buy groceries. The IRS paycheck seizure now works just like a garnishment and the seizure remains in effect, either until it is released or the taxes are paid in full. This means that unless you take immediate action to fully pay your taxes or attempt to work something out at the local IRS office, your boss will have to give the IRS a large chunk of every paycheck.

SURVIVAL RULE

If the IRS has seized your paycheck, you need to contact the IRS right away to pay the taxes in full or submit to a collection interview and negotiate an installment or payment arrangement in order to have the seizure released. (Provisions under which a release can be made are listed later in this chapter.)

A "Statement of Personal Exemptions" is sent with every Notice of Levy that seizes wages, salaries, or other income. This form is used to help your employer compute how much of your paycheck you will be able to keep. The code allows certain exemptions from IRS seizures on wages, salaries, or other income. You will be allowed to retain $75 per week for yourself and $25 per week for your spouse and an additional $25 per week for each dependent. For example, if you normally clear $250 per week and have a wife and three kids, you will be able to retain $175 ($75 for yourself and $25 for your wife, plus $75 for a total of 3 kids), and the IRS gets the balance of $75 ($250 less $175 = $75).

You are allowed at least three days to complete the statement, even if the three days extend past your payday. Your employer is instructed to exempt only $75 per week as a personal exemption if the statement is not returned timely.

The $25-per-week exemption applies to any dependent listed below who has received over half of his or her support from you for the payroll period:

- Your son or daughter, or a descendent of either.
- Your stepson or stepdaughter.
- Your brother, sister, stepbrother, or stepsister.
- Your father or mother, or an ancestor of either.
- Your stepfather or stepmother.
- The son or daughter of your brother or sister.
- The brother or sister of your father or mother.
- A son-in-law, daughter-in-law, father-in-law, mother-in-law, brother-in-law, or sister-in-law.
- An individual who is a member of your household and whose principal place of abode for the tax year is your residence.

You sign Form 668–P under penalty of perjury. Collection employees will accept as valid the number of dependents you claim unless there is substantial evidence otherwise. If a dependency exemption is disallowed, the IRS will notify both you and your employer immediately in writing.

RESTRICTIONS ON IRS LEVY POWER

Section 6334 of the code specifically lists certain items that are exempt from IRS seizure under any conditions. It is important to know what these exempt items are to protect yourself properly from arbitrary or illegal actions of a Revenue Officer or other IRS employee. Property exempt from seizure includes:

* *Wearing apparel and schoolbooks* necessary for you or members of your family. The code does not put a dollar value on this exemption. Neither the code nor the IRS regulations identify who is to make the determination of what is "necessary," and so it is to be assumed that IRS has the right to make that determination. As a matter of practice, the IRS does not normally seize everyday clothing or schoolbooks. Clothing has resale value only if it is expensive, rare, or luxurious, such as a mink coat. The code exempts only "necessary" clothing, and the IRS would not accept the idea of a mink coat as being "necessary." As a matter of practice and policy, however, the IRS does not go into homes to find such items for seizure.

* *Fuel, provisions, furniture, and personal effects.* The code provides that "if a taxpayer is the head of a family, so much of the fuel, provisions, furniture, and personal effects in his household, and of the arms for personal use, livestock, and poultry of the taxpayer, as does not exceed $1,500 in value" is exempt. The condition is that the exemption only applies to the head of a family and only exempts a *total* of $1,500, not $1,500 for each item.

* *Books and tools of a trade, business, or profession.* The exemption is for so many of the books and tools necessary for your trade, business, or profession as do not exceed $1,000 in value in the aggregate.

* *Unemployment benefits* paid under an unemployment compensation law of the United States, of any state or of the District of Columbia or of the Commonwealth of Puerto Rico. The code says "any amount" payable is exempt so the IRS cannot touch any of it. IRS policy also excludes any portion payable to dependents.

* *Undelivered mail, addressed to any person.* The code exempts any mail from seizure as long as it has not been delivered to the addressee. This statute prevents the IRS from tampering with your mailbox and possibly intercepting checks or other articles of value sent through the mail. It is unclear whether this exemption applies to packages sent by private carrier, but as a normal practice officers do not seize anything that appears to be "mail"

as it applies to written communications. Packages sent to a business by private carrier believed to contain inventory for resale would probably be seized when the entire business has been seized, notwithstanding this exemption. Revenue Officers are instructed, though, when mail is delivered to property under seizure and comes into the possession of the IRS, that it be promptly turned over to the taxpayer unopened.

- *Certain annuity and pension payments.* Exempt are annuity or pension payments made:
  - —under the Railroad Retirement Act, or benefits made under the Railroad Unemployment Insurance Act.
  - —by a special monthly pension payable by the Veterans Administration to a person whose name is on the "Army, Navy, and Air Force Medal of Honor Roll."
  - —based on retired or retained pay as an annuity paid to a survivor of a member of the Armed Forces under Chapter 73 of Title 10 of the U.S. Code.
- *Workmen's Compensation* payments paid under a workmen's compensation law of the United States, any state, the District of Columbia, or the Commonwealth of Puerto Rico.
- *Judgments for support of minor children.* If a court has rendered a judgment prior to the date of the IRS's seizure to require you to contribute to the support of your minor children, the amount of salary, wages, or other income necessary to comply with such judgment is exempt. IRS regulations require that you establish the amount necessary to comply with the order or decree. The Revenue Officer is not required to release the seizure unless he is satisfied that the amount being released will actually be applied in satisfaction of the support obligation. But the code disallows this exemption for child support if you claim the $25-dependency exemption for the same child.
- *Minimum exemption for wages, salary, and other income.* These are the personal and dependency exemptions discussed earlier.

THE SEIZURE

Serving a Notice of Levy to seize a paycheck or bank account is simple: The form is completed and either mailed or served personally on the bank or employer. Even though most levy notices are served on banks and employers, they can actually be served on any person or business entity that owes you any amount of money for any reason.

The seizure of tangible personal property or real property is more involved and complicated. The Revenue Officer must first determine that there is need to seize.

The determination to seize usually depends on the actions or inactions of the taxpayer. At some point in the collection process, contact is usually made with the taxpayer and a plan of action is specified. The Revenue Officer's decision will usually be to grant a sixty-day extension to borrow the money, negotiate an installment agreement, demand full payment, or declare the tax uncollectible due to financial hardship.

The onus of a seizure always rests on the shoulders of the tax-payer. If you do not earnestly attempt to pay off your taxes, either by trying to borrow the money or by making payments on a periodic basis, and if you do not cooperate, by not returning phone calls, not keeping appointments, or breaking agreements without explaining why, you are issuing an engraved invitation to the IRS to exercise their powers to seize whatever they can get their hands on. Revenue Officers are under a lot of pressure to close cases promptly, and they are not likely to waste much time with an uncooperative taxpayer.

Because making a seizure takes time and effort, most Revenue Officers would prefer not to do it if there is a quicker way to close the case. But in every group, there is at least one "seizure happy" Revenue Officer who enjoys exercising his legal muscle. Also, some IRS managers push their officers to make seizures for the sole purpose of enhancing their statistical enforcement profile. So the need to close a case promptly, the need to take enforcement action as retribution against an uncooperative taxpayer, and the need to accumulate seizure statistics may combine to make a seizure "irresistible."

Once the officer has determined there is a need to seize, he must ascertain what property is available for seizing and compute how much equity you have in the property. If the taxes are owed from individual income taxes (taxes owed from Form 1040 or 1040A), the most likely targets for a seizure are your automobile or house. If the taxes are owed by an employer from his or her employees' withholding taxes, the most likely targets are cash register receipts and furniture or equipment located in the public portions of the business.

Your equity in property is computed by subtracting the amount owed on the property from its fair market value. For example, if you still owe $5,000 on an automobile with a resale value of $8,000, you have equity of $3,000 in the auto. If you have a $50,000 mortgage on a house worth $80,000, you have equity of $30,000 in the house.

If the equity is substantial and far in excess of the tax liability, the Revenue Officer may decide not to seize it. After all, how would it look for the IRS to seize an $80,000 house in which you have $30,000 equity for a $2,000 tax liability? Then again, some officers are nasty enough to do just that. There is no specific rule, but the equity should be sufficient to pay the taxes and all expenses without having too much equity lost in the sale.

IRS policy prohibits Revenue Officers from seizing property when the equity in the property is insufficient "to yield net proceeds from sale to apply to the unpaid tax liabilities" (IRM 5341.2:[1]). Furthermore, any officer who seizes such property must release it immediately (IRM 5341.2:[4]). If it is determined that there is sufficient equity in the seized property to pay for the expenses of sale, but the net proceeds from the sale will be small in comparison to the tax liability, the officer and his group manager must decide if pursuing the seizure and sale is warranted (IRM 5341.2:[5]).

SURVIVAL RULE ▬▬▬▬▬▬▬▬▬▬▬▬▬▬▬▬▬▬▬▬▬

If the IRS has seized your property and your equity in the property is either insufficient to pay for the expenses of seizure and sale or small in comparison to the tax liability, you should demand that the seizure be released under the provisions of IRM 5341.2.

Before any seizure can be made, the Revenue Officer must obtain the concurrence of his group manager (IRM 5341.1:[5]). If the property to be seized is your personal residence, the seizure must also be approved above the group manager's level (IRM 5341.1:[6]). If the property is a going business, the officer must exercise every reasonable effort to collect the tax on a voluntary basis (Policy Statement P–5–34).

After determining there is sufficient equity in the property and the necessary approvals have been obtained, the Revenue Officer must prepare the appropriate papers and make the necessary arrangements.

In 1977 the Supreme Court ruled in *G. M. Leasing v. U.S.* that "a warrantless entry onto the private areas of personal or business premises of a taxpayer for the purpose of seizing property to satisfy a tax liability is in violation of the Fourth Amendment to the Constitution of the United States unless 'exigent circumstances' exist." "Exigent circumstances" exist when the taxpayer is removing property beyond the reach of the government.

The result of this ruling is a requirement that the Revenue Office obtain either a court-ordered Writ of Entry or your written permission before entering the *private areas* of your personal or business premises. Without these, Revenue Officers are allowed to enter only *upon* the *public* portion of your residence or business premises and seize property in the public area. Examples of public portions of business premises include the dining area of a restaurant and the sales area of a retail store.

Revenue Officers generally have the right to enter *onto* public or private premises to carry out their duties, including the authority to enter *onto* the premises of your private residence to seek an interview with you. But without permission they have no authority to *enter* the residence. The officer does not need to enter a personal residence to seize it. A personal residence may be seized by placing the appropriate seizure notices on the exterior of the residence. Thus the requirement to obtain a court-ordered Writ of Entry *does not prohibit* the Revenue Officer from seizing your personal residence without such a writ.

A Revenue Officer intending to seize personal property in a private area or in the private portions of your business premises will attempt to obtain your permission to enter that area by asking you to sign a "Consent to Enter Private Premises." This form is a *waiver of your Fourth Amendment rights against unreasonable searches and seizures*. There is no benefit to you if you sign the form. The Revenue Officer may try to scare you by threatening to go to court to obtain the writ, but do not be perturbed. *You will not have to go to court.*

CONSENT TO ENTER PRIVATE PREMISES

The Constitution of the United States guarantees a right to be secure from unreasonable searches of person, house, papers, and effects.

Having full knowledge of the above guaranteed rights, I, *William Robin,* consent to entry into premises located at *1503 23rd St., Alexandria, Va. 20220* by Internal Revenue Service employees for the purpose of seizure, inventory, removing property, if required, and sale of property, to collect and satisfy my delinquent tax, interest and penalty liability.

My signing of this consent to entry is not to be construed as an admission by me of the tax liability being collected.

William Robin, T/A Robin's Roost
1503 23rd St.
Alexandria, Va. 20220
54   3456

DATE: _____

Samuel J. Eagle
Revenue Officer
Samuel J. Eagle
5205 Leesburg Pike
Falls Church, Va. 22041

The Revenue Officer will then have to appear before a U.S. judge or magistrate, who *will not* summons you to appear. It is the court's responsibility to protect your rights.

The Revenue Officer may try to convince you that signing the consent form is a perfunctory process but don't believe it. No one can force you to sign it, and only the U.S. judge or magistrate can overrule your wishes. If the Revenue Officer proceeds with the seizure in a private area or in the private portion of a business premises (for example, the seizure of cash register contents) without a court-ordered writ or a signed consent by the occupant and owner of the premises, the seizure is illegal and the Revenue Officers are personally liable for damages.

SURVIVAL RULE ▬▬▬▬▬▬▬▬▬▬▬▬▬▬▬▬▬▬▬▬▬▬▬▬▬▬▬▬

You may refuse to permit any IRS employee to enter your private residence or the private portion of your business premises for the purpose of conducting a seizure, unless the Revenue Officers present a court-ordered writ authorizing such entry.

Seizures of property are always made by at least two Revenue Officers. Before making the seizure they will introduce themselves, show their identification credentials (Revenue Officers do not have badges), and make demand for full payment. If they do not receive payment in full or assurances that payment is immediately forthcoming, they will hand you IRS Form 668–B, simply titled "Levy," and either ask you to read it or read it to you. The Levy form is your official notification that your property is being seized. At that time one of the Revenue Officers will place "United States Government Seizure" stickers on the property.

If the property being seized is your personal residence, the Revenue Officers may place seizure stickers on several windows around the house. The seizure of the residence *does not* mean you must vacate the premises. You have the right to occupy the premises while it is under seizure up to the moment it is sold, at which time you may want to consult an attorney to determine if you have the right to

UNITED STATES DISTRICT COURT
EASTERN DISTRICT OF VIRGINIA

IN THE MATTER OF THE TAX
INDEBTEDNESS OF   Miscellaneous Civil
                                    Action No. 7-1512
WILLIAM ROBIN
T/A ROBIN's ROOST
1503 23rd St.
ALEXANDRIA, VA. 22020

ORDER OF ENTRY OF
PREMISES TO EFFECT LEVY

The United States of America having filed an application requesting authorization for SAMUEL J. EAGLE, a Revenue Officer
of the Internal Revenue Service, and/or other designated revenue
officers to enter the premises located at 1503 23rd St. ALEXANDRIA,
VA 22020 in order to seize property in satisfaction of unpaid
Federal taxes, together with an affidavit of Revenue Officer SAMUEL
J. EAGLE in support of that application; and the Court finding, on
the basis of the affidavit, that there is probable cause to believe that
the property or rights to property belonging to WILLIAM ROBIN
which are subject to levy by the United States, pursuant to Section
6331 of the Internal Revenue Code are located on or within the
premises described, it is ORDERED that Revenue Officer SAMUEL
J. EAGLE and such other revenue officer as may be designated
by the Internal Revenue Service, are authorized to enter the
premises described and to make such search as is necessary in
order to levy and seize, pursuant to Section 6331 of the Internal
Revenue Code of 1954. In making this search and seizure, however,
such revenue officers are directed to enter the premises during business hours or the daytime and within ten (10) days of this Order.

Thomas P. Blackbird

UNITED STATES DISTRICT COURT

Entered: April 6, 1981

Form **668-B** (Rev. February 1981)	Department of the Treasury — Internal Revenue Service
	Levy

Due from	Originating Internal Revenue District *(City and State)*
Randall B. Bower 10103 Sycamore Court Louisville, KY 40200	Louisville, KY

Kind of Tax	Tax Period Ended	Date of Assessment	Taxpayer Identification Number	Unpaid Balance of Assessment	Statutory Additions	Total
1040	12-31-79	05-18-81	42X-XX-109	$ 3,627.72	$ 186.62	$ 3,814.34

				Total amount due ▶	$3,814.34

The amounts shown above are now due, owing, and unpaid to the United States from the above taxpayer for internal revenue taxes. Notice and demand have been made for payment. Chapter 64 of the Internal Revenue Code provides a lien for the above tax and statutory additions. Section 6331 of the Code authorizes collection of taxes by levy on all property or rights to property of a taxpayer, except property that is exempt under Code section 6334. Therefore, under the provisions of Code section 6331, so much of the property or rights to property, either real or personal, as may be necessary to pay the unpaid balance of assessment shown, with additions provided by law, including fees, costs, and expenses of this levy, are levied on to pay the taxes and additions.

Dated at ___Louisville, Kentucky___ _____ September 11, _, 19 81 .
             (Place)   *(Date)*

Signature of Revenue Officer *J.B. Tamarack*	Date 09-11-81
Concurrence Signature of Group Manager *C.M. Primrose*	Date 09-11-81
Signature *(Next level of Management; required only if taxpayer's personal residence is to be seized)*	Date

___Randall B. Bower___ ____ was asked to be present during inventory. *J.B. Tamarack*
  (Taxpayer's Name)   *(Revenue Officer Signature)*

___Randall B. Bower___ ____ was present at inventory. ☐ Yes   ☒ No
  (Taxpayer or Taxpayer's Representative's Name)

Part 1 — SPf Seizure File   Form **668-B** (Rev. 2-81)

WARNING

UNITED STATES GOVERNMENT SEIZURE

This property has been seized for nonpayment of internal revenue taxes, due from _____,

by virtue of levy issued by the District Director of Internal Revenue.

All persons are warned not to remove or tamper with this property, in any manner, under severe penalty of the law.

_____ _____
Revenue Officer   Date

_____
Telephone Number

Publication No. 34 (Rev. 11-76)
Department of the Treasury
Internal Revenue Service

occupy it for another 180 days. The purchaser of seized real property will not receive a deed to the property until 180 days after the sale.

If the property being seized is an automobile, the Revenue Officer will have a commercial tow truck haul the car away to be impounded in a storage lot for safekeeping. The expenses for towing and storage will be charged back to you even though the IRS contracts for the services. Other types of personal property seized may also be removed and placed under storage.

After the seizure the Revenue Officer will then complete IRS Form 2433, "Notice of Seizure," which constitutes the official identification or inventory record of the property being seized. You will receive a copy of the forms as will any other person who may have been in possession of your property when it was seized.

While Revenue Officers try to make seizures in the presence of the taxpayer, there are times when the taxpayer is not present and the seizure is made anyway. If that occurs to you, you will find the appropriate seizure forms under your door, your doormat, or in your mailbox. Revenue Officers are also instructed to inform the local police when a car has been seized without the knowledge of the taxpayer.

The obvious purpose of seizing property is to sell it for cash and apply the cash to the tax liability. Once the seizure has been made, the Revenue Officer is required to demand full payment of the tax liability and reimbursement of expenses and costs before the property can be returned to you. Do not be misled by this demand for full payment, however. Code section 6343(a) authorizes the release of a seizure if the action will facilitate collection of the tax, and the regulations pursuant to section 6343(a) specify the conditions under which a release can be made. (These conditions will be discussed later in this chapter.) But IRS policy (5346.1:[1]) requires that when seized property is released prior to sale for less than *immediate* full payment, that "subsequent full payment *must* be provided for."

Many taxpayers believe that once their property has been seized they can't get it back. Many Revenue Officers do not make it a practice to inform taxpayers that this is not so. Even the IRS seizure forms given to the taxpayer are unclear on this point.

After seizing and removing the property for storage, officers normally wait a few days before establishing a sale date and advertising

Notice of Seizure

Name and Address

Randall B. Bower
10103 Sycamore Court
Louisville, KY 40200

Serial number
LO-21-38

Estimated expenses of seizure and sale

$ 125.00

Under the authority in section 6331 of the Internal Revenue Code, and by virtue of a levy from the District Director of Internal Revenue of the district shown below, I have seized the property below for nonpayment of past due internal revenue taxes.

Due from	Amount	Internal Revenue District *(City and State)*
Randall B. Bower 10103 Sycamore Court Louisville, KY 40200	$ 3,814.34	Louisville, KY

Description of property

	$
All that certain lot, piece, or parcel of land, together with all improvements thereon and appurtenances thereto, known as Lots 12 and 14, Block 7, Section B, of Chinquapin Lakes Recreational Park, being in Chinquapin County, Kentucky, and more particularly described in a certain plat of survey, made by John L. Holley, Certified Land Surveyor, and recorded in Plat Book 23A, Page 137, in the Circuit Court of Chinquapin County, Kentucky, on June 23, 1970.	9,000.00

For a more particular description of the above named property, reference is made to a certain deed dated May 23, 1974, and recorded in Deed Book 172-C, Page 499, in the Circuit Court of Chinquapin County, Kentucky.

The two lots listed above are unimproved with the exception of a chain-link fence. The approximate dimensions of the two lots combined are 160 feet by 140 feet.

	Total inventory value	$9,000.00

Signature of Revenue Officer making seizure	Location codes *(District and Area)*	Date
B. Tamarack	6101	10-2-81

Part 7A — To Service Center Accounting Branch immediately after seizure (yellow) Form **2433** (Rev. 4-81)

Part 6 — SPf Copy   (Pink)   Form **2433** (Rev. 4-81)

the sale. Since advertising expenses are charged back to the taxpayer, the officer will want to know if there will be any chance of release or redemption of the seized property before incurring any additional expenses. A "release" of seized property is made for *less* than full payment, whereas a "redemption" is made for full payment.

There is no legal requirement for the Revenue Officer to issue a notice of sale establishing a sale date within a specified period of time after the seizure, although it should be issued "as soon as practicable after all the necessary arrangements have been made for the sale." You will receive the original Notice of Sale.

SURVIVAL RULE ━━━━━━━━━━━━━━━━━━━━━━━━━━━━━━━

Between the time your property is seized and the date scheduled for sale, you should make every attempt possible to obtain a release or redemption of your property by arranging to pay your overdue taxes.

Sometime before the sale the officer must establish a "minimum bid price" for the property—the lowest price at which the officer will sell the property. If the property cannot be sold at that price, the IRS will "buy-in," or purchase the property for the U.S. Government at the minimum bid price and credit your tax account for that amount.

The minimum bid price is computed by a formula that starts with a determination of the fair market value of the property. The fair market value is then reduced by 25 percent, and that figure multiplied by 80 percent or more to compute the forced-sale equity. The minimum bid price is then computed by subtracting the amount of any liens prior to the tax lien (for example, a first mortgage on a house) from the forced sale equity. And in no event can the minimum bid price exceed the total taxes, penalies, interest, and other charges on the account.

The General Accounting Office has discovered that Revenue Officers have consistently over the years undervalued seized property because they were strongly discouraged from "buying-in" the property for the government. As a result of the GAO report, the IRS allows Revenue Officers to obtain an appraisal of the property from professional appraisers if necessary. Per IRM 5361.1:(4) the officer

Department of the Treasury/Internal Revenue Service

Notice of

Sealed Bid Sale

Under the authority in Internal Revenue Code section 6331, the property described below has been seized for nonpayment of internal revenue taxes due from

____Randall B. Bower, 10103 Sycamore Court, Louisville, KY____ .

The property will be sold at public sale under sealed bid as provided by Internal Revenue Code section 6335 and related regulations.

Date Bids will be Opened: ____October 2____ 19 81

Time Bids will be Opened: ____10:00____ am

Place of Sale: ____Chinquapin County Courthouse, Chinquapin, Kentucky____

Title Offered: Only the right, title, and interest of ____Randall B. Bower____ in and to the property will be offered for sale. If requested, the Internal Revenue Service will furnish information about possible encumbrances, which may be useful in determining the value of the interest being sold. (See the back of this form for further details.)

Description of Property: All that certain lot, piece, or parcel of land, together with all improvements thereon and appurtenances thereto, known as Lots 12 and 14, Block 7, Section B, of Chinquapin Lakes Recreational Park, being in Chinquapin County, Kentucky, and more particularly described in a certain plat of survey, made by John L. Holley, Certified Land Surveyor, and recorded in Plat Book 23A, Page 137, in the Circuit Court of Chinquapin County, Kentucky on June 23, 1970.   For a more particular description of the above named property, reference is made to a certain deed dated May 23,1974 and recorded in Deed Book 172-C, Page 499, in the Circuit Court of Chinquapin County, Kentucky.   The two lots listed above are unimproved with the exception of a chain-link fence. The approximate dimensions of the two lots combined are 160 feet by 140 feet.

Property may be Inspected at: ____By prior appointment with the undersigned Revenue Officer.____

Submission of Bids: All bids must be submitted on Form 2222, Sealed Bid for Purchase of Seized Property. Contact the office indicated below for Forms 2222 and information about the property. Submit bids to the person named below before the time bids will be opened.

Payment Terms: Bids must be accompanied by the full amount of the bid if it totals $200 or less. If the total bid is more than $200, submit 20 percent of the amount bid or $200, whichever is greater. On acceptance of the highest bid, the balance due, if any, will be ☒ Required in full ☐ Deferred as follows:

Form of Payment: All payments must be by cash, certified check, cashier's or treasurer's check or by a United States postal, bank, express, or telegraph money order. Make check or money order payable to the Internal Revenue Service.

Signature	Name and Title (Typed)	Date
J.B. Tamarack	J.B. Tamarack, Revenue Officer	9-12-81
Address for Information About the Sale and Submission of Bids		Phone
P.O.BOX 473-A, Louisville, Kentucky 40201		555-6789

Form **2434-A** (Rev. 8-79)

is required to advise you of the minimum bid price and how it was computed.

SURVIVAL RULE ━━━━━━━━━━━━━━━━━━━━━━━━━━━━━━━

It is important that you protect yourself from an unreasonably low evaluation of the value of your seized property. You have the right to object to the minimum bid price and the right to object to how it was computed. You also have the right to request an IRS valuation engineer, or a professional appraiser, to assist in determining the property's true forced-sale value. Be aware, though, that the costs of obtaining a private appraisal will be charged back to you.

Once the Notice of Sale has been issued, the Revenue Officer is required to sell the property within ten to forty days, except when a sale has been postponed for a maximum of one month.

Seized property may be sold either by public auction or by sealed bid. Any seized property can be released or redeemed at any time before the officer finally accepts the highest bid. Once the highest bid has been accepted, you will have lost all right, title, or interest in the personal property and may never see it again. You have no right of redemption of personal property *after* the property has been sold.

Seized property is sold "as is" and "where is." Only your right, title, and interest are sold, and the property is offered subject to any prior outstanding mortgages, liens, or other encumbrances. No guaranty or warranty is given for any reason pertaining to any aspect of the seized property.

SEIZURES OF REAL PROPERTY

Unlike other types of seizures in which personal property has to be impounded, seizures of real property do not require that the property be vacated. There have been times, though, when the IRS has seized and sold real property and the taxpayers residing on the property have refused to move, but the IRS will not get involved in conflicts between taxpayers or tenants and purchasers of seized property. In that situation the new owner would have to go to court to have the residents or former owners vacated.

Earlier it was mentioned how seized property can be released or redeemed for any reason up to the moment of actual sale. In the case of real property that has been seized and sold, the code allows the former owner one more chance to get his property back even *after* it has been sold. Code section 6337 allows the former owners, their heirs, executors, or administrators, or any other person on their behalf to "redeem" (buy back) the property at any time within 180 days after the sale.

There is one condition that must be fulfilled in redeeming seized real property *after* it has been sold by the IRS. A payment must be made to the purchaser in the amount paid by the purchaser for the property plus interest computed at 20 percent per year. If the purchaser cannot be found, payment can be made to the IRS.

What prevents the purchaser from taking over the property within the 180-day period and converting it to his own use? The highest bidder at the auction receives only a Certificate of Sale from the IRS that acts as a receipt and acknowledgment of the purchase. It is only after the 180th day that the purchaser gets a deed to the property. Conveyance of the taxpayer's right title and interest to the property is made through the deed and not the Certificate of Sale. The purchaser has no legal rights to real property until after the 180th day.

HOW TO GET A SEIZURE RELEASED

There are several effective methods that can be used to obtain a release of seized property. These methods work on any type of seizure from bank accounts and paychecks to homes and autos. Of course, the IRS will release a seizure any time the taxes are paid in full.

Code section 6343(a) authorizes the release of a seizure upon all or part of the seized property if it is determined that the action will facilitate collection of the tax liability. The regulations to this section specify the conditions that must exist before the levy can be released, and IRM policy requires that subsequent full payment must be provided for.

Releasing a Notice of Levy is not a procedure that is followed strictly according to the rule books. Many collection employees who have been delegated the authority to serve levies feel they have the authority to release them at their own discretion. Since releasing a levy does not normally require supervisory approval, collection employees can issue a release without being accountable for their actions.

But don't be mistaken. Collection employees usually only release levies when they are convinced there is a good reason to do so. For example, service of successive levies is a good reason to release a bank or paycheck levy. Another reason is when you can't pay your taxes and the levy would appear to be creating a financial hardship. However, neither the Tax Code, the regulations, nor IRM policy provide for a release of levy when it is clear that the levy is creating a financial hardship for you and/or your family. But levies are released for this reason every day, because most collection employees are compassionate enough to realize that if your situation is such that you can't pay the taxes and pay necessary living expenses at the same time, the case is "uncollectible." And if the case is uncollectible prior to levy, it is uncollectible subsequent to levy.

However, it is one situation to be able to obtain a release of a Notice of Levy served on your paycheck or bank account due to financial hardship, but it is another situation to obtain a release of a personal or real property seizure for the same reason. A seizure of personal or real property involves the participation of too many supervisors and reviewers for the Revenue Officer to exercise discretion that is not specifically allowed in the manual. Levies or seizures of any type of property may be released for full payment or for the following conditions provided subsequent full payment is provided for. Also, just because a levy or seizure has been released, it does not foreclose the possibility of future levy action.

According to IRS regulations, a levy or a seizure may be released under the following conditions:

- *Escrow Arrangement.* Rarely used, this mainly benefits businesses that have assets or inventory under seizure. The escrow arrangement ensures payment either when large tax liabilities are involved or when there are conditions peculiar to a particular case. Property is placed in escrow with a reliable and disinterested third party who assumes control of it for the purposes of protecting the property and securing payment of the liability. The escrow arrangement can be particularly effective in a situation in which the IRS has a particular asset under seizure, such as an entire business, and the taxpayer needs to have property released in order to raise money to pay the taxes.

* *Bond.* You may obtain a release of levy by delivering an acceptable bond to the IRS, conditioned upon payment of the delinquent taxes. IRS regulations specify what constitutes an acceptable bond.

* *Payment of amount of U.S. interest in the property.* This condition does not apply to seizures of monetary assets such as bank accounts and paychecks, but it is important when the IRS has seized a tangible nonmonetary asset like a car or a home. IRM policy defines the value of the government's interest in the property to mean either fair market value or forced sale value. Obviously it is to your benefit to select the forced sale value figure (if you can) since it will always be lower than the fair market value. A good case can also be made that the government's true interest in seized property is the forced sale value because the forced sale value is a better reflection of the property's distressed condition.

This provision is one that can be of the most value to you. There is no need to allow the IRS to sell your property at a forced sale liquidation price solely because you do not have the money to pay the taxes *in full* at the time of sale.

SURVIVAL RULE ▬▬▬▬▬▬▬▬▬▬▬▬▬▬▬▬▬▬▬▬▬▬▬▬▬▬▬▬▬▬

Prior to the sale of your seized property, you should attempt to obtain a release of your property by offering to pay the property's forced sale value.

* *Assignment of salaries and wages.* A seizure of a paycheck has a continuing effect until it is released by the IRS or the taxes have been paid in full.

The payroll deduction agreement must provide for the full liquidation of the tax liability and also requires your employer's approval.

SURVIVAL RULE ━━━━━━━━━━━━━━━━━━━━━━━━━━━━━━━━━━

A seizure can be released by signing a payroll deduction agreement directing your employer to deduct a specific amount from each paycheck and submitting it to the IRS on a regular schedule.

━━━

SURVIVAL RULE ━━━━━━━━━━━━━━━━━━━━━━━━━━━━━━━━━━

A seizure can be released by agreeing to and signing any type of installment or payment agreement (see Chapter 2).

━━━

• *Extension of the Statute of Limitations.* From the date the tax has been assessed, the IRS has six years within which to legally collect the delinquency. The day following the end of the sixth year the IRS has no legal authority to compel payment or enforce collection unless the statute of limitations has been extended in some manner. Revenue Officers are under strict instructions *not* to let the statutory period expire on an open case. Officers have been fired or demoted for allowing the statute to expire. When a statute has less than a year before expiring, an officer will attempt to obtain your signature on Form 900, "Tax Collection Waiver," to agree to extend the time period of the statute. If you do not sign the waiver and extend the statutory period, you may find yourself in quite a bind. Revenue Officers will use every legal power they have to collect the tax before the statutory period expires. They may begin seizing anything and everything in sight, hardship or no hardship.

They may also serve a summons to compel you to give testimony about the location of your assets. If the tax cannot be collected in full before the statute expires, the Revenue Officer may also initiate legal action to reduce the tax assessment to a judgment.

This regulation allows the IRS to release a levy that has been made before the statute expires on the condition that you sign the waiver form agreeing to extend the statutory period *before* the property is released.

• *Release where value of the interest of the United States is insufficient to meet the expenses of sale.* Although the Tax Code allows the IRS to seize property or rights to property to collect taxes, it does not prevent the IRS from seizing property in which the taxpayer has small equity. For many years, officers have seized property in which the taxpayer had *no equity.* This was solely a practice of harassment. Officers know from experience that 80 to 90 percent of the tangible property seizures never go to sale, because the taxpayer somehow comes up with the money to pay the tax delinquency and obtain a property release or redemption. Occasionally the IRS has to sell the seized property when the taxpayer simply does not have the money to pay the taxes and does not know how the property could be released without paying the taxes in full. Sometimes seized property with little or nominal equity was sold to strangers solely for payment of expenses. Since this had no effect upon reducing the taxpayer's tax liability, the seizure and sale were unjustified.

When it is clear that the sale of the property will not even pay for IRS's expenses of seizure and storage, the IRS can save face by releasing your seized property. If the officer has done his job properly, this situation would never arise in the first place, because officers are now prohibited from making seizures of property in which you have no equity. IRM 5341.2:(4) requires the officer to immediately release seized property if your equity is insufficient to yield net proceeds from the sale to apply to the unpaid tax.

But officers are still acting within IRS policies and procedures if they seize property with *nominal* equity and sell the property at a price just more than sufficient to pay the expenses.

TRANSFERRING ASSETS TO BEAT THE IRS

Many taxpayers think they can beat the IRS at its own game by either transferring their assets around or changing title to property the IRS might seize.

Transferring property to a different title can be an effective and legal means of preserving your assets, not only from the IRS but also from other creditors. But you have to be very careful because timing is a crucial element in determining whether or not the action is legal. In some situations a transfer of assets to another person or to another form of ownership could be an "earmark of fraud" if it was intended to hinder, delay, or defraud creditors. A transfer of assets may be considered a "fraudulent conveyance"—if the intention was to place the property beyond the reach of creditors to the detriment of their rights. Some states have enacted statutes making it a criminal offense to participate in a fraudulent conveyance.

This can be confusing, and so before discussing it any further, a distinction needs to be made between three separate actions. The first is the actual change in legal ownership of assets (a change in title). The second is the removal of assets from one locality to another, an action called "concealment." The third is the specific act of hiding and not reporting income to the IRS, a clearly illegal act called evasion. This discussion pertains solely to a change in ownership rights, and not to any illegal act of evasion through under-reporting of income or taxes.

CONCEALING ASSETS FROM THE IRS

Section 7206(4) of the Tax Code makes it a felony to remove, deposit, or conceal any property upon which a levy has been authorized, with the intention of evading or defeating the assessment or collection of any tax. An example of such a violation would occur if your employer purposely pays you an advance to preclude the IRS from levying upon your accrued salary. One trick that taxpayers frequently use is the transfer of their bank account. Revenue Officers are frequently frustrated by this action, and there is not much they can do about it. As long as the taxpayer actually had the bank account on the particular date that he told the IRS he had the account, perjury was not committed. (Remember that all the payment and financial agreement forms and the "Collection Information Statement," Form 433–A, are signed under penalty of perjury.) Taxpayers frequently change bank accounts, and doing so is *not* considered concealment unless the taxpayer puts his money in an account under a fictitious name, or commingles it with the account of another person or business entity. It is not uncommon for an IRS levy sent to a bank to be returned because the "account is closed." When this happens officers try to find either where the taxpayer currently banks or something else to seize.

Revenue Officers sometimes have difficulty finding a taxpayer's car. Sometimes the taxpayer even sells his car legitimately and borrows or leases one to use in getting around town. At other times the vehicle is just not to be found. This is another collection frustration because officers do not have the authority to force a taxpayer to produce property for seizure.

IRS PROCEDURES RELATING TO FRAUDULENT CONVEYANCES

Revenue Officers are given a little training in property law, and so they are supposed to be able to distinguish real property from personal property, determine title of ownership, and determine the IRS's lien priority with regard to other creditors. Obviously, before a seizure is made the officer should know what is the taxpayer's right, title, and interest in the property and how much of that right, title, and interest is encumbered by the federal tax lien. Before seizing any kind of tangible personal property or real property, the officer is required to file a Notice of Federal Tax Lien to protect the government's position against other creditors. Often a taxpayer who owes money to the IRS is also delinquent in paying other creditors.

Since possession can be a major factor in protecting the government's interest in tangible property, Revenue Officers are required to seize property if there is any indication that other creditors will also attempt to repossess or attach the property or that the taxpayer may dispose of the property to the detriment of the government.

The law does *not* prevent a person from selling his assets even if there are outstanding liens on the property. Under most state laws the liens would remain with the property after a transfer or sale has been made. The IRS would not even question the sale of property encumbered with tax liens unless it appeared that the sale was for "less than good and valuable consideration." (Consideration is the price paid for something.) But a sale of encumbered property (that is, property secured by a lien) for less than full market value could present quite a few problems. And a sale of encumbered property to a relative for less than full market value will raise even more problems.

In IRS terminology a person who disposes of his assets at such a time and in such a way as to hinder normal collection efforts is called a *transferor*, when the transfer or sale of property is made without full, fair, and adequate consideration. The person receiving the property is called the *transferee*.

In order for the IRS to look suspiciously at a sale of a delinquent taxpayer's assets, the transfer or sale must be considered to have been a fraudulent conveyance. There are three principal methods by which the IRS may proceed when a fraudulent conveyance has been made.

- The IRS may file suit in a U.S. District Court to have the transfer or sale set aside. This action reinstates the property to its original owner, the transferor, and makes it subject to seizure by the IRS. This procedure is generally the preferred remedy in federal tax cases when the IRS has a particular interest in that specific piece of property.
- The IRS may file a suit to obtain a judgment against the *transferee*. A judgment can be requested for the value of the transferred property but not exceeding the amount owed by the delinquent taxpayer.
- The IRS may begin an administrative civil proceeding to assess against the *transferee* an amount of money equal to the value of the transferred property but not exceeding the amount owed by the delinquent taxpayer. This proceeding follows the normal tax assessment route, thereby giving the transferee the right to appeal to the Tax Court. If assessed, the amount owed can be collected in the same manner as delinquent taxes.

All three of these procedures are rarely used, and the IRS is reluctant to resort to the courts for collecting taxes unless there is no other alternative. IRS policy is to exhaust all administrative efforts to collect the tax before suing, meaning that the administrative transferee assessment procedure must be tried first.

Revenue Officers who discover fraudulent conveyances are usually too busy and powerless to do anything about them. Each procedure must be run through the bureaucratic maze for approval. Court suits sometimes take years and cost the government thousands of dollars in staff time. Administrative assessments take months. So unless it is absolutely necessary to pursue collection through one of the three remedies mentioned, officers will try to collect in some other way. Some officers may proceed immediately with seizures of other property.

IMPORTANT FACTS

There are several important facts that you should be aware of before even attempting to transfer or sell your property to beat the IRS:

* Timing is important. The law assumes that you are aware of your debts and aware that tax is owed on the receipt of taxable income. It is not necessary that a return be filed and an assessment made for a transferee liability to be established. *The fact that a tax liability has accrued at the time of a transfer or sale is evidence of an impending tax debt.* In the absence of fraud or collusion, transferee liability does *not* normally exist when the transfer or sale occurs *in the tax period prior to when the tax liability is incurred.* (This may vary according to state law.) For example:

During 1981 Mr. R. A. Jones made $200,000 in the silver futures market. By the end of 1981 he still had a $200,000 taxable gain on which he owed approximately $64,000 in taxes. In January 1982, Mr. Jones transferred title of his house with equity of $75,000 to his daughter for $1,000. On April 15, 1982, Mr. Jones filed his tax return for 1981 and reported that he owed $64,000 in taxes. He never paid those taxes, and when the Revenue Officers came to collect they found that not only had he disposed of the taxable income, but he had also transferred his home for less than good and valuable consideration.

The IRS could proceed either through a civil suit or administrative assessment to recover the amount of taxes still unpaid, even though the taxes had not been assessed at the time the house was transferred. The key point here is that the income had been earned and the taxes had accrued at the time the house was transferred for less than good and valuable consideration.

If Mr. Jones had transferred the house to his daughter for less than full and adequate consideration *before* the income was earned, the IRS would have no legal right to intervene in the transfer. And, of course, Mr. Jones could have sold his house to his daughter at any time for *full* and adequate consideration and the IRS could have done nothing about it.

* In some states the law allows the IRS to seize property that has been sold to another person when the IRS has filed the federal tax lien prior to the transfer or sale. Other states will not allow this, and in those states the IRS must file suit to foreclose the federal tax lien on the property. The seizure or foreclosure of property already transferred or sold to another person must be allowed by state law and must meet other conditions of lien priorities. The subject of lien priorities is complicated and is primarily a subject for legal advice from an attorney.

The general rule is that the federal tax lien follows the property if filed prior to the transfer or sale. However, the law allows for exceptions that would prevent the IRS from enforcing its lien priority by seizure. For example, the filing of the federal tax lien will not prevent a taxpayer from selling his automobile to another person if it was sold for full and adequate consideration and the purchaser had no knowledge or notice that the federal tax lien had been filed.

* Contrary to public belief, the federal tax lien filing does *not* prevent a taxpayer from selling his real property such as a residence. It is commonly believed that the IRS has to be paid in full and the lien released *before* the property can be sold. That belief is only partially and technically correct. A taxpayer owning real property subject to the federal tax lien may find a purchaser and contract to sell the property at any time. At the property settlement, where the actual transfer takes place, the settlement attorneys will withhold sufficient funds to pay the IRS. Once the IRS has been paid and the federal tax lien released, the purchaser will receive a clear title. If there are not sufficient funds to pay the IRS in full, then the federal tax lien will not be released unless a request is made for the property to be discharged from the lien. This procedure will require an investigation by the IRS to make sure that the property, in fact, sold for full and adequate consideration.

ADVICE

* In the beginning you were told that changing title to property can be an effective means of preserving your assets not only from the

IRS but also from other creditors. This statement was not intended to encourage you to violate any laws or to create additional problems with the IRS. But my experience as a Revenue Officer has convinced me that many people could have taken steps to protect themselves in a way that not only would have been proper or legal but also would have been an intelligent tactic for financial survival.

It is estimated that there are from 12 to 15 million small businesses in this country. Judging from IRS statistics of business income tax returns filed, only 10 percent to 15 percent of these businesses are incorporated. As everyone knows, the major advantage of being incorporated is the limited liability feature. The partnership and sole proprietorship forms of business not only subject their owners to additional financial risks beyond their capital contribution, but those business forms also expose the owner's private assets to possible attachment from creditors, including the IRS.

Most of IRS's collection problems concern small businesses that don't pay IRS the taxes withheld from their employees. A substantial portion of the tangible property seizures are related to tax delinquencies of these small businesses. The IRS not only can enforce collection from the assets of the small business but often can seize individually owned assets of the business owner when the business taxes are owed by a sole proprietorship or partner. For example, consider the situation of Ralph Brown, who owns Brown's Hardware Store as a sole proprietor, and has a brand-new 1983 Oldsmobile titled in his name only. The car has over $3,000 equity because Mr. Brown put a large down payment on the purchase. He owes the IRS $2,000 for two quarters of employee withholding taxes that he cannot pay. He does not know it, but the IRS can seize his car for nonpayment of taxes incurred during his business operation. If he had titled the car either jointly with his wife or in his wife's name solely, the Oldsmobile would probably not be a target for seizure since the federal tax lien would probably not apply to the joint ownership of the car (actually, this depends upon state law) and would most certainly not apply to his wife's sole ownership. This point brings us to our next survival rule.

• In some states assets other than real property, such as a checking or savings account, can be owned as tenants by the entirety, a legal and indivisible form of ownership held only by a husband and wife

SURVIVAL RULE ━━━━━━━━━━━━━━━━━━━━━━━━━━━━━━━━━━

If you are planning to go into business for yourself or presently own a business as a sole proprietor or partner, you should seek legal advice as early as possible about how you should own your assets so that they will be protected from the enforcement powers of the IRS and other creditors.

━━

as a single entity. Fundamentally it is a form of joint tenancy with right of survivorship that only applies to the marital estate. Assets normally held as tenants by the entirety cannot be seized for a tax delinquency incurred separately by one of the spouses. However, *assets held as tenants by the entirety can be seized for a tax delinquency incurred on a tax return filed jointly.*

Many taxpayers are not aware of the possible consequences of filing a joint tax return on which there is a delinquency that cannot be paid. Most married taxpayers file a joint tax return because the tax rates are usually cheaper than the rates for filing separately. A sole proprietor files Schedule C with his joint tax return reporting business income even though the business is not jointly owned. If there are income and Social Security taxes owed by the spouse having the business income, the filing of a joint tax return makes the other spouse just as liable for their payment because taxes owed on a joint tax return are considered to be "jointly and severally liable." This means that the IRS can collect any amount, either partially or in full, from assets owned by *either* spouse and from assets owned jointly by *both* spouses.

Of critical importance is the fact that by filing a joint tax return you may be subjecting all of your assets to possible enforcement action of the IRS. As mentioned earlier, seizures of real estate are popular with Revenue Officers because they are relatively easy to do. The ideal collection problem involves married taxpayers who owe a lot of money, own real estate with a substantial equity, and who file a joint tax return. Filing a joint tax return makes it especially easy for the IRS to collect when there is jointly owned real estate involved because officers know they have more leverage to encourage the taxpayer to borrow the money or raise it in some way. Usually all they have to do is tell the taxpayers that their home can be seized and sold by the IRS at any time without even a court order.

SURVIVAL RULE ━━━━━━━━━━━━━━━━━━━━━━━━━━━━━━━━━

A taxpayer who owes more taxes than he can pay should consider filing a separate return instead of a joint return if such action would prevent the IRS from seizing any assets that are jointly owned.

━━━

Even though filing a separate return could mean an increased tax bill, it may be advisable to do so when you cannot possibly pay or borrow the money you would otherwise owe if you had filed a joint return. And filing a separate return may be a lot easier than trying to transfer your assets from one form of ownership to another. If you have any questions about whether filing a separate return would be advisable in your situation, you should discuss it with your tax practitioner or attorney.

Facing the Power of
the IRS Summons

How they get you where they want you

THE ADMINISTRATIVE SUMMONS

The IRS Summons is much like a court subpoena except that it is an administrative action not issued by a court. It is issued by an IRS enforcement official to compel a person to appear at an IRS office on a specific date and time and produce certain books and records or give certain testimony requested by the Summons. The authority to issue the Summons is granted in section 7602 of the Internal Revenue Code. Congress recognized that in many instances the IRS would be unable to administer the tax laws properly if it was unable to obtain the information needed to conduct tax investigations.

Enforcement personnel having the authority to issue Summonses include Special Agents, Revenue Agents, Revenue Officers, and Internal Security Inspectors. (The bottom of the Summons gives the name and title of the issuing officer.)

During the course of an investigation, audit, or collection procedure, the Summons may be issued to a taxpayer or other person who

Department of the Treasury
Internal Revenue Service

Collection Summons

Income Tax Return

Form 6636 (3-81)

In the matter of the tax liability of Sam Birch, 1234 S. Main Street, Alexandria, VA 22303

Internal Revenue District of Richmond

Periods Calendar years ending December 31, 1980 and December 31, 1981

The Commissioner of Internal Revenue to Sam Birch

at 1234 S. Main Street, Alexandria, Virginia 22303

You are hereby summoned and required to appear before: Mark Pine

an employee of the Internal Revenue Service, to give testimony relating to the tax liability or the collection of the tax liability of the person identified above for the periods shown and to bring with you and produce for examination the following books, records, papers, and other data:

All documents and records you possess or control that reflect income you received for the year(s)

Calendar years ending

December 31, 1980 & December 31, 1981.

These documents and records include, but are not limited to: Forms W-2, Wage and Tax Statement, Forms 1099 for interest or dividend income, employee earnings statements, and records of deposits with banks or other financial institutions.

Also include any and all other books, records, documents and receipts for income from, but not limited to, the following sources: wages, salaries, tips, fees, commissions, interest, rents, royalties, alimony, state or local tax refunds, annuities, life insurance policies, endowment contracts, pensions, estates, trusts, discharge of indebtedness, distributive shares of partnership income, business income, gains from dealings in property, and any other compensation for services (including receipt of property other than money). This includes any and all documents and records pertaining to any income you have assigned to any other person or entity.

This will enable us to prepare a Federal income tax return(s) for the year(s)

1980 and 1981

for which year(s) no return(s) has been made. A blank return(s) is attached to guide you in producing the necessary documents and records.

Business address and telephone number of Internal Revenue Service employee named above: U.S. Federal Building, 5285 Leesburg Pike, Falls Church, Va 22041

Place and time for appearance: at Rm. 602, 5285 Leeburg Pike, Falls Church, VA 22041

on the 20th day of September ,19 82 at 10:00 o'clock A M

Issued under authority of the Internal Revenue Code this 8th day of September ,19 82

Signature of Issuing Officer

Revenue Officer
Title

Signature of Approving Officer (if applicable)

Title

Part 1 to be kept by IRS

Form 6636 (3-81)

has *not voluntarily* given testimony or supplied certain books and records that are relevant and material to the conduct of a case. There are basically six situations under which the code specifies the Summons may be issued:

- When the purpose is to prepare a return because the taxpayer has failed to do so.
- When there is a need to determine if a taxpayer is liable for a tax.
- When the IRS has to collect a tax that has not been paid.
- When there is a need to ascertain whether or not a tax return has been correctly prepared.
- When the IRS must determine the liability of a fiduciary or other third party involved in a particular type of transaction with a taxpayer.
- When the purpose is to inquire into any offense connected with the administration or enforcement of the Internal Revenue laws.

Under the authority of section 7602 of the Internal Revenue Code the IRS may issue the Summons on the following persons:

- Any person liable for the tax, or any person required to perform any act under the Internal Revenue Code.
- Any officer or employee of any person mentioned above. (This usually applies when the taxpayer is a business or a corporation.)
- Any person having possession, custody, or care of books of account containing entries relating to the business of the person mentioned above.
- Any other person who may be deemed proper by the officer issuing the Summons.

As you can see, the summons power is all-encompassing. The Summons can be issued on just about anyone the IRS wishes. In practice the Summons is issued only on a person who might have information or records that would assist the service in determining a liability, preparing a tax return, or collecting an unpaid tax bill. The Summons is solely a device to obtain information. It cannot be used to make you produce assets for seizure, and it cannot be used to make you prepare a tax return.

SUMMONS FOR FAILURE TO FILE

In order to explain how the IRS uses the Summons to determine a person's tax liability, let's develop a typical situation to show the whole sequence of events that lead up to the use of the Summons. Let's suppose that you haven't filed an income tax return for the past two years and that the IRS has found out that these returns are not on file and has sent you several notices telling you of this. You are a little scared because you think you might be in trouble. But you ignore the notices, hoping the IRS will become tired of pursuing the matter and eventually drop the issue. Then one day you receive a phone call from a Revenue Officer who wants to know why you have not filed for the past two years. You tell the officer that there must be some mistake, that you have always filed your tax returns. Everybody makes mistakes, and so, could not the IRS have misfiled your returns, you ask? The officer knows there is always the possibility of a return being misfiled (even if he doubts that it could happen two years in a row). He tells you to send him a signed copy and everything will be okay. At this point you are relieved but still concerned because you know the copies don't exist.

What do you do? You tell the IRS that the copies will be in the mail soon. Several weeks go by without a word from the IRS. Just as you have forgotten about the phone call, a Revenue Officer comes knocking on your door. This guy's different. He's not smiling and he's not interested in listening to your excuses. All he wants is the returns and he starts making demands and threats. He tells you that if you don't file the returns by next Friday that he will issue you the Summons. When he leaves you are a little confused, anxious, and perplexed. You are confused because you do not know where you are going to get forms that are two years old. You are anxious because you do not know what the Summons is or what the IRS can do to you if you do not file. And you are perplexed because you don't know what you are going to do.

The following Friday passes and you have not filed the tax returns. A couple of days later you come home and find an IRS document under the door addressed to you. It's called the "Summons" and it directs you to appear at the local IRS office eleven days from now with all kinds of books and records "so that Federal income tax returns . . . may be prepared" for you. It is signed by a Revenue Officer of the IRS.

On the appointed day you show up, not knowing if they are going to take you away or show you leniency. As requested, you have brought in all your W–2 statements, canceled checks, and all records of expenditures for those two years. The officer goes through your box of records and begins to prepare your tax returns. In a couple of hours he is finished and hands you a completed return and asks you to sign it. You sign it because you think you might go to jail if you don't. The officer says thanks and says you can go. You go home relieved that they have not put you away. Your only concern now is how you are going to pay the money you owe on those returns you signed. But for this moment the big problem is over.

This was a typical example of how the IRS can use its summons authority to determine your liability without making you file the return. As mentioned earlier, the Summons cannot be used to compel you to do anything other than to give testimony or produce books and records. Section 6020 of the Internal Revenue Code gives the IRS authority to prepare tax returns. In effect, the Summons is used to compel taxpayers to produce the books and records necessary for the IRS to prepare a tax return under section 6020.

There is an important point made in Chapter 1 that needs to be reemphasized here. During the first personal contact, the Revenue Officer will ask you many questions about your income and why your tax returns were not filed to determine if fraud was present. Unless you have substantial income with an equally substantial tax liability, the officer almost always assumes that fraud is not present. Once the officer decides there has been no fraud, you will be asked to file the delinquent returns. Known in IRS parlance as "solicitation," a request to file just about kills any chance that the IRS will conduct a fraud investigation. The Criminal Investigations Division will *not* accept a case of failure to file when the officer has requested you to file. The reasoning is that you could too easily present a defense of harassment, claiming that the only reason you are being prosecuted is that the officer became mad when you did not do what the officer asked you to do. Whether this makes sense is debatable, but the fact is that the IRS will *almost never* make a criminal investigation of a failure-to-file case when the returns have been solicited. This is important for you to know because once the returns have been solicited by a Revenue Officer or any collection employee, you can feel relieved of any chances of being investigated for criminal wrongdoing. From the moment of solicitation, the die has been cast for civil enforcement.

During the first interview the officer will usually ask several other questions. He may want to know where you work, how much money you make, how long you have been working there, and what sources of income you have. You will be given a deadline for filing all delinquent returns and told that failure to comply with the deadline will be considered a refusal to file under the Internal Revenue Code. It is important that you request an extension of time to comply if you are not able to meet that deadline.

SURVIVAL RULE ▰▰▰▰▰▰▰▰▰▰▰▰▰▰▰▰▰▰▰▰▰

If you are not able to keep a filing deadline, contact the appropriate IRS employee and request additional time to comply.

A lot of unnecessary trouble can be avoided simply by keeping the communication channels open between you and the IRS. Collection employees naturally become suspicious when taxpayers fail to keep appointments or deadlines and do not call either to explain why or to reschedule another appointment or deadline. In the event that additional time is needed, the IRS will generally go along at least once and sometimes twice. Usually all you have to do is ask.

RESTRICTIONS ON THE IRS SUMMONS

The IRS has various policies restricting the use of the summons power. It is not the intention of the service that enforcement employees use the power indiscriminately. Before the Summons is issued the enforcement employee is required to consider many factors:

- The information being sought must be relevant to the completion of an assigned investigation. If the information will not lead to the completion of the case, it may not be important enough to pursue under the summons authority.
- It must be reasonable to expect the person being summoned to

have possession or knowledge of the information being sought. Employees are not allowed to use enforcement tools for "hunting expeditions," or attempts to find information that the IRS has no knowledge exists.

- IRS employees are supposed to explore other avenues of obtaining the information. For example, the Summons would not be necessary if the information could be obtained from a tax return or voluntarily from other persons.

- Employees must first exhaust all reasonable efforts to voluntarily obtain the information. At least one personal contact is supposed to be made before the Summons is issued.

- Enforcement of the Summons must be worth the time and expense of pursuing.

- Payment of fees and costs to the summoned party should be weighed against the value of the information being obtained and the amount of the tax liability involved. For example, a Revenue Officer should not issue the Summons to prepare a delinquent return if he has reason to believe that no tax would be due.

YOUR RIGHTS AS A SUMMONED PERSON

As a person summoned to appear before the IRS, you have certain constitutional and judicial rights. Among these rights are the various types of defenses that can be used to challenge the Summons. A defense is a legal reason for not complying with the Summons and can be raised by any summoned person, whether that person be the taxpayer or another person in possession of information about the taxpayer. A defense can be raised at any time, either when appearing before the IRS or when testifying before the courts. To assert a defense as a summoned person, you should appear at the interview scheduled in the Summons and make the assertion at that time. If the IRS decides to test your defense, they will go to court and ask the court to order you to obey the Summons. If your defense is valid, the court can rule against the IRS, thereby preventing them from obtaining the information requested in the Summons.

An extensive discussion of your rights and possible challenges and defenses to the Summons follows.

YOUR RIGHTS AGAINST UNNECESSARY EXAMINATIONS

Code section 7605(b) prevents the IRS from subjecting you to unnecessary examinations or investigations and provides that only one inspection of your books of account can be made for each taxable year. (The word *examination* as used here refers to an inspection of your books and records, which are compelled by the summons authority.) An exception occurs if you request the examination or if the IRS notifies you in writing that an additional inspection is necessary. The prohibition only applies to a re-examination of your books and records. It does not apply to the Summons issued to other sources, such as your bank. This statute attempts to prevent IRS harassment by restricting the number of times they can compel you to do something.

As you might suspect, the IRS has ways of maneuvering around this restriction, mainly by its interpretation of the statute. The Legal Reference Guide (LRG) of the IRM says that "The re-examination provisions of IRC 7605(b) do not proscribe [prohibit] a second examination made for a different, but authorized, purpose than the original examination." For example, the LRG points out that Tax Code section 7602 allows a summons to be served for any of several purposes: for example, determining a tax liability or collecting a tax. The IRS feels that a separate examination of your books and records for the purpose of *collecting* the tax is allowable even when there has already been an examination to *determine* the tax. They consider the second examination to be an original examination and not subject to the restriction of 7605(b).

Just so that you do not become confused about this restriction, let's review a few points that may have raised questions in your mind.

- The examination restriction applies to your books and records only, not to your tax return. While the legislative intent may have been to prevent a subsequent audit of a year that has already been audited, the courts have ruled that a re-examination (or audit) of your *return* itself is not necessarily restricted. There is a difference between your tax return and your books and records from which the return was prepared.
- A re-examination of your books and records can only occur after the IRS has sent you a written notice of their intention to conduct

a second examination. This notice provision gives them the opportunity to issue the second Summons just about anytime they need to.

SURVIVAL RULE ━━━━━━━━━━━━━━━━━━━━━━━━━━━━━━

If you have been asked twice to turn over your books and records for the same situation and for the same taxable year and you were not notified in writing that the second examination was necessary, you should challenge the second Summons under section 7605(b).

━━━

- A second examination of your books and records can be made if you fail to produce all the documents requested in the first inspection. You cannot fail to cooperate fully during the first examination and then try to challenge the Summons on the second examination based on the section 7605(b) restriction.
- The second Summons does not necessarily constitute a second examination. The IRS has the right to first serve the Summons to obtain information about what papers or documents are within your possession. The subsequent Summons may then be issued to compel the production of the pertinent books and records. In this instance the first Summons merely obtains testimony. The second Summons results in the first examination of the books and records. The Summons issued to obtain testimony is obviously distinct from the Summons issued to produce books and records.

YOUR RIGHTS AGAINST SELF-INCRIMINATION

The Fifth Amendment to the Constitution provides the privilege against self-incrimination. The privilege is a personal one, meaning that it applies only to that individual and only to the imposition of a requirement to produce incriminating testimony. The privilege extends to those papers and effects that are the private property of the person claiming the privilege or are in the personal possession of that person. Summonses issued by Revenue Officers, Tax Auditors and Revenue Agents are for civil administrative purposes and not for criminal investigations. Since the type of information sought by these enforcement officers does not usually develop into a criminal case, it is not mandatory that you as a summonsed person be informed of your rights under the Fifth Amendment.

However, the IRS can use incriminating information obtained through the use of the Summons when the information has been obtained voluntarily. Even though the Summons has been issued to compel you to testify, nothing in the process compels you to give incriminating evidence against yourself. Therefore any incriminating information IRS obtains from you under the summons process is considered to have been given *voluntarily*.

In a single year Special Agents from the Criminal Investigations Division will serve over 25,000 summonses. A large number of these will be served upon financial institutions to discover the financial transactions of taxpayers to be used in building criminal cases. Frequently there is a need to serve the Summons on taxpayers who are the subject of the criminal investigation. While the IRS believes the law does not require them to warn taxpayers of their rights when appearing in a summons interview, they do feel that there is a need to protect themselves against the defense that the information or testimony may have been given involuntarily. Special Agents are supposed to give the following warning at the beginning of a summons interview:

In connection with my investigation of your tax liability I would like to ask you some questions. However, first I advise you that under the Fifth Amendment to the Constitution of the United States I cannot compel you to answer any questions or to submit any information if such answers or information might tend to incriminate you in any way. I also advise you that anything which you say and any documents which you submit may be used against you in any criminal proceeding which may be undertaken. I advise you further that you may, if you wish, seek the assistance of an attorney before responding.

SURVIVAL RULE ▬▬▬▬▬▬▬▬▬▬▬▬▬▬▬▬▬▬▬▬▬▬▬▬▬▬▬▬

If you are given your rights by a Special Agent at the beginning of an interview, you should immediately terminate the interview and seek assistance from legal counsel.

Special Agents are required to terminate an interview immediately whenever the person being interviewed requests to have an attorney present. Another point you should know: Special Agents are *not* allowed to use language suggesting a promise of immunity, a settlement of the case, or anything that might be interpreted as intimidation or a threat.

Summonses issued by Revenue Officers, Tax Auditors or Revenue Agents rarely require the need of legal counsel. Tens of thousands of taxpayers comply each year without legal assistance. It is for this reason that you need to know the differences among the different enforcement personnel. Revenue Officers do *not* conduct criminal investigations. Revenue Agents sometimes work with Special Agents who conduct criminal investigations, but summonses issued to taxpayers during a criminal investigation are usually signed by the Special Agent leading the investigation.

The need to protect yourself against self-incrimination is obvious. IRS employees like easy cases, and the easier you make it for them the easier they can proceed with a criminal investigation. Just to be on the safe side, consider the next Survival Rule.

SURVIVAL RULE ▬▬▬▬▬▬▬▬▬▬▬▬▬▬▬▬▬▬▬▬

You may want to obtain legal assistance whenever you have been summoned and you fear that the interview could lead to a criminal investigation.

Remember though that not every case leads to a criminal investigation. If you are unaware of how the IRS conducts a criminal investigation and what kind of proof is needed to prove fraud, you have a need to be concerned. Most taxpayers comply with the Summons without legal help or because they have no reason to suspect they are in danger of being accused of performing a criminal act. If you have any doubt about your own personal situation, you should consult an attorney immediately.

YOUR RIGHT TO CONFIDENTIAL PRIVILEGE

Up to now, the discussion has been about summonses served on taxpayers, but the Summons can be issued to any *other* person deemed appropriate by the issuing enforcement officer. The most controversial summonses are those served on taxpayers' attorneys, accountants, and physicians.

Under various laws taxpayers are afforded privileges as a result of certain confidential relationships, such as the attorney-client, accountant-client, and physician-patient relationships. Each relationship brings forth its own set of problems because of the various state laws. The Tax Reform Act of 1976 gave taxpayers additional special rights regarding summonses served on their attorneys and accountants, but these special rights are in addition to other rights that may exist as a result of the confidential relationship.

- *Attorney-client privilege.* The general rule is that communications of a confidential nature may not be divulged when the communication occurred in the course of the attorney-client relationship. Although this may appear to be all-inclusive, it is not. The privilege only applies to communications made in confidence by the client for the purpose of obtaining legal advice. For example, books and records left with an attorney for the purpose of preparing a tax return are not privileged solely because they are in the possession of an attorney. The IRS may issue the Summons to an attorney to produce those books and records and go to court to obtain compliance should the attorney refuse to obey the Summons.
- *Accountant-client privilege.* The federal government does not recognize communications between an accountant and client as privileged. Any books and records left in the possession of an accountant for any purpose, even if to prepare income tax returns, are subject to the IRS Summons.
- *Physician-patient privilege.* The federal government does not recognize communications between a physician and his patient as privileged.

ADDITIONAL RIGHTS

There are additional rights granted a person summoned by the IRS even though that person may not be the taxpayer. For purposes of appearing before the IRS, *any summoned person* is considered to be a witness, even the taxpayer himself.

- As a witness, you have the right to have legal counsel present during the summons interview. You may also have any other person present to assist you. For example, you may feel more secure by having your accountant present to help with technical accounting details.

- Several federal district courts have ruled that a summoned person is entitled to have a stenographer present, and so the IRS will allow you to make a tape, stenographic or other verbatim recording of any proceeding, including a summons interview. In the event you wish to record the interview in either fashion, you should announce your intentions prior to the interview so as not to cause yourself any unnecessary delays. The IRS will also want to make a recording and may need time to arrange for the equipment to be available.

- If the summons interview results in a signed statement or affidavit, you are entitled to a copy. Very rarely does a summons interview result in this kind of a document when the interview is before a Revenue Officer or Revenue Agent. Affidavits are not needed for civil cases.

- As a summoned person, you are entitled to witness fees and travel expenses for appearing personally in response to the Summons. Also any summoned third party (someone other than the taxpayer) may receive payment for fees and costs incurred in complying with the Summons.

Internal Revenue Code section 7610(a)(1) provides for payment of witness fees and travel expenses to persons summoned to appear before the IRS. Remember that *any person* required to make an appearance before the IRS because of the Summons is a *witness.* Any witness is entitled to a fee of thirty dollars for each full day or partial day's attendance and to subsistence and travel costs at the same rates government employees are compensated for official travel. These fees are authorized by section 1821, title 28 of the U.S. Code. It is important to know that witness fees are only payable on *request.*

The provision for witness fees and travel expenses is not new, but it's doubtful that you will find many IRS employees who know about it. Even though the IRM tells the employees how payment is to be

SURVIVAL RULE ▰▰▰▰▰▰▰▰▰▰▰▰▰▰▰▰▰▰▰▰▰▰▰▰▰▰▰▰▰▰▰▰

When you have been summoned to appear before the IRS, you should make a claim for witness fees and travel expenses.

---

made, the provision is so obscure to most of them (even most tax practitioners are unaware of it) that you may even be told that witness fees cannot be paid. This is not true. If you need to quote an authority, you can:

* refer Revenue Officers to IRM 5895;
* refer Revenue Agents and Tax Auditors to IRM 4022.51;
* refer Special Agents to IRM 9369.

In addition to witness fees, section 7610(a) of the Tax Code also provides for reimbursement of certain fees and costs associated with honoring the Summons. Reimbursement is made for "such costs that are reasonably necessary which have been directly incurred in searching for, reproducing, or transporting books, papers, records, or other data required to be produced by Summons." But there are exceptions. First, no payment can be made if the taxpayer (the person with respect to whose liability the Summons is issued) has an ownership interest in the material required to be produced by the Summons. This means that if you are summoned to produce your own books and records you cannot be reimbursed for searching, reproduction, or transportation (SRT) costs. A third party who has been summoned to produce your books and records (if you are the taxpayer) cannot be reimbursed for SRT costs. This restriction is further extended to prohibit SRT payments to your accountant or attorney if he is acting as your representative. Costs are also prohibited to an officer, employee, or agent of a taxpayer (this would apply to businesses).

If a Revenue Officer determines you are entitled to payment for SRT costs, he will give you part B of the Summons assembly, which explains how to obtain reimbursement and specifies the amounts of reimbursement.

SURVIVAL RULE ━━━━━━━━━━━━━━━━━━━━━━━━━━━━━━

If you are a third party who has been issued the Summons to produce books and records pertaining to another person, you should file a claim for reimbursement of costs associated with searching, reproducing, and transporting those documents.

━━

RIGHTS OF TAXPAYERS TO STAY COMPLIANCE IN CERTAIN SITUATIONS

As a summoned person, you have the right to defend yourself against the enforcement of the Summons in court. Enforcement can be challenged on a number of grounds, including such issues as the Summons was not validly served, the information being requested is not relevant and material to the case, the Summons is ambiguous in describing the information requested, the books and records do not exist, or it is simply not possible to comply.

Before 1977 the IRS could issue the Summons to your bank or other third party to obtain information about your financial transactions without your even knowing about it. Congress recognized that a financial institution or other third party would not be as concerned about protecting your privacy as strongly as you would be. So the Internal Revenue Code was amended in 1976 to allow you rights of court intervention when the IRS has issued the Summons on certain third-party recordkeepers. The procedure was amended by the 1982 tax bill, but the concept remains of allowing you the right to contest in court the compliance of a summons by a third-party recordkeeper.

The code defines a third-party recordkeeper as a person or institution engaged in making or keeping the records involving transactions of other persons. The code specifically defines a third-party recordkeeper to be

—any bank, savings and loan, or credit union
—any consumer reporting agency
—issuers of credit cards
—brokers in stocks or other securities
—any attorney
—any accountant

In order to prevent you from using this procedure solely to delay the service's investigation, the code provides that the statute of limitations for assessment and collection of your tax shall be suspended during the period of time the matter is before the courts. The statute of limitations is not suspended when only the third-party record-keeper contests the enforcement of the Summons.

Exceptions: Congress has provided exceptions whereby taxpayers are *not* allowed the right to intervene in the compliance of the Summons served upon a third-party recordkeeper. The first exception is when the Summons is served solely to determine the identity of any person having a numbered account with a bank or other financial institution. The second exception is when the purpose of the Summons is to aid in the *collection* of an assessed liability. This would exempt most of the summonses served by Revenue Officers upon third-party recordkeepers from the intervention procedures. The third exception applies when the Summons has been issued merely to determine whether records exist, and the last exception applies to a "John Doe" Summons.

A "John Doe" Summons is used at times when the service has knowledge of a particular financial transaction that may have a bearing on someone's tax liability but does not know the identity of the persons involved in the financial transaction, thus imparting the name of a "John Doe" Summons. In the past the service would serve the Summons and the affected persons would have no knowledge that the IRS had obtained financial information about them.

Although recognizing that the IRS had a legitimate need for the use of the "John Doe" Summons as an investigative tool in appropriate circumstances, Congress believed that the issue of privacy should also be extended to those unknown individuals about whose financial transactions the IRS is seeking to learn. Under the Tax Code the IRS must get court approval before a "John Doe" Summons can be served. The court procedure is designed to protect the individual's rights by ascertaining that the IRS has a legitimate need to obtain the information requested in the Summons and is not merely on a "fishing expedition."

PENALTIES FOR FAILING TO COMPLY WITH THE SUMMONS

It is a crime for a person to refuse to appear or to produce the books and records requested by the Summons. On conviction the fine is not more than one thousand dollars and/or up to one year in jail. For this reason it is important that you appear as designated in the Summons even when you do not intend to comply with the Summons. The IRS recognizes that a criminal prosecution for summons noncompliance does not necessarily accomplish the purpose of the Summons, and so the IRS has the option of enforcing compliance by civil prosecution.

A *criminal* prosecution results in a possible fine and/or jail sentence. A *civil* prosecution provides for a court order directing you to comply with the Summons under possible punishment for contempt. The major difference is that in a criminal prosecution the IRS must prove that you willfully neglected or refused to comply. In a civil prosecution the court can order compliance without punishment, but if you fail to obey the court order, the court can issue an arrest warrant and jail you for contempt of court.

As a practical matter the IRS rarely, if ever, attempts a criminal prosecution for summons noncompliance. Even in fraud cases the element of willfulness is difficult to prove, and unless there is some obvious sign of willfulness, the IRS is not about to use government resources to pursue prosecution of something that is inherently difficult to prove anyway. As long as the possibility of criminal prosecution exists, however, the IRS knows that taxpayers are more willing to comply, mainly because of the fear of prosecution.

There was a case involving a taxpayer named George Becker, who, when summoned to produce certain books and records, told the IRS that all his books and records had been destroyed in a fire and therefore he couldn't comply with the Summons. Later the IRS asked the grand jury to subpoena the same books and records. Becker complied with the grand jury subpoena proving that the books and records had not been destroyed after all. The IRS then prosecuted Becker for willfully failing to honor the Summons. The court ruled in the government's favor and found Becker guilty of willfully and knowingly neglecting to obey the Summons.

It is doubtful a criminal prosecution for summons noncompliance would ever be pursued unless the case involved a criminal investigation and the information to be obtained by the Summons was extremely important to the investigation or unless there was a very flagrant act of noncompliance, similar to the Becker case. The usual procedure is for the enforcement officer to recommend civil enforcement in cases of noncompliance. After the initial recommendation has been made, the case file is reviewed by the IRS district counsel, who most likely would not allow a recommendation for criminal prosecution to proceed unless the case is extremely strong, meaning that there is available evidence needed to prove willfulness.

The district counsel will review the case file to evaluate several factors, such as determining if the Summons was properly served, the information being requested is material and relevant to the investigation, there is a reasonable expectation that the taxpayer has the requested information, and that the Summons was not legally defective in some way and that the IRS can meet the requirements of *United States v. Powell*, 379 U.S. 48 (1964). Under Powell, the IRS must show that:

- The investigation will be conducted pursuant to a legitimate purpose.
- The inquiry may be relevant to that purpose.
- The information being sought is not already within the possession of the IRS.
- The administrative steps required by the code have been followed.

IRS employees frequently make mistakes in the service or preparation of the Summons, and the IRS will not enforce them unless all the legal requirements and IRS policies have been met. For example, enforcement employees are *not* allowed to refer the Summons for enforcement in the following situations:

- When you or your representative have indicated a willingness to comply and have requested a reasonable extension of time within which to comply. (This emphasizes the importance of open communication at all times.)
- When you have appeared and denied under oath that you possess or control the documents requested in the Summons. There must be a "good reason" to suspect the contrary before the IRS will continue with enforcement in this situation.
- When you have refused to allow the IRS to retain custody of the

books and records, because you felt the IRS wanted to keep the material for too long and photocopying was an unreasonable alternative.

- When the books and records are demanded before you could reasonably be expected to produce them.
- When more than one examination is sought without complying with the notification requirement in Tax Code section 7605(b).

SURVIVAL RULE ▬▬▬▬▬▬▬▬▬▬▬▬▬▬▬▬▬▬▬▬▬▬▬▬▬▬▬

If you have been summoned to produce books and records that you do not possess, always appear at the time and place specified in the Summons. If you cannot or do not wish to comply, appear anyway and testify under oath why you are not able to comply with the Summons.

After the review process is completed, the district counsel will send you a letter setting up another appointment, thereby giving you another opportunity to comply. If you cannot keep this appointment, you may again request an extension of time within which to comply. In the event you do not appear or comply and do not request an extension, the matter will be referred to the U.S. Attorney General, who may initiate a civil proceeding in the U.S. District Court for enforcement.

The court will then issue you a "Show Cause Order," served by the U.S. Marshal, directing you to appear again before the IRS at a designated time to comply with the Summons or else appear at the court on a later specified date. At the court proceeding, the court *may* give you *another chance* to comply with the Summons. If you do not show up for the summons appointment *and* the court appearance, the court will automatically issue a warrant for your arrest on a charge of contempt of court.

The proceeding in the U.S. District Court provides you the opportunity to contest the enforcement of the Summons by asserting a challenge or defense to its enforcement. To accomplish this successfully it is advisable to have legal counsel because legal expertise is necessary to present a proper defense before the court. Without a proper defense the court is most likely to order you to comply with the Summons.

III

THE IRS'S SECRET
LAW

Making an Offer to Compromise Your Taxes

How to settle for as low as 10¢ on the dollar

INTRODUCTION

The Treasury Department has had the authority since 1831 to compromise money owed to Uncle Sam. The authority to compromise (or reduce) a tax liability is presently rooted in Section 7122 of the Internal Revenue Code. By submitting an offer to compromise your taxes, you are, in effect, making a deal with the IRS. You are offering to pay what you can to wipe your slate clean, to avoid future seizures of your property, and to bring your taxes down as low as you can. You are taking the initiative to get the IRS off your back and out of your life.

The offer in compromise is probably the IRS's best-kept secret. Although most IRS officials would prefer that no one knew about it, there are a few taxpayers who have used it and significantly reduced their taxes. In 1981 about two thousand offers were processed by the IRS. Unofficial estimates are that hundreds of thousands of taxpayers could have availed themselves of this technique had they only known how to take advantage of it.

A compromise is a binding settlement reached by mutual agreement of two parties. It is usually achieved after a period of discussion and negotiation. An *offer in compromise* is an amount of money offered by a taxpayer in an attempt to bring about a legal reduction in his tax liability. The Tax Code recognizes that there may be times in which it is more desirable for the IRS to accept a lesser amount in the interests of "effective tax administration."

WHEN YOU CAN COMPROMISE YOUR TAXES

There are two situations under which you may submit an offer in compromise.

• *There is a reasonable doubt that the IRS will ever be able to collect the full amount owed.* The IRS calls this "doubt as to collectibility." You can submit an offer on collectibility grounds when you sincerely doubt that you will *ever* be able to pay off the full amount owed. The IRS will accept a collectibility offer only when they, too, believe the full amount may never be paid. The first question of the IRS will be "Can this tax be collected now, and if not, could it ever be collected in the future?" A *no* answer to both parts of that question increases your chances of having an offer accepted.

This procedure is not to be confused with the procedure discussed in Chapter 2 referred to as "currently uncollectible." In that procedure the IRS will suspend *all* collection action based on your current inability to pay, with collection activity theoretically expected to be resumed at a later date when your ability to pay improves. A suspension of collection is based on your financial hardship resulting in an inability to pay, even in small monthly installments. But your tax liability remains a valid debt, even if your financial hardship continues. The offer in compromise, however, is based not only on your *current* financial hardship but also on your *prospective* financial hardship. The procedure also results in a legal reduction of your tax liability to an amount the IRS agrees is basically "all they're ever going to get."

• *There is a reasonable doubt that you even owe the tax.* The IRS calls this doubt as to liability. When there is a "bona fide" dispute

SURVIVAL RULE ▬▬▬▬▬▬▬▬▬▬▬▬▬▬▬

You should submit an offer to compromise your taxes when you cannot pay in full what you now owe and there is little chance that you will ever be able to pay the balance.

about a question of fact or law with respect to the merits of a tax liability, there is an opportunity for you to submit an offer to compromise your tax liability. The most likely timing of an offer on doubt as to liability will be any time *after* assessment; prior to assessment of additional taxes there are legitimate appeals procedures that make the offer unnecessary.

This should not be confused with the situation in which you receive an erroneous bill, either because your payment was not credited to your account or the IRS computer caused a billing mix-up. When you are inadvertently sent a bill for taxes you do not owe, the IRS will attempt to straighten out the problem when you bring it to its attention. It is not the practice of the service to use the compromise procedure as an alternative to normal procedures of abating taxes that are clearly not owed.

The compromise is also different from the settlement negotiated during an appeal of an audit. Issues frequently come up during audits that are not clearly defined by IRS regulations or the Tax Code. Often called "gray areas," these are issues in which either you or the IRS could be right. The IRS might be motivated to negotiate a compromise of a proposed audit assessment if they are reluctant to litigate the issue in the courts, particularly when they are afraid of the possibility of having a court overrule the IRS and establish a precedent that they do not like. A negotiated settlement of a proposed audit assessment might well mean a compromise: You give in on a few issues and the IRS gives in on a few issues. But the settlement in an audit appeal is entirely different from the liability compromise discussed here. Although a compromise involves an offer of money for a settlement of a reduced liability, an appeals settlement may result in a reduced tax liability *without* an offer of money.

SURVIVAL RULE ▬▬▬▬▬▬▬▬▬▬▬▬▬▬▬▬▬▬▬▬▬▬▬▬▬▬▬▬▬▬

You should submit an offer to compromise your taxes when there is a reasonable doubt that you owe either all or part of the taxes the IRS has assessed against you.

OBJECTIVE OF AN OFFER IN COMPROMISE

The service's objective in accepting an offer is to expedite tax collection with the least possible loss or cost to the government. Theoretically the compromise provision is designed to benefit both you and the IRS. The benefit to you is obvious: You no longer have to pay as much as the IRS originally wanted you to pay. The benefit to the IRS may not be as obvious to you, but you can be sure they are not about to compromise a tax liability unless the benefit is obvious to them. With liability issues, taxpayers must show that a reasonable degree of uncertainty exists in the service's position. With collectibility issues, the IRS might just come out ahead with an offer because the taxpayer may offer assets that are not reached by the federal tax lien.

Officially the IRS recognizes the compromise as a legitimate collection tool. But in this case, national policy regarding offers differs from local implementation. Every IRS official is charged with the responsibility of bringing in the optimum amount of revenue under the powers and resources available to him. Many district and regional officials believe that the offer provision in the Tax Code is contrary to their responsibility "to maximize the revenue." To many Revenue Officers, it is an issue of equity and fairness. How can one justify taking enforced collection against one taxpayer while compromising the liability of another? The tax system is founded on voluntary compliance, and some officials see the offer provision as something that could undermine that compliance, believing that if the public knew about the compromise authority, they surely would not understand it. So the result is a mixed application of the law. An offer that may be acceptable in one district may not be acceptable in another.

SITUATION: SUBMITTING AN OFFER BASED ON DOUBT OF COLLECTIBILITY

Q. *I owe quite a bit of money because of a large gain I made by selling my business last year. This year I used the money to pay my wife's hospital bills. I am retired on a small pension, I'm too old and sickly to get a job, and I don't think I'll ever be able to pay the money I owe. What can I do to get out of this mess?*

Your situation appears to meet the criteria for the IRS to accept an offer based on doubt as to collectibility. In accepting offers based on collectibility factors, the IRS must not only consider your present income but must also consider your future earning capacity or income potential. A senior citizen living on a pension who has no assets and little potential of earning money in the future has a good chance of having an offer accepted.

Although the IRS refuses to outline the exact circumstances under which an offer would be an appropriate collection tool, it considers any of the following as warranting consideration of the credibility of an offer based on doubt as to collectibility.

* Liquidation of your assets and the payments from your present and future income will *not* result in full payment of the tax liability.
* Your spouse, who is *not* liable for the tax, has property that you may use to raise money for the offer to compromise your tax debt.
* You have an interest in assets that the IRS cannot seize because it is not covered by the federal tax lien. For example, if you owe the taxes separate from your spouse, but you own your house as "tenants by the entirety" and the IRS cannot seize the house under state law, the IRS will still consider a minimum of 20 percent of the net equity in the property as your interest and will demand payment of this interest as consideration for the offer.
* You have relatives or friends who might be willing to lend or give you the funds needed for submitting an offer.

The IRS will only accept an offer after considering your "maximum capacity to pay." If you are unable to pay in full or unable to meet monthly payments now but there is some likelihood that you *will* be able to pay in the future, the IRS will merely suspend collection efforts until such time as you are better able to pay. (See Chapter 2.) If you cannot pay now, the IRS must consider the prospects of your being able to pay in the future. The IRS will make a determination of your future earning potential by evaluating such factors as your age, job experience, health, education, skill level, financial profile, and just about anything else that is relevant (like the possibility of your sick, rich brother dying and leaving his fortune to you).

In determining your maximum capacity to pay, the IRS will determine if your offer consists of all that you could possibly offer. You will be asked to complete Form 433, "Statement of Financial Condition," an eight-page document that details your entire financial condition. This form will be scrutinized carefully by a Revenue Officer who will personally investigate every item you have listed. After the officer makes his recommendation, several higher-management officials must review and approve the offer. Each reviewer will be attempting to determine if the amount of money you are offering is the maximum your financial condition will allow you to offer.

In order to compromise your taxes, you have to offer a definite and specific amount of money. The amount offered cannot be frivolous. You cannot offer to give the IRS $10 to compromise a $1,000 liability, and you cannot give them $100 to compromise a $10,000 liability. But you might be able to compromise a $1,000 liability by offering $100 or compromise a $10,000 liability by offering $1,000 if:

- This is all the money you have or could borrow.
- It represents all the equity in your assets.
- You are willing to make certain concessions to the IRS about your future earnings.

In order for you to be able to make a legitimate offer (one that is not frivolous or nominal or made with the intention of delaying collection action), you need some cash. If you have no cash and you cannot borrow it commercially from the equity in your assets, then you need to find a relative or friend who will either give you or lend you the money for the purpose of submitting an offer.

SITUATION: COMPROMISE BASED ON
DOUBT AS TO LIABILITY

Q. *I recently got a bill from the IRS for over $1,000, owed from my 1980 income tax return. I actually got a refund for my 1980 taxes, and so I went down to the IRS office and asked them to check this out. They told me that my 1980 tax return was audited for unreported tip income received while I was a waitress at the local steak house. I never even knew about the audit. They never contacted me, and even though I moved from the apartment where they sent the audit notices, I still stayed in town. So they didn't try very hard to find me. Now I'm told that to contest this I have to pay the tax and file a claim for a refund. I think that's absurd. I'll admit to owing some taxes since I never reported any tip income, but I don't owe as much as they figured. Their estimate of unreported tip income was based on the restaurant's gross earnings, of which three-quarters of their sales occur during the night. I only worked the day shift and didn't earn as much tip income as the waitresses who worked nights. How can I handle this?*

Your situation appears to be a good case for submitting an offer to compromise based on doubt as to liability. Since you were not available when the IRS audited your tax return, you had no chance to contest the merits of the standard the auditors were using in computing the unreported income. And obviously, because you had moved and did not receive the IRS correspondence proposing the assessment, you had no opportunity to appeal it through administrative or judicial channels. Your situation appears to present a "bona fide" dispute about the amount of taxes you should legally owe.

Most audit issues are rather clear-cut, and the IRS has a strong basis for showing taxpayers where they are clearly mistaken. The IRS recognizes, though, that some issues are not clear-cut and that a small percentage of cases contain a basis for a "mutual doubt," or a possibility that either a portion or all of the liability might not be legally owed. For example, the "mutual doubt" could arise because your supporting documentation may have disappeared, your books and records may not have been complete, you may not have "constructively received" income you were entitled to receive, or other extenuating circumstances may have arisen.

If you believe that you have a "bona fide" dispute and there may be a degree of doubt about whether you owe the tax, you may want to submit an offer to compromise the liability. If so, you should know these points:

- A doubt of liability must be supported by tangible evidence of the facts and not by the mere possibility or suspicion of doubt as to the amount legally due. The evidence must raise a "serious and well-founded doubt about the correctness of the liability, but the doubt is not sufficient enough to form a basis to abate the liability."
- When a doubt becomes "mutual," that is the IRS recognizes there is some doubt, the amount acceptable by the IRS will depend on the degree of doubt found in that case.
- The IRS will *not* compromise a liability solely because you have aroused public sympathy or because your situation appears to be similar to another case in which an offer was accepted. The IRS does not use precedent as a rule of equity when accepting offers. (Just because Joe Lewis did it, doesn't mean you can.)
- A compromise can only exist when there is room for concessions. Both parties must be willing to give up something. If it is clear to the IRS that you owe the tax, there is no room for concessions.
- There is no basis for a compromise on the merits of the liability when the liability has already been challenged and affirmed by either the U.S. Tax Court, or other court of competent jurisdiction.

In the event that you have been assessed a tax based on a standard or a rule of law that may not apply in your case, you should offer a reasonable amount of money, based on the facts and circumstances of the case and not on unsupportable assumptions or allegations. For example, in the situation described, the taxpayer should try to reconstruct a reasonable amount of tip income by asking the restaurant to supply her with an estimate of daily sales during the hours she worked. (Businesses usually make cash register readings several times a day.) Then those sales should be divided evenly by the number of waiters and waitresses working during those shifts to arrive at an equal amount of sales per employee. Then a reasonable estimate of tip income could be computed by multiplying 10 percent to 15 percent of the per-employee daily sales and then totaling the amounts to arrive at an estimate of her tip income. This would result in the computation of an amount that is reasonable and representative of the degree of doubt in that case.

SURVIVAL RULE ■■■■■■■■■■■■■■■■■■■■■■■■■■■■■■■■

If you do not owe the tax, the IRS owes you an explanation, and if the assessment cannot be supported, ask the IRS to abate the tax (cancel it out or wipe it off the slate). You do not have to submit an offer to reduce a tax liability that is clearly not owed.

COMPROMISING PENALTIES

Penalties such as those assessed for the failure to pay or the failure to file can be compromised under the same code section as the tax is compromised. But if you can establish "reasonable cause," you can request that the penalties be abated and no compromise is even necessary. (See Chapter 3 for more on this.)

In the absence of reasonable cause, the code assumes that there is "willful neglect," and penalties must be charged for failing to comply with the rules. But a penalty may be compromised when there is clearly some doubt about the situation giving rise to the penalty or some dispute exists over whether an excuse is actually reasonable cause or willful neglect. Whenever the situation falls somewhere in between reasonable cause and willful neglect, a basis for compromise exists. (Chapter 3 includes an extensive discussion on compromising penalties.)

IRS POLICIES ON COMPROMISING TAXES

The IRS cannot refuse to consider your offer. Several years ago a high regional official put the word out that he didn't like offers, that he didn't want to see any, and if one was submitted, the employee was to give it back to the taxpayer. Since this policy was oral, it was only discovered by the National Office when they did a comparison study of how regions handled offers. The study also revealed many regional variations in the number of offers received and the number of offers accepted. This study showed that there were inconsistencies among the regions in applying national policy and criteria, although IRS policy is that all offers must be given consideration and review based on the merits of the case.

If you submit a legitimate offer but the amount offered is not adequate, you must be given the opportunity to increase the offer. You may want to increase the offer when it appears that your offer will not be accepted because the amount of money you are offering is too small. A larger offer may give it more favorable consideration.

An offer must not be rejected arbitrarily and capriciously by the IRS. Although this is the policy it is not always followed. Offers are frequently rejected on nothing more substantial than the fact that "the boss doesn't like offers." Some Revenue Officers are under pressure to reject perfectly valid offers just because higher management will not approve them. Employees who don't uphold management policies don't get promoted.

The one technique that officers frequently use is to tell the taxpayer that they have reviewed the case, their supervisor has reviewed it, and the recommendation will be made to reject it. Then the officer will suggest to the taxpayer that he may want to withdraw the offer because if it is rejected now his chances of another offer being approved in the future are decreased. Usually the taxpayer withdraws the offer without even requesting a final written determination. I have always found it difficult to accept the premise that once the offer has been rejected the chances are poorer that it will be accepted in the future.

SURVIVAL RULE ▬▬▬▬▬▬▬▬▬▬▬▬▬▬▬▬▬▬▬▬▬▬▬▬▬▬▬▬

Never withdraw an offer in compromise on the premise that it will be rejected. Only withdraw the offer if you intend to submit a second offer with an increased amount of money. Always request a written response from the IRS to your offer.

If the IRS rejects the offer, you should receive a letter explaining why it was rejected. Of course the IRS could send you a letter stating that the rejection is "in the government's best interests." That's the catch-all phrase that is used when the IRS cannot think of any better reason. Sometimes it is used legitimately on public policy grounds. The service will not accept an offer if the compromise would generate adverse public opinion that would result in criticism of the service. For example, offers will probably be rejected from persons known to be involved in criminal activity.

The real problem with most offers is not in finding reasons to reject them (although that may be true in some places) but in finding reasons to accept them. The IRS has no obligation to accept an offer and believes that the taxpayer is given a privilege even to be allowed to submit one.

PREPARING THE OFFER

An offer must be submitted on Form 656, "Offer in Compromise." This is the formal way to do it. Without Form 656 the Revenue Officer might think you are trying to bribe him or "make him an offer he can't refuse."

SURVIVAL RULE ━━━━━━━━━━━━━━━━━━━━━━━━━━━━━━━

Always submit an offer on Form 656 and never, never *mention the word* offer *to an IRS employee without specifying you want "to compromise" your tax liability. It is important that the IRS employee doesn't think you are trying to bribe him with the offer.*

━━

All field employees are given training in bribery awareness and are taught that a bribe can be, and usually is, subtle and covert. To prevent any misunderstanding, always clarify your intentions.

Form 656 must be completed and signed by both parties if a joint income tax return is involved. Either the amount being offered or a deposit must be attached to the form at the time it is submitted. If an offer is based on "doubt as to liability," it should be given to a Tax Auditor, Revenue Agent, or anyone in the Examination Divison. It can be submitted at any stage of the audit process. If the offer is based on "doubt as to collectibility," it should be given to a Revenue Representative, Revenue Officer, or anyone else in the Collection

Form **656**
(Rev. July 1979)

Department of the Treasury — Internal Revenue Service

Offer in Compromise

To be Filed in Duplicate

For Office Use Only

Offer is — *(Check applicable box)*
☐ Cash *(Paid in full)*
☐ Deferred payment

Serial Number _____

(Cashier's stamp)

Amount paid
$ _____

Names and Address of Taxpayers
David & Mary Whistler
3419 S. Norview Avenue
Norfolk, Virginia

Social Security and Employer
Identification Numbers 103-X5-6788 104-2X-677X

Date 3-31-79

To: **Commissioner of Internal Revenue**

1. This offer is submitted by the undersigned proponents (persons making this offer) to compromise a liability resulting from alleged violations of law or failure to pay an internal revenue liability as follows: Failure to pay income taxes, *(State specifically the alleged violation involved, the kind of unpaid tax liability, and each period involved)* plus statutory additions, for the calendar years 1974, 1975, and 1976.

2. The total sum of $ 8,500.00 _____ paid in full or payable on a deferred payment basis as follows:[1] Payable within thirty (30) days of notice of acceptance of this offer.

with interest at the annual rate as established under section 6621(a) of the Internal Revenue Code (subject to adjustments as provided by Code section 6621(b)) on the deferred payments, if any, from the date the offer is accepted until it is paid in full, is voluntarily tendered with this offer with the request that it be accepted to compromise the liability described above, and any statutory additions to this liability.

3. In making this offer, and as a part of the consideration, it is agreed (a) that the United States shall keep all payments and other credits made to the accounts for the periods covered by this offer, and (b) that the United States shall keep any and all amounts to which the taxpayer-proponents may be entitled under the internal revenue laws, due through overpayments of any tax or other liability, including interest and penalties, for periods ending before or within or as of the end of the calendar year in which this offer is accepted (and which are not in excess of the difference between the liability sought to be compromised and the amount offered). Any such refund received after this offer is filed will be returned immediately.

4. It is also agreed that payments made under the terms of this offer shall be applied first to tax and penalty, in that order, due for the earliest taxable period, then to tax and penalty, in that order, for each succeeding taxable period with no amount to be allocated to interest until the liabilities for taxes and penalties for all taxable periods sought to be compromised have been satisfied.

5. It is further agreed that upon notice to the taxpayers of the acceptance of this offer, the taxpayers shall have no right to contest in court or otherwise the amount of the liability sought to be compromised; and that if this is a deferred payment offer and there is a default in payment of any installment of principal or interest due under its terms, the United States, at the option of the Commissioner of Internal Revenue or a delegated official, may (a) proceed immediately by suit to collect the entire unpaid balance of the offer; or (b) proceed immediately by suit to collect as liquidated damages an amount equal to the liability sought to be compromised, minus any deposits already received under the terms of the offer, with interest on the unpaid balance at the annual rate as established under section 6621(a) of the Internal Revenue Code (subject to adjustments as provided by Code section 6621(b)) from the date of default; or (c) disregard the amount of the offer and apply all amounts previously deposited under the offer against the amount of the liability sought to be compromised and, without further notice of any kind, assess and collect by levy or suit the balance of the liability, the right of appeal to the United States Tax Court and the restrictions against assessment and collection being waived upon acceptance of this offer.

6. The taxpayer-proponents waive the benefit of any statute of limitations applicable to the assessment and collection of the liability sought to be compromised, and agree to the suspension of the running of the statutory period of limitations on assessment and collection for the period during which this offer is pending, or the period during which any installment remains unpaid, and for 1 year thereafter. For these purposes, the offer shall be deemed pending from the date of acceptance of the waiver of the statutory period of limitations by an authorized Internal Revenue Service official, until the date on which the offer is formally accepted, rejected, or withdrawn in writing.

7. The following facts and reasons are submitted as grounds for acceptance of this offer: We are unable to pay these taxes.

(If space is insufficient, please attach a supporting statement)

8. It is understood that this offer will be considered and acted upon in due course and that it does not relieve the taxpayers from the liability sought to be compromised unless and until the offer is accepted in writing by the Commissioner or a delegated official, and there has been full compliance with the terms of the offer.

If this offer is paid in full at the time it is filed, show in item 2 the amount only. If this is a deferred payment offer, show (a) the amount deposited at the time of filing this offer; (b) any amount deposited on prior offers which are applied on this offer; (c) the amount of each deferred payment, and the date on which each payment is to be made. (Amounts payable after the filing date of the offer, including amounts payable upon notice of acceptance, are deferred payments.)

Under penalties of perjury, I declare that I have examined this offer, including accompanying schedules and statements, and to the best of my knowledge and belief it is true, correct and complete.

Signature of Proponent

Signature of Proponent

I accept the waiver of statutory period of limitations for the Internal Revenue Service.

Signature of authorized Internal Revenue Service official

Velma Veery

Title	Date
Revenue Officer	4-2-79

Form 656 (Rev. 7-79)

Division. An offer submitted on the collectibility issue must be accompanied by Form 433, "Statement of Financial Condition." Both Forms 656 and 433 must be signed under penalty of perjury.

Form 656 is a contract between you and the IRS and can be enforced under the laws of contracts. For example, a legal contract entails mutual agreement, adequate consideration, the capacity to make the contract, a legal subject, and there must be an offer and an acceptance. The purpose of the terminology on Form 656 is to assure that these elements are present along with some other important provisions.

An explanation of the various paragraphs on the offer form follows.

LINE 1: Identifies the type of taxes involved. This must be clearly stated.

LINE 2: Specifies the amount of the offer. If the offer is to be made in installment payments (it does not have to be in one lump sum), space is provided to list the payment schedule. Interest will continue to accrue on the balance of any unpaid offer until it is paid in full. Interest charged by the IRS is subject to change every six months and is compounded daily.

LINE 3: You agree that:

- The IRS can keep any and all payments or credits already made to the account being compromised. This is important because you cannot make a payment on a delinquent liability, submit an offer later, and expect to have that payment applied to the offer. *A previous payment cannot later be shifted for inclusion in the offer.* All payments and credits must be applied to the tax liability until a completed Form 656 has been received. An oral intention to make an offer carries no legal weight. If you intend to submit an offer, make it clear to the Revenue Officer that you intend to do so and save your payments for the offer. There have been many cases in which taxpayers gave the IRS all the money they had but were later unable to make an offer because they had no money left.

- The IRS can keep any future refunds as long as the refunds when added to the amount offered do not exceed the original amount owed. This provision does not have to become a problem to you *if* you take appropriate steps to minimize excessive tax overwithholding during the year. The waiver of future refunds should be crossed out if you are submitting an offer based on doubt as to liability.

LINE 4: None of the payments will be applied to interest until *all* the taxes and penalties have been paid first. This is important for you to know because interest is deductible on your tax return, but penalties are not. Even interest you pay the IRS is deductible. Remember, though, that you won't have any interest deductions until the final payments. When the final payments are made, have the IRS figure out for you how much interest you paid.

LINE 5: You agree that while the IRS is considering your offer you will not contest in court the amount of the liability being compromised. If you are submitting an offer that will be paid in installments (called a deferred offer), you must make each payment as specified or the IRS may:

- sue for the balance due on the offer.
- sue for the amount of liability being compromised.
- completely disregard the offer and proceed with collection without further notice of any kind.

LINE 6: You agree to a suspension of any statute of limitations applicable to the assessment and collection of the liability you are proposing to compromise. The suspension runs during the entire period the IRS is considering your offer, including the period of time that installments have not been paid, plus an additional one year. The statute of limitations on collection is six years from the date the taxes are assessed. By merely submitting an offer you are giving the IRS at least an additional year to collect the original liability.

LINE 7: This is where you indicate the grounds under which you are submitting the offer. The first thing you write is either "Doubt as to Liability" or "Doubt as to Collectibility." In cases of doubt as to liability, you must specify the reasons why you are making the offer.

LINE 8: This line informs you that you are still legally liable for the full amount of your unpaid taxes until the offer has been accepted and there has been full compliance with all the terms of the offer. The hidden point the IRS makes here is that the act of submitting the offer does not mean the IRS has to withhold any further collection efforts. Under National Office policy, collection efforts will be suspended unless the officer decides that your offer is frivolous—the amount is so small that the IRS thinks you are not serious and may be submitting the offer with the sole purpose of delaying collection actions. But even then the IRS must notify you that they consider the offer frivolous and that they intend to proceed with further collection efforts.

When preparing and submitting an offer, you will want to follow the checklist below that officers use initially for reviewing offers.

- The elements of contract law are present.
- The offer is submitted on the most current Form 656.
- The offer form is prepared properly; your identification number is included, the type of tax is correctly and specifically identified, the sum offered is specific as to amounts and dates, and you have signed and dated the offer.
- Form 433, "Statement of Financial Condition," is attached to all offers based on doubt as to collectibility.
- You have agreed to the waiver provisions.
- On collectibility offers the sum offered represents your "maximum capacity to pay."

DETERMINING MAXIMUM CAPACITY TO PAY

An adequate offer to compromise based on doubt as to collectibility must represent your "maximum capacity to pay." Although the IRS does not really have a formula for determining your maximum capacity to pay, they do define it as "all that can be collected from the taxpayer's equity in assets and income, present and prospective." The definition is stretched to include "assets or income that are available to the taxpayer, but beyond the reach of the Government" (IRM 5743.1:[1]).

When an offer in compromise is submitted based on doubt as to collectibility, the offer must be accompanied by Form 433, "Statement of Financial Condition and Other Information." This eight-page document literally exposes the soul of your financial condition. Revenue Officers will automatically reject any collectibility offers that are not accompanied by Form 433. If you are making a serious attempt

Form **433**
(Rev. April 1979)

Department of the Treasury — Internal Revenue Service

Statement of Financial Condition and Other Information

(Please file in duplicate with offer in compromise)

Please furnish the information requested in this form with your offer in compromise, if the offer is based in whole or in part on inability ᵗᵒ pay the liability. If you need help in preparing this statement, call on any Internal Revenue office. It is important that you answer all que. ᵒns. If a question does not apply, please enter N/A. This will speed up consideration of your offer.

1a. Name(s) of Taxpayer(s)	b. Social Security Number	c. Employer Identification Number
David & Mary Whistler	103-X5-6788	54-X012X1

d. Business Address	e. Bus. Tel. No.	2. Name and Address of Representative, if any
3802 S. Norview Ave Norfolk, VA	659-0879	Frank Martin 182 Main St.
f. Home Address	g. Home Tel. No.	Norfolk, VA
7719 S. Norview Avenue Norfolk, VA	659-1987	

3.	Kind of tax involved	Taxable period	Amount due	Amount offered
a.	Income	1974, 75, 76	$25,401.00	$8,500.00
b.				
c.				
d.				
e.				

4.	Due and unpaid Federal taxes, *(except those covered by this offer in compromise)*		
	Kind of tax	Taxable period	Amount due
a.	None		
b.			
c.			

5. Names of banks and other financial institutions you have done business with at any time during past 3 years—

Name and address	Name and address
a. Norfolk National Bank 800 Main St., Norfolk, VA	b.
c.	d.

e. Do you rent a safety deposit box in your name or in any other name?

☐ No ☒ Yes *(If yes, give name and address of bank)* Norfolk Nat'l Bank, 800 Main, Norfolk

6. If income withholding or employment tax is involved, please complete 6a through f

a. Were the employees' income withholding or employment taxes, due from employees on wages they received from employment, deducted or withheld from the wages paid during any period shown above? ☐ Yes ☐ No

b. If so, was the tax paid or deposited to the Internal Revenue Service? ☐ No ☐ Yes

c. If deducted but not paid or deposited to IRS, how did you dispose of the deducted amounts?

d. Has business in which you incurred such taxes been discontinued? ☐ No ☐ Yes

e. If so, on what date was it discontinued?

f. How did you dispose of assets of discontinued business?

7. Offer filed by individual

a. Name of Spouse	b. Age of Spouse	c. Age of Taxpayer
Mary	54	58

d.	Names of dependent children or relatives	Relationship	Age
(1)	Sandra	Daughter	21
(2)	Gail	Daughter	20
(3)			
(4)			
(5)			
(6)			
(7)			

Form **433** (Rev. 4-79)

to compromise, you should make sure you fill in every block on the form completely and honestly. If the IRS discovers that you left anything out, the offer will be automatically rejected.

Form 433 lists the following items:

- A statement of assets and liabilities as of the date the offer is being submitted
- All life insurance policies including present cash surrender value and cash loan value
- Accounts and notes receivable
- Fair market and liquidation values of merchandise inventory, real estate, furniture and fixtures, trucks, automobiles, and any type of securities
- A statement of income and expenses for the past two years

Once the offer is submitted it will be assigned for investigation to a Revenue Officer specifically trained in offers in compromise. The investigation will include a comprehensive analysis to ascertain your ability to pay, the priority of the federal tax lien in relation to other creditors, and the liquidating value of your assets. This information will be used to determine whether it is in the government's best interests to accept your offer.

The starting point for considering your maximum capacity to pay is the evaluation of all your assets based on their liquidating or quick sale value. The quick sale value is the amount that would be realized from the sale of your assets in a short period of time. (This is different from the forced sale value previously discussed.) The IRS will define the equity in your assets as "the quick sale value less any encumbrances against the assets which have priority over the federal tax lien."

As you can see there is enough information required on Form 433 for any officer to attempt to determine your maximum capacity to pay. Before accepting the offer, the investigating officer may require you to:

- borrow money on any assets you own that may have some equity, such as your car and house.
- turn over the cash you have, such as your checking accounts and savings accounts.

- sell any stocks and bonds that have equity but cannot be used as collateral for borrowing.
- sell any "luxury items" that the IRS determines you don't need, particularly if you are making monthly payments on them. Freeing up additional money to apply to the taxes is the first thing that the officer looks for. For example, if you are making $400-a-month payments on a boat, you might as well kiss the boat good-bye. The Revenue Officer will surely tell you to sell it, or he will seize it and sell it for you. Pleading that you will lose money on the sale won't do much good either.

Requiring you to accept a collateral agreement is one method that is frequently used to ensure that the IRS is collecting "maximum capacity." A collateral agreement is a contractual agreement made specifically for you to provide additional consideration for acceptance of the offer. The IRS frequently requires it as a method to minimize the amount of taxes that are lost through the compromise. Often it brings in additional sums that are not immediately obtainable in any other manner.

There are four types of collateral agreements:

- *Future Income Agreement.* This is the most common type of collateral agreement. A future income agreement will typically provide for yearly payments ranging from 20 percent to 50 percent of your annual income that exceeds your "ordinary and necessary living expenses." These agreements usually run for a period of not more than five or six years.

The IRS recognizes that many taxpayers want to compromise their taxes in order to enhance their ability to increase their income. Because of a large tax liability and a filed federal tax lien, they may be unable to secure a job paying a substantial salary or to obtain the credit necessary to expand a present business or finance a new one. The IRS believes that once the compromise is accepted and the taxpayer's income increases, the government should be able to recoup part of this increase in earnings by means of the future income agreement.

When an offer is accepted by the IRS, the filed federal tax lien is released, thereby removing the biggest obstacle restricting a taxpayer's business endeavors or preventing him from increasing his earning capacity. With a future income agreement, an increase in income also benefits the government since it leads to an increase of payments to the IRS.

The main difference between submitting an offer with a future income agreement and merely paying the taxes off in monthly installments is the effect upon the government's filed tax lien. In cases in which the taxes are paid in monthly installments (see Chapter 2), the government does not release its filed tax lien until the liability is paid in full or the liability cannot be collected because the statute of limitations has expired.

- *Agreements Reducing the Basis of Assets.* This is an agreement to forgo a tax benefit by agreeing to a reduction in the basis of certain assets. This results in your paying higher taxes in the future, but it enables the government to recoup a portion of the taxes lost through the compromise.

- *Agreements Waiving Losses and Investment Credits.* In this agreement you give up your right to certain tax benefits that accrue as a result of a net operating loss, a capital loss, or unused investment credit. This agreement is only used when you are either operating a business or are making plans to operate one. In effect, you waive your right either to carry back or to carry forward these items, thereby resulting in an increase in your tax liability.

- *Agreements Waiving Bad Debts.* Again, this agreement is used only for those in business. Accounts and notes receivable that become uncollectible are deductible in the year they become worthless. Waiving the deduction for a bad debt also results in an increased tax liability during the year the debts are determined to be worthless.

WHEN THE TAX LIEN IS RELEASED

The IRS will release the federal tax lien when the following conditions have been met:

- All payments specified in the offer have been paid, including all installments.
- All assets required to be assigned or turned over to the govern-

ment under the terms of the offer have been so assigned or turned over.

- All other terms and conditions of the offer have been met, with the exception of the collateral agreement. The collateral agreement remains in force under the contractual agreement. The release of the government's tax lien will serve to protect the purpose of the collateral agreement, which is to benefit from any future increase in your income.

RETURNING YOUR MONEY

Internal Revenue Code section 7809(b) guarantees that the IRS will return your money if your offer is subsequently rejected. The money is supposed to be kept in a special deposit fund account and is not transferred to the Treasurer of the United States until the offer has been accepted. However, a favorite ploy used by Revenue Officers is the attempt to have the deposit of a rejected offer applied to the delinquent taxes. The deposit *cannot* be applied to the delinquent taxes unless *you agree* and authorize the application in writing. You should know that for the period of time the IRS is considering your offer, you do not receive any interest on the money.

ADVICE FOR SMALL
BUSINESS OWNERS

Paying Business Taxes in Installments

How a little a day keeps the IRS away

INTRODUCTION

The IRS says that "nonpayment of taxes withheld from employees' wages is the most serious delinquency problem facing the IRS." Statistics show that over 26 million employment tax returns are filed each year by business employers who report and pay quarterly the Social Security and income taxes withheld from their employees. Of this total, almost 10 percent are filed late, resulting in fines or penalties of almost $400 million. A reasonable extrapolation from these delinquency penalty assessments would indicate that more than $1 billion in employment taxes are paid late to the IRS each year.

Of the more than 12 million businesses in this country that file income tax returns, over two-thirds withhold taxes from their employees and file employment tax returns quarterly. The major corporations rarely present a problem for the IRS, but when they do, the problems are monstrous. For instance, W. T. Grant went bankrupt owing the IRS over $80 million in unpaid employee withholding taxes.

IRS collection efforts primarily focus on the small business taxpayer. As a group small business owners have the lowest compliance rate with the tax laws, barely over 57 percent. This means that nearly half of the small business taxpayers are late in filing returns or in paying what they owe. This is understandable considering that the small business is frequently under-capitalized, subject to serious cash-flow problems during periods of economic uncertainties, and faces continuous governmental regulation on all levels. The prospect of opening a small business today and having it survive at least five years is statistically slim.

This chapter and the next are written especially for small business owners who need to know how to protect themselves from the clutches of IRS's enforcement power.

PAYING EMPLOYMENT TAXES IN INSTALLMENTS

The Internal Revenue Manual allows Revenue Officers to arrange with small business owners to pay their taxes in periodic installments. But there are problems implementing those procedures.

Because the district and regional IRS offices place such a high priority on the collection of employment taxes, officers in the field are given marching orders by their immediate bosses to "get tough" with delinquent businesses, even if this means seizing and selling the businesses' assets. But most officers would prefer *not* to seize a business because of the time involved. An officer can easily spend twenty to forty hours on a properly conducted business seizure.

As mentioned in earlier chapters, your filing and payment history is important when decisions are made about whether you get an installment agreement or are subjected to seizures. If as a business taxpayer you have a history or a pattern of tax delinquency, you will not be handled with kid gloves. A chronic delinquent is supposed to be read the "riot act." But if you know IRS procedures and cooperate with the Revenue Officer, you can make your life a lot easier and possibly stay in business as well.

Before discussing installment agreements, you need to understand this IRS terminology as it applies to installment agreements:

- *Delinquent taxes* are those for which a bill has already been sent, meaning that the tax return has already been filed and the amounts have already been assessed.

- *Accrued taxes* are those taxes that are already legally due but that have not been billed because the tax returns were not yet filled, even though the due date for filing may have passed. Accrued taxes also include withheld taxes that have not yet been deposited, and the required date for deposit has passed. (Once deposited in a bank the money is forwarded to the IRS.)
- *Current taxes* are withheld taxes that are not yet due for deposit and any amounts withheld after the date of contact by a Revenue Officer.

At the initial interview, the Revenue Officer is required to determine the cause of the business delinquency. This question is a formality. Most taxpayers reply with the stock answer of a "cash-flow shortage." Even though a cash-flow shortage is really just the symptom of a business problem and not a cause, few Revenue Officers understand the difference.

Another point that has to be dicussed at the initial interview is the requirement to file a Notice of Federal Tax Lien to protect the government's priority over other creditors. (See Chapter 5 for an explanation of the federal tax lien.) An officer must determine if a federal tax lien should be filed within thirty days of receipt of the case. A federal tax lien will normally be filed if the outstanding liability is more than two thousand dollars. In order for the Revenue Officer to withhold filing the federal tax lien, he must obtain written approval from his manager whenever the liability exceeds five thousand dollars. Most managers in the collection division are reluctant to stay filing unless it can be clearly shown that filing would hamper future collection efforts. As a business owner, you should realize that the filing of a notice of lien could have a detrimental effect on your business operations by injuring your credit rating. The filing itself could also jeopardize your ability to borrow money by using your assets for collateral. At your first opportunity you should ask the Revenue Officer to withhold filing the tax lien.

The officer will demand full payment, and if full payment is not immediately made, he will either ask you to come into the office for a collection interview (see Chapter 2) or conduct the interview right there on your business premises. Information must be obtained to complete IRS Form 433–B, "Collection Information Statement for Businesses." Although this form is designed for business taxpayers, most Revenue Officers would prefer to have a financial statement prepared by an accountant.

The IRS does have an *automatic installment agreement* procedure for business taxpayers similar to the one for individual taxpayers (see Chapter 2). The only problem is that the Internal Revenue Manual does not precisely specify how businesses qualify. The only indication is that the delinquent taxes must be below an undisclosed amount and that the account must be in notice status (also see Chapter 2). For businesses that do qualify the IRS will allow up to twelve months to pay in full, and the only requirement is that you must sign Form 433–D, "Installment Agreement." (Form 433–D is also discussed in Chapter 2.) There is only one way to find out if you qualify for this type of installment agreement—you must request it.

SURVIVAL RULE ━━━━━━━━━━━━━━━━━━━━━━━━━━━━━━

> *If you are unable to fully pay your business employment taxes when demanded by a Revenue Officer but can make regular periodic payments and pay in full within twelve months, you should request an automatic installment agreement, "under the provisions of IRM 5231.52:(4) and Law Enforcement Manual, part 5, section 213."*

It certainly will not hurt to ask for the agreement. If you qualify, you will have saved yourself a lot of headaches. Make sure when you request the installment agreement to repeat the part of the Survival Rule in quotations. It will send any Revenue Officer who may not be aware of these provisions scurrying to the manual to find out what you are talking about.

In the event that you do *not* qualify for the automatic installment agreement, you should try for the next best thing: the *negotiated installment agreement* for business taxpayers. This can be done only after the officer has analyzed your financial statements on Form 433–B and has determined your ability to pay. If the determination is made that you have the ability to pay all delinquent and accrued taxes, you will be asked for immediate payment. If you are unable to pay immediately, then you better make it crystal clear that you cannot. Otherwise, you should be prepared for such enforced collection action as levy, seizure, or assertion of the 100 percent penalty. (This will be covered in the next chapter.)

IRM 5231.52:(5) specifies the following when a business taxpayer cannot pay all delinquent and accrued taxes:

1. If it is determined that the taxpayer cannot pay operating expenses and, at the same time, pay current taxes, deferring action on delinquent and accrued taxes would serve no useful purpose. Under these conditions, appropriate collection actions such as levy, seizure, or 100 percent penalty should be taken immediately to protect the interest of the government.
2. If it appears that the taxpayer can pay current taxes and, given a reasonable period of time, pay both accrued and delinquent taxes, the installment agreement procedures in IRM 5231.53 should be followed with available funds being applied in the following priority order to:
   —current taxes
   —accrued taxes
   —delinquent taxes

The IRS subscribes to the old "shoot 'em out of their misery" principle, and is adamant that business taxpayers be immediately brought into compliance with the tax laws by paying all current taxes. This causes a big problem for Revenue Officers when the business can pay either delinquent or current taxes, but *not* both. This situation happens more frequently than any other. It only makes sense that unless the business has had some dramatic turnaround, which would improve its cash position, the business will *not* have enough money to pay both delinquent and current taxes.

SURVIVAL RULE ━━━━━━━━━━━━━━━━━━━━━━━━━━━━━━━━

When you cannot pay in full your delinquent taxes and you do not qualify for an automatic installment agreement, you should attempt to negotiate an installment agreement based on your ability to make periodic payments.

━━━

The negotiation process to work out an installment agreement involves give-and-take face-to-face discussions between you and the Revenue Officer. The Revenue Officer has the authority and the power to seize and sell any and all of your business assets, everything from bank accounts to cash registers and office equipment. The more assets you have, the more leverage the officer has over you. The more assets you have that are not secured by liens of other creditors, the more the officer is going to "hang tough."

There is a great amount of inequity and unfairness built into the whole process. A good, solid company with lots of unsecured assets experiencing a temporary business slowdown may catch more "heat" from the Revenue Officer than the under-capitalized, highly secured business with few assets. Again it's a question of leverage and assertion of control. Many Revenue Officers need cases over which they can exercise their authority because they often have so many cases in their inventory with no easy solutions. So don't be surprised to find out that you have been given forty-eight hours to pay up while the guy next door has been given twelve months to pay.

Sometimes an installment agreement is the only way the tax can be collected. To be in a position to negotiate an installment agreement, you need to show three things:

- You cannot *fully* pay now, but you do have the money to pay current taxes.
- Your borrowing potential is either nonexistent or very limited.
- You can make periodic payments timely and not go into default on the agreement.

The negotiation process involves the settlement of these three questions:

- Should an installment arrangement be made?
- How much should be paid and when should it be paid?
- Over what period of time will it take to liquidate the liability?

An analysis of your financial statement may yield the answers to those questions. But analyzing a financial statement of a business is not easy, and it takes most Revenue Officers years to become comfortable with their ability to do so. Officers are not required to have an accounting background, and the IRS tries to teach them what they need to know about financial statement analysis. Unfortunately the National Office has not yet found a way to have Revenue Officers apply objective standards in the decision-making process. As a result, the answers to the above three questions usually come from the subjective give-and-take between you and the Revenue Officer.

The first question you will be asked after the Revenue Officer is convinced that you cannot immediately pay in full is: "How much can you pay?" The next question is "When can you pay it?" From your answers to those questions the Revenue Officer will try to work out in his own mind whether your answers are honest and sincere and whether they constitute a proposal acceptable to his boss.

The IRM requires that an installment agreement must be approved by the immediate manager when the tax liability exceeds two thousand dollars, the agreement extends for more than one year, or the taxes are employee withholding taxes owed by a business still in operation. The manager must consider whether the installment agreement is appropriate for the amount being proposed, that is, whether *his* evaluation of the financial information in the file shows that the amounts being proposed are too high or too low. Most likely the supervisor will be looking to see if the payments are too low.

Every Revenue Officer who has had experience with this process knows what his group manager's quirks and idiosyncracies are. Each manager has his own philosophy of how things should be and are to be done. Some managers will make it almost impossible for an installment payment to be approved. They will keep telling the Revenue Officers to ask their taxpayers to supply more financial data, until even the taxpayers' accountants will be at wit's end trying to figure out what's going on.

Sometimes the problem is not with the Revenue Officer's manager but with a higher official, such as a branch chief or a division chief. Some districts require that all business taxpayer installment agreements be approved on the higher management level. The problem is that this kind of interference doesn't result in the approval of installment agreements either. Instead, the officials are almost afraid of approving them, afraid that a review by a regional official will show that they missed something.

This bureaucratic muddle causes many Revenue Officers to try to forget the whole idea of even proposing a business installment agreement. The nitpicking that can occur simply takes too much of their time and causes friction between them and management.

Even though it can be a headache for a persistent business owner, the negotiating process may mean the difference between survival and bankruptcy. It may very well pay to put up with all the hassles that come with the negotiation process. Just remember that most Revenue Officers would prefer not to seize a business because it takes a lot of time and a lot of work. But experience has shown that in nine out of ten business seizures the business owner somehow manages to come up with the money, and this knowledge will always be in the back of the Revenue Officer's mind during negotiations.

For further information about the collection and seizure process, a business owner should read Chapter 2 and Chapter 5. The suggestions and recommendations made in those chapters are not only applicable to business owners but also may be crucial to the survival of the business.

Protecting Yourself from the 100 Percent Penalty

How the IRS pierces the corporate veil

INTRODUCTION

The IRS can not only seize and sell all a corporation's assets for nonpayment of the corporation's taxes, but through a civil procedure called the 100 percent penalty the IRS can assess against a "responsible" *person* the amount of unpaid employee income and Social Security taxes as a personal penalty for failure to pay them to the IRS. The authority for the 100 percent penalty is section 6672 of the Internal Revenue Code.

Section 6672 of the Code applies to any "trust fund taxes." Income and Social Security taxes withheld from employees' paychecks are called trust fund taxes because they are, by law, held in trust by the employer to be paid at a later date to the government. Trust fund taxes can also include other collected taxes, such as excise taxes. A failure to pay any tax can be a crime if it is willful as defined under the criminal statutes. But because the IRS cannot possibly prosecute every small business owner who doesn't pay the IRS, the collection of delinquent employment taxes is normally handled as a civil matter.

The 100 percent penalty is an additional enforcement tool that enables the IRS to contend with the problem of the limited liability benefit granted by the corporate charter. It is called a "100 percent penalty" because the IRS attempts to collect 100 percent of the taxes that were withheld from employees' paychecks but not paid to the IRS.

In order to collect the unpaid tax the IRS attempts to discover who the responsible persons were who were charged with the duty of paying the IRS and didn't. Then the IRS determines if the responsible persons were willful in not paying the IRS by determining if the persons paid other creditors instead of the IRS. Once the responsible persons have been identified and the element of willfulness has been determined to exist, the IRS administratively assesses the amount of unpaid employee withholding taxes against the responsible persons as a *personal tax liability*. Those responsible persons are then liable for the full amount of the unpaid withholding tax, and their assets are subject to the seizure and sale powers of the IRS just as if the taxes had been incurred individually. The 100 percent penalty is most always used with corporate tax liabilities, even though in some circumstances it can be used against limited partners in a partnership.

DECIDING WHO IS RESPONSIBLE AND WILLFUL

When the corporation fails to pay its outstanding withholding tax liability upon demand, an investigation by the IRS begins. In some districts Revenue Officers will begin the 100 percent penalty investigation even though the corporation is still operating and may be paying its delinquent taxes on the installment plan. In other districts the investigation is begun only after all other alternatives have failed, including payment arrangements and seizure and sale of the corporate assets. But beginning the investigation early is usually done to make an important point with the corporate officers and to "put the fear" of the IRS into them.

When determining who had the responsibility for paying the payroll taxes the IRS can investigate any *officer, shareholder,* or *employee* of the corporation who was either under a duty to perform the act of paying the IRS or had the power to direct the act of collecting, accounting for, and paying the withholding taxes. The responsibility for performance must also coincide with the timing of the nonperformance. For example, J. R. Jones was Treasurer of AXE Manufacturing, Inc., from September 1979 through March 1981. Starting in April 1981 AXE became delinquent in paying its employees' withholding taxes. Mr. Jones had no responsibility after March 1981, and so therefore the IRS could not assess the 100 percent penalty against him.

Determining responsibility is not always easy. Sometimes corporate officers change roles and titles, and sometimes the responsibilities either are shared or there is no distinct division of authority. What frequently occurs is that one corporate officer will blame another corporate officer, and in the end no one admits responsibility.

So the IRS must decide who was responsible for paying the withheld taxes and does so by examining the evidence. The first action the Revenue Officer does is to requisition photocopies of the employment tax returns from the IRS service center. The signature of the corporate officer on the bottom of the return leads the Revenue Officer to suspect that person first.

The next step is to summons the corporation's bank for the signature cards and corporate resolution covering the company's checking account. The corporate resolution establishes which officers were assigned by the corporation's board of directors the responsibility and authority for disbursement of funds. The signature cards show which individuals had the right to sign checks on the corporate checking account. If the signature cards and the corporate resolution point to the same person who signed the employment tax return, the case begins to get stronger against that person.

The Revenue Officer's next action is to interview the corporate officers who may be involved. The interview consists of completing a standard interview sheet that attempts to determine responsibility. Many of the questions concern the history of the corporation's financial affairs.

During the interview the Revenue Officer will try to find out who has possession of the canceled checks. If he has to, the Revenue Officer can serve a summons on the corporate officers to produce them. Corporate officers are usually reluctant to produce the canceled checks because the checks are the strongest evidence supporting responsibility.

The Revenue Officer will want to photocopy those canceled checks that show a disbursement of funds to pay other operating expenses during the time that the federal withholding taxes weren't paid. The checks not only help to establish responsibility but also willfulness. The Revenue Officer is likely to say "Aha! See there. You had the money to pay the IRS but instead you paid someone else." The canceled checks are probably the most incriminating of all documents.

The Revenue Officer may also have to examine more evidence to support his determination of responsibility. For example, the State Corporation Commission will identify the corporate officers and the board of directors at the time of the last annual filing. The corporate by-laws and minutes of any meetings between the directors will also be examined where available. Resignation letters are important in determining dates when responsibility ceases. Public records may have to be checked for evidence of corporate responsibility, and creditors may have to be contacted for information to determine who had the responsibility for ordering supplies and incurring indebtedness.

It is important to stress that the IRS is not just looking for one responsible person but responsible *persons*. If an analysis of the actual operation and control of the corporation's affairs discloses that more than one person had the responsibility for paying the employee withholding taxes, all those persons will be assessed the same amount of 100 percent penalty. This does *not* mean that the amount of withheld taxes is divided equally among the responsible persons. Instead it means that each responsible person becomes liable for the *full* amount of withheld taxes not paid.

If the Revenue Officer cannot conclusively determine which person is responsible, the policy of the service is to assess the tax against the President, Secretary, and Treasurer. The IRS is not about to be stumped in determining who the responsible persons are. Even though the IRM requires that the investigating Revenue Officer support his assertion (recommendation for assessment) either by evidence or documentation, the "shotgun penalty" approach has been used many times. In the shotgun penalty approach the Revenue Officer assumes that *all* the corporate officers are guilty and proceeds to assert the penalty against all of them. This is the "guilty before proven innocent" tactic. IRS managers have been known to support this approach because it closes cases quickly. However, it is a definite violation of due process and your constitutional rights. It requires the corporate officer to prove that he is innocent rather than the IRS to prove that he is guilty. A taxpayer who may have been an innocent individual in the operation of the business because he had no direct authority could easily fall prey to the shotgun penalty approach. And it has happened many times.

Whenever multiple assessments of the 100 percent penalty are made, the IRS is *not* interested in collecting the tax in multiples of 100 percent. Instead the IRS only wants to collect the original 100 percent plus interest. (Since this is a penalty, not a tax, the IRS cannot charge a failure-to-pay penalty on the assessment of a 100 percent penalty.) This can sometimes be difficult, especially when the corporate officers live in different parts of town or in different parts of the country.

SURVIVAL RULE ▬▬▬▬▬▬▬▬▬▬▬▬▬▬▬▬▬▬▬▬▬▬▬▬▬▬

An assessment of multiple 100 percent penalties against several responsible persons makes each person liable for payment of the complete and full amount of tax assessed. Therefore you should protect yourself by making sure that your business has clear lines of responsibility and that they are adhered to.

▬▬

Corporate officers have been known to get together and affix responsibility and liability among themselves on a pro rata basis, thinking that that agreement will save them from the IRS. Those kinds of agreements may be legally binding ("may be" is used with caution) among the signatories, but they are *not* binding on the IRS. The IRS is not required to honor the agreement and may legally collect the full amount owed in any portion that it can. One corporate officer may actually be more liable and have more culpability than another, but after assessment the IRS will go to the person who has the best means of paying, no matter how unfair it may be.

Once the responsibility issue has been settled, the test of willfulness is applied to each of the responsible persons. The test of willfulness as it applies to the 100 percent penalty is a civil one, not the same as the test used in criminal cases. The IRS states that "willfulness implies a state of mind of the individual which generally must be proved by circumstantial evidence." In a civil case there is no need to prove evil intent or that there was a bad motive involved in not paying the government the amount of taxes withheld from employees' wages. Instead, all that needs to be shown is "that the responsible party was aware of the oustanding taxes and deliberately declined to pay them over or has knowledge they are not being paid."

The IRM further states that "the penalty should be asserted where the money required to be withheld from employees as taxes, in lieu of being paid over to the government, is knowingly and intentionally used to pay operating expenses of the business or other debts with a freedom of choice as to payment."

THE RIGHTS OF A RESPONSIBLE PERSON

There are administrative due process and appeal rights involved with the 100 percent penalty investigation. The investigating Revenue Officer must make a written report to his group manager specifying against whom he is making the recommendation for assertion of the 100 percent penalty. If the group manager approves the recommendation (and he most always does), you will be notified of the proposed penalty if you are considered to be a responsible person. On *proper* request, you will be granted conference and appellate privileges prior to assessment of the penalty.

The first notification designating you as the responsible person will come on IRS Letter 1153(DO), also known as the "10-Day Notification Letter." The letter accompanies Form 2751, which specifies the amount of penalty being proposed for assessment.

SURVIVAL RULE ▬▬▬▬▬▬▬▬▬▬▬▬▬▬▬▬▬▬▬▬▬▬▬▬▬

Do not sign Form 2751 if you disagree with the assessment of the 100 percent penalty and if you wish to appeal the IRS decision to assess the penalty against you.

Form 2751 gives you an opportunity to agree with the decision so that the IRS may proceed with the assessment. Frankly I don't know why anyone would agree outright to sign this form. Even if there are

Form **2751**
(Rev. Nov. 1980)

Department of the Treasury—Internal Revenue Service

Proposed Assessment of 100 Percent Penalty

(Sec. 6672, Internal Revenue Code of 1954, or corresponding provisions of prior internal revenue laws)

Report of Corporation's Unpaid Tax Liability

Name and address of corporation

Catalpa Products Inc.   12635 Wilshire Blvd.   Los Angeles, CA 90024

Tax Return Form No.	Tax Period Ended	Date Return Filed	Date Tax Assessed	Identifying Number	Unpaid Balance of Assessment	Penalty
941	9-30-81	12-02-81	1-04-82	95-3170XX2	$ 11,729.40	$ 10,442.84
941	12-31-81				16,216.25*	11,736.53
					*Tax only	
					Total Penalty	$ 22,179.37

Agreement to Assessment and Collection of 100 Percent Penalty

Name, address, and social security number of person responsible
John E. Barberry 321-XX-9215   211 Reedie Drive   Brentwood, TN 37007

I consent to the assessment and collection of the total penalty shown, which is equal either to the amount of Federal employment taxes withheld from employees wages or to the amount of Federal excise taxes collected from patrons or members, and which was not paid over to the Government by the corporation named above; and I waive the privilege of filing a claim for abatement after assessment.

Signature of person responsible   *John E. Barberry*   Date 9-9-82

Form **2751** (Rev. 11-80)

no other individuals responsible, the option of signing Form 2751 at this stage only benefits the IRS. The sooner they can report corporate accounts uncollectible and the sooner they assess the penalty, the happier they will be. On a 100 percent penalty assessment the IRS doesn't start charging interest on the unpaid balance until ten days after assessment. Unlike other taxes whereby a return is required to be filed, a delay in the 100 percent penalty assessment does not result in additional interest charges to the responsible person. So unless you just want to get the whole thing over with, the IRS does not make it worth your while to sign Form 2751 agreeing to the assessment.

If you do not respond to the ten-day letter, the IRS will send you a thirty-day letter on IRS Letter 1154(DO). It is a formal notice advising you of your appeal rights. Instructions pertaining to those appeal rights are on the reverse side of the form. Basically you have the option of appealing the assessment through the appeals office.

SURVIVAL RULE ▬▬▬▬▬▬▬▬▬▬▬▬▬▬▬▬▬▬▬▬▬▬▬▬

Make sure that you follow the instructions precisely when making an appeal. The procedure requires a written request and must be initiated within the thirty-day period from the date of Letter 1154(DO).

The appeals procedure will not be discussed in detail here because it is complicated. But if you get confused along the way about your rights of due process make sure either the Revenue Officer or his group manager explains to you completely what your rights are.

Other important points are:

* You have the right to qualified representation during the appeals process by either an attorney, a CPA, or an individual enrolled to practice before the IRS.
* If the administrative appeals process does not satisfy you, or if you wish to bypass the administrative appeals process, you may take your case to the U.S. Court of Claims or to the U.S. District Court. Generally you must pay at least a portion of the tax and file a claim for refund with the IRS before proceeding with this route.

FIGHTING SUSPICIOUS IRS ACTIONS

The 100 percent penalty procedure can be tricky, and if you are not careful it can cost you more money than you realize. Experienced Revenue Officers are aware of certain things that may benefit you, but they are not about to tell you what they are. It is their job to protect the government's interest by "maximizing the revenue," and so what may be to your benefit may not be to the government's benefit.

HOW NOT TO PAY THE 100 PERCENT PENALTY

The IRM states that "it may be suggested to persons determined to be responsible for nonpayment of the trust fund portion that they have the option of paying the trust fund liability on behalf of the corporation, instead of having the liability assessed against them under 100 percent penalty procedures." This sounds good until the Revenue Officer tells you that payment must be by cash, cashier's check, or by certified check drawn on the corporation's bank account, if it is still open. Then you will be told to include a written statement certifying that payment is being made *by the corporation* for application to the trust fund liability. This procedure may be detrimental to you for several reasons:

- Your statement will preclude your right to sue for a refund at a later date. The corporation cannot sue for a refund because the corporation legally owes the tax. The IRS wants the written statement from you because it shows that the corporation is paying the tax and not you, a possible responsible officer. Several responsible officers have made payments to the IRS from their own funds to prevent the assessment of a 100 percent penalty and then sued for a refund after the statute of limitations for assessment of the penalty had expired. This turned out to be a clever ploy by the responsible person, but quite a gamble.
- Your contribution of personal funds to the corporation may be considered by the IRS as a contribution to your capital account as a shareholder unless a loan agreement is made. If you actually lend the money to the corporation with the expectation of a recovery, then when the business folds you *may* be able to deduct the amount of the loan on your tax return as a bad debt. As a

contribution to your capital account the money may only be deducted when the corporation goes defunct and the value of the stock becomes worthless. A loss from worthless stock is subject to the limitation on capital losses, which currently is three thousand dollars per year.

SURVIVAL RULE ▬▬▬▬▬▬▬▬▬▬▬▬▬▬▬▬▬▬▬▬▬▬

If you decide to personally pay a corporation's employment tax liability to prevent the IRS from assessing the 100 percent penalty against you, make sure that the money is a loan to the corporation and not considered as a contribution to your capital account. If you find this confusing, you should check it out with your tax practitioner or accountant.

USING INABILITY TO PAY AS AN ESCAPE

The factor of collectibility can be the basis for *nonassessment* of the 100 percent penalty against the responsible officer(s) but only in those cases in which the future collection potential is obviously nonexistent because of advanced age and/or deteriorating physical or mental condition.

SURVIVAL RULE ▬▬▬▬▬▬▬▬▬▬▬▬▬▬▬▬▬▬▬▬▬▬

If the IRS is about to assess the 100 percent penalty against you, and even though it may be clear that you were the responsible person, you should make a written request for nonassessment of the penalty if your financial situation shows that you cannot pay the penalty now and there is little likelihood that you will be able to pay in the future.

Your written request for nonassessment should be made "under the provisions of IRM section 5542.3." If the investigating Revenue Officer agrees with the request, it has to be approved not only by his boss but also by the branch chief and the division chief. A Collection

Information Statement (Form 433-A) will be required (see Chapter 2).

Even though the IRM provides for nonassessment of the 100 percent penalty for reasons of noncollectibility, it is hardly ever done because few persons held responsible for the tax ever ask that the penalty be waived. Some IRS collection managers are reluctant not to assert the penalty, because then the IRS essentially shuts off any hopes or expectations of recovering the revenue. The argument is always made that one cannot foresee the future and who knows if someday the responsible person will inherit a bundle of money from a deceased relative or maybe even win the jackpot in the "Publisher's Clearing House Sweepstakes."

THE MOST IMPORTANT LOOPHOLE YOU SHOULD USE

The IRS has a set procedure for determining how much a responsible person is to be assessed. The procedure is designed to maximize the revenue for the government, and so it is in your best interest to know how to minimize your potential loss of revenue by taking advantage of a certain little "loophole" that almost every Revenue Officer knows about but won't mention.

The loophole is rooted in IRS Policy Statement P-5-60, a portion of which reads as follows:

In determining the amount of the 100 percent penalty to be assessed in connection with employment taxes, any payment made on the corporate account involved is deemed to represent payment of the *employer* portions of the liability (including assessed penalty and interest) *unless there was some specific designation to the contrary by the taxpayer.* [Italics mine.]

Payments made by a corporation on its delinquent employment tax liability are normally applied first to the non-trust-fund portion of the liability—the employer's contribution to Social Security, and interest and penalties. Only when the non-trust-fund portion has been paid entirely is any portion of the payment applied to the trust-fund portion covering employees' withholdings.

The important point in that policy statement begins with the word *unless.* By reducing the amount of the unpaid trust-fund portion of the corporate liability, you reduce the amount of the 100 percent penalty that may be asserted and assessed against you. And the only way to do that is to take advantage of Policy Statement P–5–60 by *designating that each and every voluntary payment be applied to the trust-fund portion of the corporation's liability.*

SURVIVAL RULE ▬▬▬▬▬▬▬▬▬▬▬▬▬▬▬▬▬▬▬▬▬▬▬▬▬▬▬▬

> *If your business is having financial troubles and you make subsequent payments to the IRS on delinquent withholding taxes, always include a written letter with each payment specifying that the money be applied directly to the trust-fund portion of the liability.*

▬▬

Make sure that your letter is dated and signed and that it refers to the number of the check. Always keep a copy of the letter just in case the IRS loses the original. The right to designate how the money is to be applied has to be exercised when the payment is made. Exercising this right may not only save you money in the long run, but it may also result in a nonassessment of the 100 percent penalty against you.

HOW TO COMPROMISE THE 100 PERCENT PENALTY

In Chapter 7 the concept of compromising your taxes was discussed. One of the grounds for submitting an offer to compromise is for a reasonable doubt of collectibility. Since the 100 percent penalty is used by the IRS when it determines that the tax is not collectible from the corporation, the law also gives a corporate taxpayer or responsible officer the right to compromise the unpaid portion of the delinquent employment tax liability on behalf of the corporation— which will preclude assertion and assessment of the 100 percent penalty against a responsible person. But don't expect anyone from the IRS to tell you about this either.

Under what circumstances should one submit an offer? When there are only enough corporate assets remaining to *fully pay the trust-fund portion* of the liability. If you have designated your payments, then you will probably have no need to submit an offer. But if you have made payments to the IRS without designating how they were to be applied, you have funds remaining that could be applied to the delinquent taxes, and together all the payments will cover the trust-fund portion of the liability, then you should consider submitting an offer to compromise the tax.

The IRS is mostly interested in recovering the amount of trust-fund taxes withheld from employees' paychecks. If the IRS cannot collect the non-trust-fund portion, it is written off as uncollectible. The IRS places such emphasis on recovering the trust-fund portion, because the employee actually gets a W–2 from the corporation showing the total amount of taxes withheld. It makes no difference to the employee that his corporate employer never paid his withheld taxes to the IRS. The IRS will honor the W–2 giving the employee full credit for the amount of tax withheld. If the IRS cannot collect the trust-fund portion from the corporation or the responsible person, the loss is absorbed by the government, not the employee.

The IRS will consider the idea of an offer in compromise if enough money can be paid on the account to effectively cover all the *trust-fund portion* of the outstanding tax.

You have two options when considering submitting an offer. First, the corporation and its responsible officers may submit a joint offer covering both the taxes assessed against the corporation and the 100 percent penalty not yet assessed. Second, separate offers may be submitted by each responsible officer and the corporation to compromise the 100 percent penalty not yet assessed. The purpose of such an offer is to preclude assessment of the 100 percent penalty.

Before deciding whether to submit an offer you should reread Chapter 7 and the portion of Chapter 3 that discusses penalty offers. There are several ramifications involved, and it is also a good idea to discuss these ramifications with your tax advisor or investigating Revenue Officer.

An offer may be submitted by a corporation even *after* the 100 percent penalty has been assessed against the responsible persons. The 100 percent penalty assessment will be abated if an amount equal to the *unpaid trust-fund portion* of the corporation's tax liability is accepted in the form of an offer in compromise.

PROTECTING YOUR TAX REFUNDS FROM THE 100 PERCENT PENALTY

When the 100 percent penalty is assessed against you as a responsible person, the IRS will automatically put a freeze in the computer that will prevent any future refund checks from being issued to you. This means that until the 100 percent penalty is fully paid, all income tax refund checks are prevented by the computer from being released. The money is then applied to the unpaid balance of the 100 percent penalty assessment.

This procedure will definitely cause you a problem if you file a joint income tax return with your spouse. An income tax refund check issued from a joint return is payable only to both spouses. Although the check is indivisible, the IRS continues to take a joint refund check and apply it to the 100 percent penalty liability of one person, who is most likely to be the husband.

This practice occurs for administrative reasons, not legal ones. Legally the IRS doesn't have a leg to stand on. But it happens when the IRS puts a freeze on the responsible person's Social Security number, and since the primary number used in filing a joint return is usually the husband's, the refund check is then frozen. There are several ways in which this freeze might be legally and ethically circumvented.

- Consider filing separate returns for as long as it is economical to do so. When separate income tax returns are filed, only the refund amount belonging to the responsible person will be frozen and applied to the 100 percent penalty. A refund will be sent to the other spouse if that tax return shows a refund. Remember that the law allows a couple who has filed separate tax returns three years in which to amend the returns by filing jointly. However, you cannot first file jointly and then amend to file separately; the IRS will not allow it. So if initially you want to file separate returns to recover a large portion of your refund and then, after the 100 percent penalty has been paid, file an amended return to change the filing status to joint filing, you may do so within three years of the initial filing. It may be to your advantage to later refile jointly if it will increase your refund.
- There is no law that requires you to be overwithheld during the year on your income taxes. You can adjust your withholding so that you would either owe a little, break even, or receive only a nominal refund. By doing this you increase your net pay during the year when you can best use it to pay bills. If you have already been making monthly payments on a 100 percent penalty liability,

there is no need to give the IRS more than required, which is what happens when they freeze your refunds and apply them to the 100 percent penalty. On the other hand, if you want your refund check applied to the 100 percent penalty, then no further action is required on your part.

Index